A Mazing of the Text

Currents in Comparative Romance Languages and Literatures

Tamara Alvarez-Detrell and Michael G. Paulson
General Editors

Vol. 75

PETER LANG
New York • Washington, D.C./Baltimore • Boston • Bern
Frankfurt am Main • Berlin • Brussels • Vienna • Canterbury

Margaret M. Bolovan

A MAZING OF THE TEXT

The Search for Signification
in the Labyrinth of French Poetics

PETER LANG
New York • Washington, D.C./Baltimore • Boston • Bern
Frankfurt am Main • Berlin • Brussels • Vienna • Canterbury

Library of Congress Cataloging-in-Publication Data

Bolovan, Margaret M.
A mazing of the text: the search for signification
in the labyrinth of French poetics / Margaret M. Bolovan.
    p. cm. — (Currents in comparative Romance languages and literatures; vol. 75)
Includes bibliographical references and indexes.
1. French poetry—History and criticism. 2. Labyrinths
in literature. I. Title. II. Series.
PQ401.B58   841.009'15—dc21   98-48969
ISBN 0-8204-4069-8
ISSN 0893-5963

Die Deutsche Bibliothek-CIP-Einheitsaufnahme

Bolovan, Margaret M.:
A mazing of the text: the search for signification in the
labyrinth of French poetics / Margaret M. Bolovan.
–New York; Washington, D.C./Baltimore; Boston; Bern;
Frankfurt am Main; Berlin; Brussels; Vienna; Canterbury: Lang.
(Currents in comparative Romance languages
and literatures; Vol. 75)
ISBN 0-8204-4069-8

Cover illustration: Pinwheel labyrinth at Chantilly Gardens (seventeenth century),
adapted from Jacques François Blondel, *Cours d'architecture civile ou Traité de la
decoration, Distribution et construction des bâtiments contenant les leçons
données en 1750, et les années suivantes*, ed. M. Patte, Paris 1771–1777.

The paper in this book meets the guidelines for permanence and durability
of the Committee on Production Guidelines for Book Longevity
of the Council of Library Resources.

∞

© 1999 Peter Lang Publishing, Inc., New York

Printed in the United States of America

FOR
E. L. B.

Contents

Illustrations

Introduction

Enter the Labyrinth

Mais, ô la belle palme et quel trésor de gloire
Pour celui qui, cherchant la plus noble victoire,
D'un si grand labyrinthe affrontant les hasards,
Saura guider sa Muse aux immenses regards,
De mille longs détours à la fois occupée,
Dans les sentiers confus d'une vaste épopée!
André Chénier, "L'Invention (Poème)"

The most famous labyrinth of legend is that which housed the Minotaur in Crete. When Theseus entered the labyrinth, he was prepared to traverse its bewildering paths, defeat the Minotaur, and thereby liberate his people. Theseus was guided in his quest by the love of Ariadne and the wisdom of Daedalus, both of which were manifest in the ball of thread unraveled as he wandered through the halls of the prison-maze.

The labyrinth was built by Daedalus at the command of King Minos to house and to hide the Minotaur, the illegitimate and monstrous offspring of Queen Pasiphaë and the bull from the sea.[1] This labyrinth was a "maze none could escape from,"[2] filled with "innumerable winding passages."[3] In only two instances have people exited from the labyrinth. Theseus found his way out again with the aid of Ariadne's thread. As a result, Daedalus, along with his son Icarus, was imprisoned in the labyrinth for having supplied Ariadne with the thread and the knowledge to use it. The ingenious Daedalus built wings for himself and for Icarus.[4] Daedalus flew to freedom. The impetuous Icarus, however, flew too close to the sun, and his wings melted, sending him to his death in the sea.

Tracing the etymology of labyrinth is itself an intricate undertaking. In the middle ages the common explanation was that the labyrinth was derived from *labor intus* [labor lies within].[5] For John Ruskin, the term relates to a "rope-walk," placing the emphasis on the guiding thread.[6] Popular etymology in twentieth-century sources connects "labyrinth" to "labrys," the double-bladed axe.[7] Maze, on the other hand, is likely of Scandinavian origin and denotes bewilderment or confusion. The Norwegian *mas* becomes Old English *mase*. The two words came together over time because of similar connotations, and the distinction between labyrinth and maze blurred. Matthews, for instance, argues that there is little or no distinction between the terms (MML 1). Still, the disparity between the two concepts varies from writer to writer, and the term "maze" does not carry all of the connotations associated with the Cretan myth, nor does it evoke the range of symbolism attached to the mythic signifier "labyrinth."

The Cretan labyrinth was not the first mythical maze.[8] Indeed, in Greek and Latin texts, Daedalus' construction is often compared to the elaborate Egyptian labyrinth after which it is said to have been modeled. This labyrinth, which was located just above Lake Moeris in Egypt, is first referred to by Herodotus in the fifth century B.C. (MML 7). Pliny, who believed the Egyptian structure to be the oldest and most renowned labyrinth, used the phrase "viarum illum inexplicabilem errorem" ["bewildering maze of passages"] to describe its complexities.[9] Nevertheless, western poets know the image primarily through the Cretan myth and the retelling of this myth in the works of classical writers such as Ovid and Virgil. The labyrinth has enormous potential as a mythic symbol, potential which has been exploited by numerous writers over the centuries. In French poetics, the labyrinth has been used to signify many, often contradictory, concepts at once: the human condition, the poetic text, a prison, a tomb, an entrance to the underworld, the search for the ineffable, an initiation, the renewal of life. Sometimes it represents death or hell; other times it denotes the search for truth and the path to salvation or greater understanding.

Though the shape of the figure differs in every manifestation, the labyrinth is generally recognizable with its complex pathways winding or spiraling out from a fixed center.[10] The figure of the labyrinth combines the attributes of the vortical whorl[11] with the interweaving of the braid.[12] Like a spider's web, to which it is often compared, the labyrinth involves a fusion of the linear and the circular. Though visually, the labyrinth is sometimes more rectangular in shape, metaphorically, the labyrinth is generally described as circular, in the same manner as Heidegger's path of experience—"a circular happening through which what lies in the circle becomes exposed."[13] The labyrinth is a conception of the interlacing of absence and presence perpetually in the process of unfolding.

The term is constantly being rearticulated to express new meanings. Given the wide range of significations associated with the labyrinth, there is great diversity in the way labyrinthine themes are manifest in various poetic works. In the labyrinthine text, numerous intertwining paths are contained in a single form, and with a stream of constantly shifting images, the poet recreates the ordered chaos of the maze.

Poetry which employs images and structures of the labyrinth simultaneously involves the poet's contemplative wanderings or deeper descents into self in a search for meaning.[14] An internal journey is generally inherent in the labyrinthine text. At the same time, as a mythic symbol, the labyrinth extends outside of any individual work, and intertextual analysis becomes an essential component of the search for signification. As intertexts, these writings again and again enter the textual dialogue. Each use of the labyrinth builds upon and plays off of those that have come before it. Certain texts, especially Virgil's *Aeneid*, Ovid's *Metamorphoses*, Dante's *Inferno*,[15] and Petrarch's *Canzoniere*,[16] have had a profound impact on the understanding of and use of labyrinthine imagery in French poetry.

This study seeks to unravel the labyrinthine threads left in the "mille longs détours" of poetic discourse, primarily certain French poetic texts of the sixteenth to the twentieth century. Several of these texts contain explicit references to the labyrinth; others reveal mere traces of the Cretan myth, but are structurally and/or symbolically labyrinthine in their own respect. The seminal threads uniting all these poetic endeavors reside both in the reconceptualizations of the labyrinth and in the labyrinthine search for signification which the writer and the reader undertake in approaching the text.

Previous Studies of the Labyrinth

When entering such a multifaceted maze, it is prudent to examine the paths which have been trodden before. There are abundant renderings of labyrinths—on coins, tombstones, and church floors, in paintings and illustrations, and maze-gardens, and as a result, there are numerous studies on the visual image of the labyrinth. Three of the most impressive books which catalogue labyrinths and mazes in the visual arts are Paolo Santarcangeli's *Le Livre des labyrinthes: Histoire d'un mythe et d'un symbole,*[17] Hermann Kern's *Labirinti: Forme e interputazioni: 5000 anni di prenzenza di un archetipo,*[18] and W. H. Matthews' *Mazes and Labyrinths: Their History and Development.* These three works concentrate on figures and representations from prehistory to the present day and shed light on the myths and rituals surrounding these images.

That the structure, themes, and metaphors associated with the labyrinth have had an impact on contemporary thought is evident given the great profusion of labyrinthine imagery in twentieth-century literary dialogue.[19] In its most basic usage, the labyrinth conjures up images of winding passages and the loss of direction. The symbol of the labyrinth is itself a maze leading the reader into a confusing web of often incongruous meanings. Modern and postmodernist protagonists exist within labyrinthine cities; they are entrapped in labyrinths of love, politics, and intrigue; they search within the labyrinth of self for their own center of being and encounter the Minotaur in various guises of self and other. Two critical works have dealt specifically with the metaphor of the labyrinth in twentieth-century fiction: Wendy Faris' *Labyrinths of Language*[20] and Donald Gutierrez's *The Maze in the Mind and the World: Labyrinths in Modern Literature.*[21] Faris' study focuses on the labyrinth as a symbolic landscape and narrative design for modern fiction. She asserts that the labyrinth is not merely a persistent figure in contemporary thought, but also a model for narrative structure and a "distinctive sign of writing, reading, and thinking in our era" (2). To illustrate the central place of the labyrinth in the twentieth century, she examines a number of novels, including James Joyce's *Ulysses*, Michel Butor's *Passing Time*, Alain Robbe-Grillet's *In the Labyrinth*, several works of Jorge Luis Borges, Umberto Eco's *The Name of the Rose*, and André Gide's *Theseus*.

Donald Gutierrez, in his study, also analyzes the metaphor of the labyrinth in the twentieth-century experience in literature. The novels he explores do not always have explicit labyrinths in them. Instead, he asserts that the literature discussed embodies figurative mazes: "complex or chaotic social conditions, biological or sexual necessity, physical or social confinement or uncertainty" (viii). He focuses on British and American fiction, primarily novels, including Henry James' *The Jolly Corner*, E. M. Forster's *A Passage to India*, James Joyce's *A Portrait of an Artist as a Young Man*, Henry Miller's *Tropic of Cancer*, and D. H. Lawrence's *Lady Chatterly's Lover*. In all of these works, Gutierrez argues, the labyrinth serves as a master metaphor.

The most thorough examination of the labyrinth as a metaphor and image is Penelope Reed Doob's *The Idea of the Labyrinth from Classical Antiquity through the Middle Ages*. She examines the literary, conceptual, and metaphorical backgrounds of the medieval idea of the labyrinth. Using a wide range of classical and early Christian texts, Doob shows how the labyrinth developed into a sign of complex artistry, impenetrability, and difficult intellectual and verbal processes.

As a literary historian, Doob examines the evolution of labyrinthine ideas and metaphors, connecting what is found in medieval literature not only to classical texts but also to the visual arts and to the myths, legends, and rites which have influenced their creation. Several of the texts she discusses, notably Boccaccio's *Geneology of the Gentile Gods* and the anonymously authored *Ovide moralisé*, replicate the Cretan labyrinth explicitly and illustrate the rich metaphorical potential of its characters, plot, and structure. Other texts, like Boccaccio's *Il Corbaccio* and the two anonymous works *The Assembly of Ladies* and *La Queste del Saint Graal*, draw creatively upon the plot of the Cretan legend. While there are no references to Theseus or the Minotaur in the later texts, there is a presentation of the world as a perilous maze wherein the characters live and love precariously with great labor and much energy. Doob's text culminates in an examination of the labyrinthine aesthetic which connects three works: Boethius' *Consolation of Philosophy*, Dante's *Divine Comedy*, and Chaucer's *House of Fame*. She perceives an intertextual link between these works and suggests that each receives its ideas of the labyrinth from the previous texts and builds upon these concepts.[22]

In another general approach to the image of the labyrinth in literature, archetypal critics view the significance of the Cretan myth in relation to the overriding pattern of mythic quest. Northrop Frye, Joseph Campbell, and Mircea Eliade all attempt to identify universal symbolic archetypes of the collective unconscious in literature. In an archetypal analysis, the labyrinth, the Grail Quest, the descent into hell, and other heroic wanderings are all understood as versions of the same pattern, and Theseus is viewed as one manifestation of the "hero with a thousand faces." Myth in this conception functions as the structural foundation of literature which makes communication of meaning possible.[23] Because motifs such as heroic ordeals, the labyrinthine journey, and metamorphosis are archetypal, people want and need to express these concepts, and mythic symbolism therefore appears constantly in literary works. Northrop Frye and Mircea Eliade use the concept of the labyrinth as an especially pervasive image of the quest in their writings.

Myth and Ritual Significance

The labyrinth has been a significant mythical symbol in diverse cultures around the world since prehistoric times. Mazes and caves were often associated in classical and medieval literature.[24] Boccaccio, for example, conceived of the Cretan maze as a series of caves.[25] Not every cave has labyrinthine tunnels connecting numerous caverns, and not every labyrinth is subterranean, but often the two images intertwine. Some Roman authors even argue that the Cretan labyrinth of the myth is actually based on the caverns of Gortyna or other caves or quarries of Crete. When the French botanist G. P. de Tournefort visited the Gortyna caverns on Mount Ida in 1700, he was quite convinced that he was in fact visiting the Cretan maze. He described the caverns in some detail in "Voyage du Levant." The cavern, of which he writes, is so devious that

> If a Man strikes into any other Path, after he has gone a good way, he is so bewildered among a thousand Twistings, Twinings, Sinuosities, Crinkle-Crankles and Turn-again Lanes, that he could scarce ever get out again without the utmost danger of being lost.
>
> (MML 24)

The primal cave denotes the maternal matrix of the womb and represents security, peace, and absence of danger; at the same time, it also is related to the grotesque, the mysterious, the unknown, and death. All of these attributes apply equally well to the subterranean labyrinth. Both images are used to represent a rebirth or an initiation and a yearning for greater awareness. There are similarities even between the labyrinth and Plato's cave, from within which the light of the sun serves as a guiding thread to the outside world.[26]

In order to understand contemporary significations of the labyrinth, it is essential also to examine the religious implications of the symbol. The labyrinth, as a mythic image, belongs to the sacred knowledge of a people. Taken in the context of the society which created them, myths, and their accompanying rituals, serve important religious roles and are the "very foundation of social life and culture."[27] Myth does not contain the logical truth of *logos* but rather the absolute truth of the sacred. *Mythos* is associated with the human need to know, to understand, to have some measure of control. According to Eliade, this control is gained to some extent through the recital of myth and the ritual reenactment of sacred events. In the myth of the labyrinth, the sacred truths which are addressed include birth, initiation, death, and rebirth.

In Greek antiquity, the relationship between the labyrinth and death was explicit. On a Roman tomb in Tunis, for example, a large labyrinth mozaic has an inscription beneath it which reads, "Here, enclosed, he loses his life" (DIL 73). Often it is the Minotaur at the center of the labyrinth which actually symbolizes death. Even if a protagonist finds his or her way to the center, unravelling the mystery of the inescapable labyrinth, the Minotaur is there waiting with his double-bladed axe. The tomb is often presented as the final labyrinth in this life.

However, death is only one of the ritual meanings associated with the labyrinth. Theseus manages to enter the Minotaur's home, travel its passages, and escape. Henri Jeanmaire asserts that the story of Theseus' ordeal in the labyrinth actually stems from ancient Greek rituals of initiation.[28] Theseus is used as the model for the young person undertaking a rite of passage, a symbolic rebirth into adulthood. These early Greek rituals themselves can be traced back to even older initiation ceremonies during which a cavern is ritually transformed into a labyrinth symbolic of the Earth-Mother, out of which we are born and to which we return when we die. Scholars have noted labyrinthine initiation rituals in diverse cultures, both ancient and contemporary.[29]

Mircea Eliade has identified a labyrinthine initiatory structure which in most cases will "more or less clearly imply a ritual death followed by resurrection or a new birth."[30] This symbolic death and rebirth involves a descent into Hell where its monsters are confronted. Initiation ceremonies involving the labyrinth prepare participants both for sacred life here on earth and for rebirth after death. The labyrinth therefore signifies the womb as well as the tomb. In some instances the labyrinth represents the road which the soul or spirit must follow to enter the afterlife or to reach reincarnation. Ariadne's thread might then be conceived of as the umbilical cord which leads the hero to symbolic rebirth.

The labyrinth in funerary myths is generally related to a dangerous passage into the bowels of Mother Earth.[31] Often coming of age initiation rituals involve an imitation of a hero's journey to the land of the dead and back again. In Western myth and literature, numerous personages make this voyage, including Theseus, Heracles, Aeneas, Ceres, Dionysos, and Dante, and these voyages are generally described in distinctly labyrinthine terms. Virgil's *Aeneid* is full of labyrinths both explicit and implicit, and though he never refers to Hades as a maze, it can easily be interpreted as such. Petrarch, for example, writes of Virgil's Hades: "I knew that the 'descent to Avernus was easy,' the gate of the labyrinth was wide, and that the way out was hard and difficult to find."[32] In Book 6, Aeneas comes to the temple of Apollo built by Daedalus. On the door to the temple, Daedalus had sculpted the story of the Cretan labyrinth. The fresco illustrates how Ariadne, with the advice of Daedalus, helped to guide Theseus out of "the treacherous windings of the labyrinth" (121). The labyrinth in this context is connected not only to death and war but also to love and guidance.

Dante also peoples his *Inferno* with characters from the Cretan myth, and not coincidentally, the persona is guided through the labyrinth of hell by Virgil. The Minotaur and Minos serve the significant function in Dante's text of reinforcing the image of Inferno as a labyrinth. In fact, the Minotaur seems to believe that he is still inside the construct of Daedalus, and for all practical purposes he is. When Dante and Virgil approach, the Minotaur in his semi-intelligence makes a rather insightful mistake, believing Dante to be his nemesis come to kill him again:

> My wise guide cried to him: "Perhaps you think
>   you see the Duke of Athens come again,
>   who came once in the world to bring your death?
>
> Begone, you beast, for this one is not led
>   down here by means of clues your sister gave him;
>   he comes here only to observe your torments."
>
> The way a bull breaks loose the very moment
>   he knows he has been dealt the mortal blow,
>   and cannot run but jumps and twists and turns,
>
> just so I saw the Minotaur perform. (XII: 16–25)

The relationship between Dante and Theseus is instantly recognized by the Minotaur. Not only are they both maze-walkers, they are also guided and protected by higher powers, destined to escape from a labyrinth which for others is inescapable.

Minos' role in Inferno is a distorted reflection of his function in the Cretan myth:

> There stands Minòs grotesquely, and he snarls,
>   examining the guilty at the entrance;
>   he judges and dispatches, tail in coils.
>
> By this I mean that when the evil soul
>   appears before him, it confesses all,
>   and he, who is the expert judge of sins,
>
> knows to what place in Hell the soul belongs;
>   the times he wraps his tail around himself
>   tells just how far the sinner must go down. (V: 4–12)

As he did as king and judge in Crete, Minos assigns each person to their place. Here, however, his judgement is secondary. The people have already been judged by God; Minos is merely an ornament of the Inferno. He has also become quite monstrous and brutish in appearance. Though Dante never explicitly refers to hell as a labyrinth, not surprisingly, his contemporaries often read it as such. Boccaccio, Francesco da Buti, and Benvenuto all interpreted Inferno as a labyrinthine cave (or series of caves).[33]

Several rituals are directly related to the Cretan myth. The relationship between ritualistic dance and the labyrinth is well documented.[34] In classical and medieval literature, dance is often referred to in association with the labyrinth. In the *Iliad*, for example, Homer refers to the dancing floor built by Daedalus for Ariadne in Crete which has a maze pattern upon it. Theseus and his companions also perform a labyrinthine dance in Delos after their escape from Crete. In this dance, Theseus "imitated the confused and twisting journey of the labyrinth with the boys and girls who had escaped with him, singing as they danced first in one circuit, then winding back."[35] This dance which spread to Greece and Italy was known as the crane dance.[36] Plutarch later noted that in his time a labyrinthine dance was still being performed in Delos.[37] Similarly, Robert Graves identifies the labyrinth with the partridge dance, an erotic spring dance in which devotees wore wings and danced in a spiral (316). In medieval France, a number of dioceses practiced Easter rituals which involved labyrinthine dances.[38] Inevitably, these dances are tied to seasonal change and the rebirth associated with spring.

The Greek funerary games are also connected to the image of the labyrinth. In describing funeral games held in honor of Aeneas' deceased father, Virgil writes,

> There was a labyrinth with a tortuous path
> Running between blind walls and treacherous
> With a thousand twists and turns, whose baffling maze
> Defied the following of any trail:
> No man could solve it, no man retrace his step.
> The course of these Trojan boys was not unlike it
> As they wove in and out in mock attack
> And mock retreat. (VA, 5: 111)

In both the dance and the funeral games, the participants of the ritual symbolically repeat the passage of Theseus through Daedalus' maze. In this manner they participate in the sacred and prepare themselves to pass through the labyrinth of life and death.

For Christian writers, the labyrinth of death was not impenetrable. With the guidance of baptism and communion, one could escape to eternal life. Indeed, medieval carvers often "placed mazes on baptismal fonts" as emblems of this guidance through the labyrinth of life and death (DIL 74). In 1621, Claude Paradin wrote of the emblematic labyrinth:

> par ce labyrinth. . . se pouroit entendre que pour rencontrer la
> voye, & chemin de vie eternelle, la grace de Dieu nous adresse:

nous mettant entre les mains le filet de ses saincts commandemens.
A ce que le tenans & suivans tousiours nous venions a nous tirer
hors des dangereux foruoyemens des destroits mödains.[39]

Indeed, in medieval France, as in other parts of Europe, the labyrinth
was appropriated as a symbol by the church. Labyrinths were engraved
on the floors and walls of many churches and were associated with
various rituals. These religious mazes were known as "Chemin de
Jérusalem," "daedale," or "meandre." The center of these labyrinths
was called "ciel" or "Jérusalem."[40] Theseus generally came to be
associated with Christ.[41] In the Christian maze, there is only one path
to salvation, and Grace takes the place of Ariadne's thread.

As the term "chemin de Jérusalem" implies, these labyrinths
symbolize the concept of pilgrimage. The twisting paths of the maze
represent the sinful world, and at the center, the destination—celestial
paradise. Those who were incapable of actually making a pilgrimage
to Jerusalem could do so on their knees following the maze on the
floor of the church, or with their fingers tracing a wall labyrinth. Such
miniature pilgrimages were perceived as penitence.

Searching for Mythic Signification in Poetic Discourse

Criticism which examines mythic signification in poetry is quite
diverse and draws on a variety of sources from numerous disciplines,
including anthropology, linguistics, psychoanalysis, religious studies,
and literary theory. Within this body of theory, there is no set
definition of myth, nor is there a common approach to literary
analysis. Among the major approaches that literary theorists have
taken in addressing myth, the most common include myth as
archetype, as literary genre, and/or as linguistic process.

Myths around the world have a startlingly similar group of
motifs, characters, and actions. This has led many critics to focus
their studies on identifying archetypal patterns of myth. Some critics
argue that rather than being the result of dispersals and borrowings,
these parallels have arisen because myths answer basic human needs

and are grounded in inherent structures of thought. So while myths might be expressed in specific, historical forms, they are based on archetypal patterns. Thus Joseph Campbell can argue that in a particular myth "the problems and solutions shown are directly valid for all mankind."[42] This vein of literary theory known as archetypal criticism is founded largely on the work of Jung, though critics such as Northrop Frye and Mircea Eliade have developed these archetypal conceptions of myth in their literary and religious discourses.

While archetypal critics try to identify universal symbolic patterns or discover the collective unconscious in literature, other critics assume that myth can be better approached as literature.[43] In this context, myths are viewed as evolving and synthesizing over time so that they contain layer upon layer of meaning and metaphor. Classical stories, poems, and epics are not myths themselves, but literary retellings of the myths. The literary record of these myths is vast, so there is a reservoir of intertextual material for the poet. Mythical symbols and motifs are quite common in literature. Though initiatory patterns have lost their ritual reality, and mythic symbols, to a large extent, "have been emptied of their religious content" (ER 128), the structures and the images have been preserved. The mythology surrounding the labyrinth provides ample symbols and imagery for poetic expression.

Poets exploit this creative reservoir in several manners. Many poets consciously draw on traditional myths of the past but transform these myths to express the contemporary cultural consciousness. Characters or motifs are often taken directly from mythology and modified to suit the poet's needs. Marguerite Yourcenar uses Phaedra and Theseus in "Phèdre ou le désespoir" (YF 31–37), but they are characters quite distinct from those found in Ovid. Many of the same themes and images from the Cretan myth are retained in Yourcenar's text, but everything is recontextualized. The subway system is invested with the attributes of the labyrinth, and it is Phèdre who must descend into its depths.

Writers also use mythical allusions to enhance their poems. Joachim Du Bellay, for example, employs the image of Icarus to refer to his own plight as a poet. These references are at times obvious, but except in letters to Ronsard, Du Bellay does not mention Icarus explicitly. Instead, he uses images of wings, flight, and falling. He attempts through the numerous passages of his text to reach the ineffable love of Olive, but he is fearful of donning wings. Such images were familiar to Du Bellay's intended audience as the Icarian flight was a common theme in French Renaissance poetry.[44]

Other works contain mythical structures invented by the writer which nonetheless bear parallels with traditional myths. Racine's *Bajazet* contains no direct references to the myth of the Cretan labyrinth—such allusions would seem out of place in the Turkish setting. Nonetheless, the structure and themes of the labyrinth inundate the text. An archetypal analysis could perhaps account for such parallels, but the labyrinth motif is also well-known to Racine through his readings and translations.[45]

Another approach to the relationship between myth and poetry concentrates on the mythopoeic process itself. As early as the eighteenth century, the Italian scholar Giambattista Vico asserted that there existed an "essential unity of poetry and myth, rooted not in rite or belief, but in the nature of language."[46] Some modern critics have followed this line of thought, concentrating their analysis on the symbolic and metaphorical language from which both myth and poetry arise.[47] Myth and poetic discourse both are regarded as coming out of and reflecting a fluid universe. Vico saw *logos* as the word of logic and *mythos* as *parlar naturale*, the "verbal signifier for things,"[48] similar to Edenic language before the fall. Mythopoeia thus refers to the dimension of the imagination, the realm of metaphor and metamorphosis.

In its earliest uses, the image of the labyrinth was largely ritualistic and was connected to issues such as rebirth, initiation, and seasonal renewal. Modern images of the labyrinth often retain these connotations in the linguistic sediment, but they are generally more directly concerned with the search for signification. The labyrinth invariably involves a quest for truth, self-knowledge, or love. Such a quest can range from Saint-Amant's spiritual wanderings to Phèdre's descent into the labyrinth of self in Yourcenar's *Feux*. The search for signification is never easy, given the multifaceted nature of the labyrinth.

Classical and medieval labyrinths, whether they be visual, literary, or internal, are generally conceived of as having a center. This center is the ultimate destination, for here the hero will find pure understanding, unconditional love, or salvation. In the Christian tradition, the center does not exist merely as a goal, rather it resides within the self as a soul. The soul is that core element of the self which is not confined by the self. When the body dies, it is this soul which is supposed to live on. The center of the self has no direct physical manifestation; it cannot be located in the body, nor is it subject to the perpetual substitution of thought and language. The center is the ineffable original presence which can never be reached except in death. Therefore, in theory, the soul/center would guarantee the presence of self because it is outside the play of *différance*. Likewise, in the center of the labyrinth, there will be an absence of any secondary significations, leaving only presence itself or conversely, as in the Kabbalah, nothingness. A metaphorical space such as the center of the labyrinth is clearly not meant for mortal eyes, which partially explains why it is so difficult to reach. Arriving at the center of the labyrinth often means certain death (though consequently it may also signify immortality) or, at the very least, metamorphosis. Even a mythic hero like Theseus needs aid to defeat the death which awaits him in the labyrinth.

One of the most intriguing ideas associated with the labyrinth is that of the excluded center. Labyrinths are supposed to have a center, yet in most instances, it is unattainable. To search for center or truth within a discursive formation is therefore an exhaustive and never-ending effort which involves pealing back layer upon layer of historical meaning *ad infinitum*. Such is the search for center that it only leads back upon itself—there is nothing at the center except yet another quest.

Sometimes the poet may even become entrapped in his or her own work. The literary artist, as creator, generally has a view from above the labyrinth; like Daedalus soaring above his creation, the poet sees the text in its entirety, whereas the hero placed in the labyrinth sees only the passages ahead and behind. However, in many versions of the Cretan myth, Daedalus, the artist, the creator of the labyrinth, is imprisoned in his own construction by an angry King Minos.[49] The figures of Daedalus and Theseus partially converge in such instances. When the poet searches for self meaning, he or she becomes both the architect of the labyrinth and a wanderer in the maze.

For the poet who embarks on a search for self, the labyrinth often becomes a maze of self-reflecting images. In the process which Jacques Lacan refers to as the "stade du miroir,"[50] the image of self is created in relation to the similarities and distinctions between self and other. Unable to locate a center, the subject disregards this instability and ineffability and seeks a unified self image by reflecting on its differences from the Other. The persona in Mallarmé's *Igitur*,[51] for example, constantly gazes at his own reflection in both actual and metaphorical mirrors, and there is a constant chain of signifiers denoting the persona and its mirrorings. With each new signification the former Igitur is both absent and present. In the "hasard infini des conjonctions" every object in the poem is connected by shadows and reflections of one kind or another. This idea is reinforced by the metaphor of the Arachnean thread in the spiraling staircase. The self-reflecting image is also a major theme in both Saint-Amant's "Le Contemplateur"[52] and Théophile de Viau's "La Maison de Sylvie."[53] The world is itself a kind of convex mirror, "la plaine liquide."[54] There is a labyrinth of shifting images of self and other, and movement is the only constant in the transitory world presented in these poems, where images are not merely transitory, they are transformed. Edward Nolan has noted that within the confines of the labyrinth the "mirror phase" is fully operational: "the minotaur, whatever else it is, will, if perceived carefully enough by Theseus, reveal itself as a fulfilling mirror, as the completion of the self in the other."[55] The Minotaur at the center of the labyrinth is at the same time an object of the search, a reflection of the subject, and an inexplicable being. The subject is perceived in the Other, but as the other is a constantly changing chain of signs, the reflected image is not fixed. The result is a shifting specular image of self.

Another essential duality of the labyrinth is that it can be unicursal, multicursal, or a combination of both. André Peyronie suggests that

> There are two types of labyrinth: those with a single passage (which were the only ones to be represented pictorially until the middle of the sixteenth century), and those with several passages containing intersections and offering possibilities for choice, error, etc.[56]

In the unicursal labyrinth there is one path which twists and turns but which inevitably leads to the center if followed. The route is indirect in such a labyrinth, but with perseverance, the hero will always reach the center. To the contemporary mind, such a maze is hardly labyrinthine at all, but in the medieval and classical mind, it was the predominant visual image (see Figure 1).

The essential trait of the multicursal maze is that it contains dead ends and false paths. Consequently, there is an obligation to choose at each intersection. The possibilities for error and deviation are innumerable. In the multicursal labyrinth there is an obligation to choose one's way of life, and consequently, there is confusion and doubt. Choice and responsibility often take the place of the determination and faith which are necessary in the unicursal model (see Figure 2).

Artistic renderings of the unicursal labyrinth have been in existence since prehistoric times, but Paolo Santarcangeli suggests that multicursal labyrinths made their first appearance in the Baroque period (401). In the realm of visual arts, this assertion is to a great extent valid, but in myth and literature, the distinction is not so obvious. The labyrinth in classical myth and literature is often described in such a way that it would have to be multicursal. Even in medieval Christian literature, in which only a single path leads through the labyrinth to salvation, the image of the multicursal maze persists. Doob devotes an entire chapter, in her study on medieval labyrinths, to addressing the conflict between the unicursal labyrinth-as-visual-symbol and the multicursal labyrinth-as-concept. Her explanation is that just as one signifier was used to denote both the symbolic and the conceptual, so was one emblematic form used for both unicursal and multicursal labyrinths.[57] This distinction is less problematic since the sixteenth century, as both types of mazes begin to appear in the artistic realm, and the multicursal maze eventually becomes the predominant image. The contemporary writer draws on both images.

Despite obvious differences, unicursal and multicursal labyrinths were for centuries denoted by a single signifier. Roland Barthes' discourse on the mythic sign offers some insight into this and other dualities associated with the labyrinth. Barthes suggests that while a signifier would generally be an empty form waiting to be filled by a signified (the concept), the mythic signifier has always already acted as a linguistic sign and it retains traces of the former meaning. These two aspects of the signifier exist simultaneously.[58] The mythical concept is made up of all the connotations and ideas that can be associated with the signifier in a given situation. Barthes stresses that such a concept has an open character:

> en fait, le savoir contenu dans le concept mythique est un savoir confus, formé d'associations molles, illimitées. [. . .] c'est une condensation informe, instable, nébuleuse, dont l'unité, la cohérence tiennent surtout à la fonction. (226)

Numerous connotations can be attached to a single mythic signifier. So the labyrinth, for example, can at the same time be unicursal and multicursal; it can have a center, but the center may be ineffable. It can be both a place of wandering and a place of confinement.

The labyrinth already serves as a linguistic sign full of meaning. When the poet uses this sign as a mythic signifier in a poem, the former meanings do not entirely disappear, but the form is at the same time filled with a new signification. The term "labyrinth" is constantly being rearticulated to express new meanings, with the old significations at least partially obscured in the circuitous passages. Yet traces, vestiges of former significations, will remain hovering at the fringes of each rearticulation. If the poet wishes to use the labyrinth to denote a particular view of death, the new mythic signification will reflect this image, but it will also contain to varying degrees many of the previous connotations. The text in this conception can be likened to a spider web with its "entrelacs perpétuel."[59]

Barthes has also asserted that "the labyrinth is so well-conceived a form that what can be said about it easily falls short of the form itself."[60] How can words do justice to a symbol in which are united contraries such as death and rebirth, confusion and truth, confinement and wandering? It is not surprising that the labyrinth is often used as a metaphor for the very linguistic system which seeks to describe it. Language can easily be envisioned as a multicursal maze full of twists and turns. The labyrinth is a place of shifting signification and perpetual movement.

If the labyrinth as signification is then used as a signifier for the poetic text, the metaphor of the labyrinth gives shape to the unstable everflowing text, and at the same time, it gives a deconstructive instability to what is offered as real. In the poetic text that is the labyrinth, the thread of words forms the lines of passage while the text gives it order and boundedness. A poem, or any form of discourse for that matter, is created through the weaving of words.[61] These words may be followed by various readers in different directions through the passages of the text. The idea of the myth as a guiding thread offers an interesting image when this myth is woven into a poetic text. As a linguistic thread, it may be followed by the reader either to search for or to deconstruct meaning.

Chapter 1

Longing for the Ineffable:
The Icarian Flight in Du Bellay's *L'Olive*

Elements of the Cretan myth often appear in French literature of the sixteenth century, and labyrinths have adorned the floors of many French churches since medieval times, yet in the 1550s the signifier "labyrinth" was just beginning to enter the French lexicon. The term was used occasionally in neo-Latin poetry and discourse. However, those who wrote in French tended to use euphemisms, such as *dédale* or *maison dédale*, to signify the Cretan maze. Though the mythical symbol was well-known, it was not until the poets of the Pléiade began using the term that "labyrinth" became an established image in French vernacular poetry.

By the early 1550s, "labyrinth" had entered the repertoire of the Pléiade poets, and it surfaces in their works as both a symbol and a rhetorical figure. Ronsard in *Amours de Cassandre* (1552) and Olivier de Magny in *Les Amours* (1553) both name the labyrinth and employ the image in relation to love and its many contradictions. Amadis Jamyn, Jean de Boyssières, Etienne Pasquier, and Philippe Desportes similarly utilize the labyrinth as a symbol for the imprisonment of love.[1] But in France, this period's most intriguing renderings of labyrinthine imageries are to be found in the writings of Joachim Du Bellay.[2]

In *Divers jeux rustiques* (1558) Du Bellay writes:

Les cueurs humains un labyrinthe sont,
Qui maints destours, maintes cachettes ont,
Où l'on se perd, qui n'a le fil pour guide
D'un bon esprit et jugement solide. (XXIII: 17–20)

Love is likened to the labyrinth with its many detours, and the lover who does not have a thread for guidance is bound to get lost. The Cretan myth and love are here intertwined in the poetic imagery employed by Du Bellay. A similar relationship is developed in *Poésies diverses*:

> Comme dans les erreurs de Crete
> Parmy tant de chemins tortus
> De ses pas se trouve deçeuë
> Et ne peut retrouver l'issuë
> du labyrinth' de tes vertus. (XVII: 152–6)

In this instance love alone does not lead the poet onto the tortuous paths. Rather it is the poet's perceptions of the beloved's virtues which thrust him into the labyrinth and lead him into error. The bewilderment of the poet is then fueled by both his inability to express her beauty and his unrequited desire. The use of "erreurs" to denote the labyrinth is quite significant in *L'Olive* as the diverse metaphorical and literal meanings of *erreur* constitute the labyrinthine structure of the text.

There are only two other instances in his *oeuvre* where Du Bellay mentions the labyrinth by name. In *Les Antiquités de Rome* "son vieux labyrinth' la Crete n'oublira" (II. 8) is proferred as one of the seven great wonders of the world. The second instance, "Hymne de la Surdité," sheds more light on Du Bellay's use of the figure. In this poem, the labyrinth is utilized as a symbol for the ear:

> Comme l'oeil, le sentir, et ce nerf sinueux
> Qui, par le labyrinth' d'un chemin tortueux,
> Le son de l'air frappé conduit en la partie,
> Qui discourt sur cela, dont elle est avertie. (XV: 45–48)

In the poem, Du Bellay provides a detailed anatomical description of the aural cavity. The conception of the ear as labyrinth provides insight into Du Bellay's use of the mythic image.[3] Sounds or words enter the passageway of the ear, and "le son de l'air frappé" is metamorphosed into ideas and images in the brain. Near the end of the poem, the discourse of the brain has gained wings and taken flight—"discours aellez volent à l'environ" (XVI: 242). Du Bellay's own deafness gave him an invested interest in this subject, and in "Hymne de la Surdité" he laments his own lack of hearing. Words become lost in the labyrinth of his ear never to reach their destination; still, his own written discourse builds wings in an effort to soar above the barriers and twisted pathways.

In the sonnet sequence *L'Olive* (1549),[4] the labyrinth remains unnamed yet omnipresent. Du Bellay tends to signify mythological figures through their attributes, characteristics, and even tangentially related elements. He often goes to great lengths to avoid naming a figure,[5] yet the Cretan maze is constantly evoked through synecdoche, metaphor, antonomasia, and periphrasis. The place in which the poet finds himself is a "prison doulce" (Sonnet XXXIII), a "chemin plein d'erreur variable" (Sonnet XLIII) and a "grand erre" (Sonnet LVIII). The sonnets are replete with paths, flight, ascent and descent, death and immortality, prisons and detours, centers and escapes. There is no shortage of labyrinthine imagery in *L'Olive*.

The labyrinthine motif in *L'Olive* is evoked most explicitly in the interplay of diverse significations in the semantic field of *erreur* and *errer*. The classical poets had already connected error with the figure of the labyrinth. Virgil, for instance, refers to the Cretan maze as the "irremeabilis error" ["a wandering from which one cannot return"] (DIL 30). Petrarch also takes this path when he explores "giovenile errore" in the *canzoniere*, and he utilizes metaphorical and literal error throughout his poetry.[6] Renaissance poets were confronted with two distinct values associated with "errer": one signifying movement and the other behavior.[7] The first sense was connected with wandering, the second with straying from the correct path. In the poetry of Petrarch's *Canzoniere*, Pontus de Tyard's *Les Erreurs amoureuses*,[8] and Du Bellay's *L'Olive*, error is used to exploit this double-voicedness, and love is offered as the primary force which obscures reason and leads man to "errer."

Furthermore, Du Bellay utilizes several labyrinthine discourses which flourished in sixteenth-century French literary dialogue: the

Renaissance revitalization of Icarian flight, Petrarchan labyrinths of love, the poetic quest for the ineffable, and the poetic practice of *imitatio*. In *L'Olive*, Du Bellay interweaves these literary threads, and at the same time he rearticulates the discourse and brings it to new heights.

Icarian Flight

A variety of mythical characters are alluded to in *L'Olive*, but Icarus holds a special position in this mythology because his character is utilized by Du Bellay to reflect on his own poetic practice. Numerous classical writers tell the tale of Daedalus and Icarus and how they escape from the labyrinth using wings constructed from fallen feathers. Du Bellay's allusions to the myth evoke several related concepts in *L'Olive*: the motif of the pen as feather (poetic flight), the effort to describe Olive's attributes which are often equated with the sun (poetic aspirations), fear of his inability to capture her virtues in words, which could result in a fall (poetic impasse or failure), and the contrast between his efforts and the successes of his predecessors (poetic immortality).

Correlations between flight and the poetic arts have a long literary history. In Plato's *Phaedrus*, for example, the lover feels wings growing on his soul and longs to fly upward.[9] Du Bellay exploits this imagery in his writings. The use of wings to symbolize poetic flight appears first in *La Deffence*, where after recounting the work of the poet, Du Bellay asserts: "Ce sont les esles dont les ecriz des hommes volent au ciel" (DDI 106). In *L'Olive*, vocabulary and imagery associated with flight appears frequently and is coupled with a neoplatonic aspiration towards things of the spirit. Beginning with Sonnet LVIII, at the center of the sequence, a neoplatonic conception of flight in pursuit of the ideal becomes a major movement in *L'Olive*:

> De mon esprit les aesles sont guidées
> Jusques au seing des plus haultes Idées
> Idolatrant ta celeste beaulté. (ll. 9–11)[10]

Although flight imagery does occur before this point, it is from the center on endowed with Platonic overtones. Whereas the poetic wanderings of the self had previously taken him on paths by land and by sea, the poetic voice now takes to the heavens.

The writers from whom Du Bellay borrowed most extensively, Virgil, Ovid, Horace and Petrarch, all utilized the story of Icarus. In Book VIII of the *Metamorphoses*,[11] Ovid recounts the story of Icarus and Daedalus in some detail. Daedalus serves as the guide for his son as they seek to escape from Crete. Daedalus the craftsman, the genius, is able to soar without over-reaching the strength of his wings. Icarus, on the other hand, is young and impetuous and wants to soar ever higher. Though Daedalus warns him several times, Icarus cannot resist an impetuous flight towards the sun. Though he only has to follow the path of his father to escape the labyrinth, he is tempted to reach the sun:

> When the boy Icarus began to enjoy the thrill of swooping boldly through the air. Drawn on by his eagerness for the open sky, he left his guide and soared upwards, til he came too close to the blazing sun, and it softened the sweet-smelling wax that bound his wings together. The wax melted. Icarus moved his bare arms up and down, but without their feathers they had no purchase on the air. Even as his lips were crying his father's name, they were swallowed up in the deep blue waters which are called after him.
>
> (OM 185)

Writers of the Italian Renaissance saw Icarus as a ready figure for their poetic efforts, and the story of Icarus appears in works by Dante, Petrarch, Ariosto, Sannazzaro, and Boccaccio, among others. Petrarch especially connects Icarus to poetic practice:

> I thought I was skilled enough in flight
> (not by my power, but by his who spreads my wings)
> to sing worthily of that lovely knot
> from which Death looses me, with which Love binds me.

> I found myself much more slow and frail in operation
> than a little branch bent by a great burden,
> and I said: "He flies to fall who mounts too high,
> nor can a man well do what the heavens deny him." (307: 1–8)[12]

The skill to fly and the ability to write poetry worthy of his love are correlated in this sonnet. The poet soon finds that his abilities do not equal his subject and alludes to the fate of Icarus. The relationship between the image of flight and the poet's pen is made more explicit in the next lines of the sonnet:[13]

> Never could any pinion of wit,
> let alone a heavy style or tongue, fly so high as Nature did
> when she made my sweet impediment. (307: 9–11; PRD 486)

The feather is connected not only to flight here, but also to the writer's pen and in a negative sense becomes a symbol of the writer's inadequacy. The flight of the feather/pen parallels the writer's frustrated attempts to soar. The poet will never be able to reach with his writing the natural beauty of the beloved.

The Icarian imagery found in Petrarch's sonnets influenced and was imitated by Du Bellay, who also identifies with and feels a certain empathy for Icarus and his doomed attempts to soar. Like Icarus, Du Bellay is striving to reach the unattainable. The myth of Icarus comes to symbolize both the inaccessibility of the love-object and the poet's endeavors to capture her beauty.

Du Bellay's use of the Icarian figure and flight imagery was also influenced by his contemporaries. French Neo-Latin writers made use of the myth, but it was the Pléiade poets who really popularized the myth in France. Though, in general, sixteenth-century French poets did not view Icarus in a positive light, he often appears in the poetry of the period. In fact, the myth of Icarus is used as an intertext in sixteenth-century French literature more frequently than the story of Theseus' ordeal in the labyrinth.[14] The earliest renderings of the flight of Icarus in the French Renaissance were generally imitations or "poetic translations" of earlier Italian poems. For example, Sonnet CLXVII of Ronsard's *Amours* is based on a poem by Ariosto, and Desportes' *Icare est cheut ici le jeune audacieux* is a rendering of Sannazzaro's *Icaro cadde qui*.[15]

Though the references to Icarus in French verse are occasionally explicit, often the allusions are as vague as a wing or a feather. Ronsard, in his Horatian ode which ends Book IV of the 1550 odes, writes: "Tousjours, tousjours, sans que jamais je meure / Je volerai tout vif par l'univers."[16] Again in his *Derniers vers*, Ronsard signifies upon his own writing with the allusion to Icarus: "ma plume vole au ciel pour estre quelque signe."[17] In *Délie*, Scève uses the image of the feather to express his humility: "ma plume au bas vol de son aele" (CCXXVII).[18]

Du Bellay not only borrows from and imitates other poets' use of Icarian imagery, but in some sonnets he also makes conscious allusions to those poets he imitates. In Sonnet CV of *L'Olive* both Scève and Petrarch are specifically evoked:

> L'Arne superbe adore sur sa rive
> Du sainct Laurier la branche tousjours vive,
> Et ta Delie enfle ta Saone lente.[19]

Petrarch is presented as the "esprit divin" whose poetry lives on, while Scève is the "cigne nouveau, qui voles en chantant" of whom Du Bellay writes. The two poets are evoked through the images of their beloveds. The feather, which Petrarch and Scève had both used as a symbol of inadequacy in the face of the ineffable, becomes in Du Bellay's sonnet a symbol of their poetic glory:

> J'aime, j'admire & adore pourtant
> Le hault voler de ta plume dorée.
>
> [. . .]
>
> Mon Loire aussi, demydieu par mes vers,
> Bruslé d'amour etent les braz ouvers
> Au tige heureux, qu'à ses rives je plante. (CV: 7–8, 12–14)

The feather/pen image not only soars when applied to Petrarch and Scève, but it has also been transformed into gold (DD 407). At the same time, Du Bellay is planting his own Olive tree by the shores of the river. In this way Du Bellay asserts the richness of the efforts of his two predecessors, while suggesting that his verse will rival theirs. Yet he then tempers this assertion with the image of the sun burning him and the sea waiting with arms open. Du Bellay portrays himself as the Icarian figure, contrasted with the intertextual references, who like Daedalus are more astute fliers.

Avian imagery is utilized frequently in *L'Olive*. In Horace and Ovid, Icarus has often been connected to the metamorphosis of the poet into a swan. In his *Odes*, Horace writes:

> On no ordinary or flimsy feather shall I be carried in double form through the liquid air, a poet, nor shall I stay any longer on earth; conquering envy, I shall leave the towns. The son of poor parents, summoned by you, I shall not die, beloved Maecenas, nor shall I be imprisoned by the waters of the Styx. Already now the rough skin is forming on my legs, and I am changing above into a white bird, and light feathers are appearing on my fingers and shoulders. Now better known than Icarus, son of Daedalus I shall visit the shores of the moaning Bosphorus, the Gaetulian Syrtes, and the Hyperborean plains. (Book II, Ode 20)[20]

The poet in his metamorphosis compares himself to Icarus, becoming even more famous for his flight. In this ode as well as Ode IV.2, Horace contrasts Pindar, the poet who is successful in his flight (and is metamorphosed into a swan) with Icarus, whose flight had ended in disaster. Pindar soars effortlessly like a swan, but other ambitious poets who do not share his genius and try to follow his path with artificial wings end up in a watery grave.[21] Du Bellay borrows this imagery in Sonnet LIX, in which the narrator drowns like Lëandre trying to reach his lover, metamorphoses into a swan, and then sings the praises of his lover:

Moy, que l'amour a faict plus d'un Lëandre,
De cest oyseau prendray le blanc pennaige,
Qui en chantant plaingt la fin de son aage
Aux bordz herbuz du recourbé Mëandre. (LIX: 1–4)[22]

Du Bellay rearticulates Horace's imagery, but more importantly he
has also adapted the concept of the metamorphosis into a swan as "a
symbol of immortality gained through poetry."[23] According to the
legend of Lëandre, the swan sings immediately before death. So the
poet dies trying to reach his love, but in dying he manages to give
flight to her praises and impart immortality upon her.

Also of interest is the context in which the swan is dying—along
the twisting banks of the Meandre. The Meandre river is often
associated with labyrinths due to its winding path. In *Metamorphoses*,
Ovid writes:

> Just as the playful waters of the Maeander in Phrygia flow this way
> and that, without any consistency, as the river, turning to meet
> itself, sees its own advancing waves, flowing now towards its
> source and now towards the open sea, always changing its
> direction, so Daedalus constructed countless wandering paths and
> was scarcely able to find his way back to the entrance, so confusing
> was the maze. (Book 8: 162–8)

The link between the winding river and the Cretan labyrinth is well
established, and in Du Bellay's sonnet the two myths are intertwined.
The dying swan, flying away from the river towards the sun, parallels
the flight of Icarus, who rising from the labyrinth, soars too high only
to plummet into the sea.

While the swan represents a symbol of the poetic ideal to which
Du Bellay aspires, he often worries that he will prove to be an Icarian
figure whose wings will eventually melt:

Quel cigne encor' des cignes le plus beau
Te prêta l'aele? & quel vent jusq'aux cieulx

Te balança le vol audacieux,
Sans que la mer te fust large tombeau? (Sonnet CXV: 5–8)[24]

The swan in this instance refers to the poet Ronsard, who, in a sonnet addressed to Du Bellay, asserts that he has avoided the fate of Icarus despite being warned that he was aiming too high:

Par une cheute subite
Encor je n'ai fait nommer
Du nom de Ronsard la mer
Bien que Pindar j'imite.
          ("A Jouachim Du Bellai Angevin," ix: 165–68)

While Ronsard compares himself positively to Pindar (contrasting himself with Horace who had used the Icarian image to highlight his inadequacy) Du Bellay in Sonnet CXV develops an imagery closer to the Horatian model.

In the entire sequence of *L'Olive* there is a flawed Icarian close.[25] The "cheutes eternelles" of Icarus come to represent Du Bellay's own fear of failure as he attempts to understand and communicate Olive's significations:[26]

Mais (ô moy sot!) de quoy me doy-je plaindre,
Fors du desir, qui par trop hault ataindre,
Me porte au lieu ou il brusle ses aesles?

Puis moy tumbé, Amour, qui ne permet
Finir mon dueil, soudain les luy remet,
Renouvelant mes cheutes eternelles. (Sonnet XXXVII)[27]

The poet fears failing and generally stresses "his own inadequacy," but he is also frightened by the possibility of his success (SDI 78), and of reaching such great heights that his wings will be burned.

Du Bellay is aware that he is being guided by Ronsard. He is Icarus to Ronsard's Daedalus. Daedalus, of course, leads and encourages Icarus, but does not himself fall into the sea (SDI 80–81). The daedalian figure, the poet/craftsman, can soar like the swan. While he is sure of Ronsard's ability to fly, Du Bellay is less certain of his own attempts.

Several years after the publication of *L'Olive*, Du Bellay employs the same imagery with a slightly altered emphasis in *La Complainte du Desesperé*:

> Alors que parmy la France
> Du beau Cygne de Florence
> J'alloys adorant les pas,
> Dont les plumes j'ay tirées
> Qui des ailes mal cirées
> Le vol n'imiteront pas. (ll. 67–72)[28]

Here, in an admixture of arrogance and insecurity, Du Bellay asserts that though he imitates the poetry of Petrarch, he will not imitate the flight and fall of Icarus (SDI 83). While both the arrogance and the insecurity had appeared in *L'Olive*, the poetic voice in the earlier work is not as confident of success. At times in *L'Olive*, Du Bellay suggests that he will equal or surpass the flight of his guide, but then his assertion is tempered with an image of Icarus. When the poet endeavors to fly too high, he is inevitably spurned by Olive or confounded in his attempts to describe her "face excellente."

Petrarchan Labyrinths of Love

The image of the labyrinth and even characters from the Cretan myth were used by Dante in *La Commedia* and by Boccaccio in *Geneology of the Gentile Gods*. But the literary predecessor who had the most significant influence on Du Bellay was Francesco Petrarch. The labyrinth is a central image in Petrarch's work.[29] In *Liber sine nomine* the labyrinth is used extensively as a metaphor for Avignon and its sexual perversions. Avignon is referred to as the fifth labyrinth, a hell on earth created by the lust and deviations of its inhabitants:

> Here is the dreadful prison, the aimless wandering in the dwelling place of shadows, [. . .] tyrannical Minos, and the voracious Minotaur, memorial of forbidden love—but no healing medicine, no love, no charity, no promises worthy of trust, no friendly counsel, no thread as a silent guide to mark the twisted path, no Ariadne, no Daedalus.[30]

The labyrinth is presented as a "prison," a place of "aimless wandering," and a memorial to forbidden love. Avignon, Petrarch asserts, has all the negative qualities of the Cretan labyrinth, but the city is missing the love, counsel, and guidance and other positive elements associated with Ariadne and Daedalus. As such it has become an evil and inescapable trap.

In the *Canzoniere,* Petrarch presents the reader with quite a different *laberinto*. Unlike the lustful prison-maze of Avignon, the *Canzoniere* are created by Petrarch's love for Laura. He enters the labyrinth of his own desire:

> Mille trecento ventisette, a punto
> su l'ora prima, il dì sesto d'aprile,
> nel laberinto intrai, né veggio ond' esca.
>
> One thousand three hundred twenty-seven, exactly
> At the first hour of the sixth day of April,
> I entered the labyrinth, nor do I see where I may get out of it.
>
> (211: 12–14; PRD 364)

But if Petrarch's labyrinth of love for Laura is less lustful and less perverse than the prison-maze of Avignon, it is no less entangling. Errors, knots, prisons, and blindness are recurrent in Petrarch's labyrinth. The narrator's life has been "a long wandering through a blind labyrinth" (224: 4; PDR 380). According to Gaetano Cipolla the labyrinth is the primary emblem for the passion of love in Petrarch's *Canzoniere*.[31] The name Laura itself is related to the Greek word for "passage" (MM 175). Petrarch creates a network of signs around Laura and her polysemous name: "lauro," "l'aura," "l'aurora," "allora." It is this amorous labyrinth which is imitated by Du Bellay.

As the first French sonnet sequence written ostensibly for the love of a woman, Du Bellay's *L'Olive* has often been credited for the success of the love sonnet in sixteenth and seventeenth-century French literature.[32] Although Sonnet I is actually written in imitation of Ariosto's *Quel arboscel che'n le solinghe rive*,[33] the intertext which Du Bellay purposefully calls to mind, and which he hopes to rival in his quest for poetic immortality, is Petrarch's *Canzoniere*. In the preface and within the text itself, Du Bellay clearly asserts that *L'Olive* follows but is not limited by the Petrarchan tradition:

Je ne quiers pas la fameuse couronne,
Sainct ornement du Dieu au chef doré,
Ou que du Dieu aux Indes adoré
Le gay chapeau la teste m'environne. (I: 1–4)

Du Bellay evokes the image of the laurel and, by extension, Petrarch's *Canzoniere*. The famous crown which Du Bellay rejects is the laurel wreath of Apollo. This wreath, an important image in Petrarch, was appropriated from Ovid's *Metamorphoses*. Ovid associates the wreath with Apollo's unsatisfied desire for Daphne who was metamorphosed into a laurel plant (TP 18). The laurel wreath is also symbolic of poetic glory in both Ovid's account and in Petrarch's praise of Laura (TOS 47). Thus, in just two lines, Du Bellay has evoked Petrarch's *Canzoniere*, Ovid's *Metamorphoses*, unrequited love, and poetic glory. But Du Bellay rejects the laurel wreath, and he refuses as well the ivy crown of Bacchus in lines three and four.[34]

In the second stanza, the chain of substitutions and the poetic wandering continues. As with the laurel of Apollo and the ivy of Bacchus, Du Bellay evokes and then rejects Venus' myrtle (DD 403):

Encore moins veulx-je que l'on me donne
Le mol rameau en Cypre decoré:
Celuy qui est d'Athenes honoré,
Seul je le veulx, et le Ciel me l'ordonne.

Du Bellay signifies through periphrasis the plants and their corresponding imageries in order to situate his praise for Olive. He indicates the paths that have been taken before and then deviates from them. Three mythological allusions, three plants, three emblems of glory—all rejected. In their stead he chooses the olive tree of Minerva and Athena.[35] The poet seeks and will honor in his verse the woman for whom this plant is an emblem.

In the final stanza, Du Bellay, who has up to now used periphrasis and allusion, evokes the laurel by name:

> Orne mon chef, donne moy hardiesse
> De te chanter, qui espere te rendre
> Egal un jour au Laurier immortel.

Though Petrarch's Laura is often alluded to in this sonnet and throughout *L'Olive*, the most direct allusion, the laurel, only appears five times.[36] However, Petrarch is imitated and alluded to continuously.

A wonderful example of how Du Bellay arranges sonnets to accentuate the intertextual relations can be found in Sonnets XXXIII and XXXIV. In the first of these there is a rather close imitation of one stanza of a Petrarch sonnet. Du Bellay writes in the second quatrain of Sonnet XXXIII:

> O l'an heureux, le mois, le jour & l'heure,
> Que mon coeur fut avecq' elle allié!
> O l'heureux noeu, par qui j'y fu' lié,
> Bien que souvent je plain', souspire & pleure!

This compares quite well with the first quatrain of Petrarch's Sonnet 61:

> Benedetto sia 'l giorno e 'l mese et l'anno
> e la stagione e 'l tempo et l'ora e 'l punto
> e 'l bel paese e 'l loco ov' io fui giunto
> da' duo begli occhi che legato m'ànno.[37]

Although this is not a translation, the relationship is clear. Also in Du Bellay's Sonnet XXXIII, the narrator for the first time in the sequence is granted a kiss from Olive—a rare occurrence indeed. In Sonnet XXXIV, Du Bellay revels in this triumph when he proclaims:

> Avoir esté par vous vaincu & pris,
> C'est mon laurier, mon triomphe & mon prix,
> Qui ma depouille egale à leurs trophées. (ll. 12–14)

On one level the trophy he celebrates is the kiss of Sonnet XXXIII, but at the same time, he is boasting of his rearticulation of the Petrarchan intertext.

   In the last sonnet of the sequence, Du Bellay again returns to the image of Laura:

> Montre le moy, qui te prise & honnore,
> Pour mieulx haulser la Plante que j'adore
> Jusq' à l'egal des Lauriers tousjours verds. (CXV: 12–14)

Interestingly, just as in Sonnet I, the laurel appears in line 14, and the imagery is expressed in parallel terms. In each of these instances, the major thrust of the sonnet is to render Olive (and her praise-singer) equal to Petrarch's Laura, and thus to immortalize both her beauty and his poetry. Du Bellay asserts that the work will immortalize Olive by singing her praises and making her more famous than Petrarch's Laura. The text becomes the avenue of Olive's immortality.

   The beloved is honored, revered, despised, and dissected. Olive is omnipresent, but she is also surprisingly absent, as she only appears by name twice in the entire sequence. Olive, the name, is conspicuously present through its absence in the text contrasted with its overwhelming presence in the title. She appears constantly either as an idealized notion (metaphorical and mythical) or a substituted part—hair, eyes, a branch, a tree. She is beyond the poet's reach—an inaccessible Other. In L'Olive the heart leads the lover in his amorous wanderings. The pure waiting of desire leads the poet *errant* to quest for "un objet désigné le plus souvent par son absence."[38] The slippage of meaning reflects the process of erring as both wandering and going astray in the labyrinth of love, and the numerous signifiers for Olive lead the reader in all directions through the network of the text.

Giving Presence to the Ineffable

L'Olive is not concerned solely with labyrinths of love and desire. There is another thread which runs through Du Bellay's entire *oeuvre*, a poetic quest—an "unending and increasingly 'laborious' poetic struggle towards an ideal" (TP 43). Du Bellay searches constantly for a poetic style of his own and a poetic ideal which would be capable of carrying his love for Olive. In investigating love from numerous angles, through circuitous, repetitive passages, Du Bellay creates a labyrinth of words.

At the same time, when Du Bellay explores the various approaches to Olive's love, he is delving into the realm of the metaphysical. Olive embodies the neoplatonic ideal of absolute beauty and becomes part of the ineffable center of the labyrinth. Du Bellay's unreachable goal involves the immortalization of Olive in poetry and encompasses the realization of a poetic ideal. Jerry Nash has identified the theoretical conception *illustratio* at work in Du Bellay's sonnet sequence, and he traces its usage backwards from Du Bellay to Quintilian and Cicero. Theoretically, *illustratio* has three senses: to illuminate the object and seek to give presence to the ineffable; to make clear the mind of the subject; and to help the reader see this bright metaphorical presence.[39] Each of these significations is apparent in *L'Olive*. Both the beloved and poetic perfection are connected to *illustratio*. Du Bellay suggests the hope of illuminating the object of contemplation and reaching the ineffable. However, this poetic ideal is presented as ever elusive. Du Bellay recognizes a universal flux which makes reaching a static ideal impossible. Constant variation and movement render poetry and love inexplicable.

The goal of the poet-wanderer would be found in the "face excellente" of Olive. However, it cannot be apprehended by mortals. Faced with the indescribable beauty of Olive, Du Bellay wonders:

> Auray'-je bien de louer le pouvoir
> Ceste beauté, qui decore le monde,
> Quand pour orner sa chevelure blonde
> Je sens ma langue ineptement mouvoir? (Sonnet VIII: 1–4)[40]

He finds himself lacking in his efforts to find words worthy of his beloved, and in the end, he dies without ever saying a word. The poet who seeks to capture the essence of Olive in verse, the hero who searches for the secrets of the labyrinth, and the knight who embarks on a quest for the Holy Grail all share in common a laborious wandering in the face of the ineffable. Du Bellay presents the poet's dilemma as Icarian in nature: "Tu sers d'exemple, à qui ose aspire / Trop hardiment à chose non mortelle" (LI: 13–14). Indeed, the poet will never succeed in grasping the untouchable love object, nor in discovering her higher meaning. The poet's endeavors are rendered "mes entreprises vaines?" (LV: 8). Though Du Bellay imitates the classic works of the foremost poets and artists, art by its very nature can never equal the perfection of the Beloved's beauty:

> L'art peult errer, la main fault, l'oeil s'ecarte.
> De voz beatez mon coeur soit doncq' sans cesse
> Le marbre seul, & la table, & la charte. (Sonnet XIX: 12–14)[41]

The acts of creating are linked to the multiple meanings of error. The poet searches, and the poet is capable of being misled, faltering or deviating, but the beloved's beauty provides a map.

In Du Bellay's poetry, metaphor and myth wander along numerous paths searching for the words which might incarnate these ideals. However, his quest for the ineffable love object leads to a "literary dilemma of the impossible" (NB 15–16), in which he experiences an ineptitude in attempting to express his thoughts to Olive:

> Mais ce m'est bien une douleur plus forte,
> Que je ne puis de ma tristesse enclose
> Tourner la clef, lors que je me dispose
> A vous ouvrir de mes pensers la porte. (Sonnet XXX: 5–8)[42]

The beloved is indescribable, and the writing is itself unable to convey her beauty. Throughout the sequence there are reflexive references to "mes vers," and the literary index is unusually high.[43]

The concept of the poet's powerlessness is emphasized in *L'Olive* with the use of the term "power" and especially its negative manifestations. Various forms of *non-pouvoir* appear fifty-six times in the sequence.[44] This powerlessness is amplified by the depiction of the poet as a prisoner in the inescapable system which his poetry reveals. The narrator is bound and imprisoned by his unreturned love for Olive, by his attempts to describe Olive's ineffable beauty, and by the very nature of the world.

Du Bellay has been drawn into this prison by his own neoplatonic literary pilgrimage, but he has also been led into the labyrinth by Olive's irresistible beauty (KO 56). It is his inability to describe Olive which gives Du Bellay the most frustration. In the labyrinth of words through which he searches to reach Olive, his descriptions constantly err. It is generally Olive's beauty which carries the blame for Du Bellay's condition:

> Lors je fu' pris: & ne me prenoy' garde
> Qu'en mile noeuds lié je me regarde
> En la prison d'une beauté celeste. (LXXXV: 9–11)

Like Daedalus, Du Bellay finds himself a prisoner of his own construction. The poet wonders why he remains in a prison from which it seems he could escape:

> Que songes-tu, mon ame emprisonnée?
> Pourquoy te plaist l'obscur de nostre jour,
> Si pour voler en un plus cler sejour,
> Tu as au dos l'aele bien empanée? (CXIII: 5–8)

Perhaps such a flight would not be an escape at all but would only lead to another labyrinth, or even worse, he might meet the fate of Icarus. But there is also another reason: the obscurity of the day pleases Du Bellay. This is a pleasurable prison he has made for himself, a labyrinth from which he dare not escape for fear of losing the contemplation of his beloved:

> O prison doulce, ou captif je demeure
> Non par dedaing, force ou inimitié,
> Mais par les yeulx de ma doulce moitié,
> Qui m'y tiendra jusq'à tant que je meure. (Sonnet XXXIII: 1–4)

Du Bellay has perhaps been thrust into the labyrinth of love, but the textual labyrinth, through which he wanders in contemplation, is of his own construction. Du Bellay often seems to relish in the prison he has constructed for himself.

Throughout the sequence the narrator wanders on land, sea, or sky:

> Penser volage & leger comme vent,
> Qui or' au ciel, or' en mer, or' en terre
> En un moment cours & recours grand erre,
> Voire au sejour des ombres bien souvent. (Sonnet XLIII: 1–4)

But in the second quatrain of the sonnet, the object of affection becomes an unattainable goal: "Celle beauté tousjours devant toy erre, / Et tu la vas d'un leger pié suyvant" (ll. 7–8). So while Olive is the object of Du Bellay's sonnets, a spiritual quest is undertaken, a quest which encompasses Olive, but which aspires towards the eternal. The poet in his meditations is much like a wanderer, a sailor, or a bird soaring through the sky, and his wanderings are described in terms strikingly labyrinthine:

> Pourquoy suis-tu (ô penser trop peu sage!)
> Ce qui te nuist? pourquoy vas-tu sans guide,
> Par ce chemin plein d'erreur variable? (Sonnet XLIII: 9–11)[45]

Unfortunately, the narrator does not have with him the ball of thread which can lead him back out of the labyrinth. "Erreur variable" is similar to the contemporary notion of *différance*, but with the emphasis placed on wandering signification and the possibility of going astray, rather than on difference and deferral.

Part of the reason why Olive can never be captured and expressed is that the beauties of the "femme aimée" merge with those of nature. Du Bellay writes:

> Si tu la vois, tu verras le soleil
> Du beau visage, à cetuy la pareil,
> Que l'Ocean de ses longs braz enserre. (Sonnet LXXX: 9–11)

The segments of imagery merge into one grand image of beauty. When Du Bellay searches for Olive's love, he is delving into the realm of the metaphysical.

Connections among Olive's perfect beauty, the poet's expression, and natural imagery are first apparent in Sonnet VI:

> Comme on ne peult d'oeil constant soustenir
> Du beau Soleil la clarté violente,
> Aussi qui void vostre face excellente
> Ne peult les yeulx assez fermes tenir. (Sonnet VI: 1–4)

The poet who attempts to look on her great beauties will be wounded, even blinded. Her beauties are comparable to the sun, since no one can behold their brilliance without being blinded, or burned as Icarus was when he flew too close to it. As Du Bellay proclaims in Sonnet XCVIII: "Ne voyant point le Soleil qui m'eclere."[46]

Du Bellay has borrowed from Ariosto's tenth madrigale "Occhi, non vi accongete" the idea that the face of the "femme aimée" is "du beau Soleil la clarté violente"; anyone who regards it for too long or too closely will be blinded by its light.[47] After describing his beloved's dazzling face, the poet-lover questions his ability to praise his beloved adequately, since he cannot even gaze on her as he would like:

Regardez doncq' si suffisant je suys
A vous louer, qui seulement ne puys
Vos grands beautez contempler à mon gré. (Sonnet VI: 9–11)

This sonnet with its preponderance of terms for powerlessness is
indicative of the poet's inability to describe Olive: "ne peult," "Ne
peult," "nuysante, si [. . .] aveugle," "ne puys," "Que si mes yeulx
avoient un tel pouvoir" (NB 16). The use of negative enumeration to
create a progression in the poem had become a common practice
among the Italians, and it was being adopted by poets of the Pléiade
(NB 19).

Whereas the sun represents that part of Olive which is blinding in
its beauty, and which might burn the wings of the poet, the poetic
thoughts and reflections, on the other hand, are more often
connected with water imagery. Icarus when he fails to reach the sun
and the ineffable falls into the sea where he drowns.

Of the prominent nature images in his sonnets, a large number
are associated with water. Water inspires the poet and reflects his
thoughts and sensibilities and at the same time represents *profondeur*.
The feeling of *profondeur* is enhanced by the use of diaphoric images.
For example, Du Bellay employs a juxtaposition of opposites when he
writes:

O fleuve heureux, qui as sur ton rivage
De mon amer la tant doulce racine,
De ma douleur la seule medicine,
Et de ma soif le desiré bruvage! (Sonnet LXXVII: 1–4) [48]

The dialectic between "amer" and "doulce" helps to create a tension
that further emphasizes the poet's entrapment between desire and
suffering. The only medecine which can relieve his suffering and the
only drink which can quench his thirst is unattainable.

Water can be conceived of as reflective of the thought and
sensibilities of the poet:

> Tu ne sens point, quand tu te reposes,
> Plus s'irriter de flotz tempestueux
> Contre tes bords, qu'en mon coeur fluctueux
> Je sen' de ventz & tempestes encloses. (Sonnet XLVIII, ll. 5–8)

The poet's sentiments and the ocean's movements intertwine. The "flotz tempestueux" and the poet's "coeur fluctueux" flow in unison as he searches for reflections of himself, as well as Olive, in the eternal.

Sitting on the bank of a river in reverie, the poet guides the reader on an inner journey, his thoughts meander like the river. The poet searches for sources of inspiration, and often he finds them in allusions to water:

> Loyre fameux, qui ta petite source
> Enfles de maintz gros fleuves & ruysseaux,
> Et qui de long coules tes cleres eaux
> En l'Ocean d'une assez vive course. (Sonnet III: 1–4)

This quatrain stresses the river's movement: "Through verbal action and enjambement, the stream swells into the river and the river flows into the ocean."[49] The water emerging from the spring is similar to the inspiration of the poet, whose thoughts flow and flow, meandering until they reach the ocean. Ultimately water comes from and returns to its source, evoking the cyclical movement of nature. The ocean has also been referred to as the "commencement des choses."[50]

The correspondence between the poet's desired object and the vague contours of the ocean creates a sense of *profondeur*. Because the poet's vision of Olive has merged with nature, his longing for her becomes ineffable. Her essence now joins the rivers flowing through the Loire Valley to meet the ocean and its eternal movement:

> Toy, qui courant à voile haulte & pleine
> Sage, ruzé & bienheureux nocher,
> Loing du destroict, du pyrate & rocher,
> Voles hardy ou le desir te meine. (Sonnet LXXX, ll. 1–4)

Sailing in the ocean of thought, Du Bellay contemplates the "doulce voix" and "beau visage" of his love, but this quickly leads to thoughts of death and of immortality.

The object of affection is always already unattainable:

> O mile fois le bien aimé des Dieux!
> Qui sans mourir, & sans voler aux cieulx,
> Peult contempler le paradis en terre! (Sonnet LXXX, ll. 12–14)[51]

Indeed, the poet cannot grasp the ineffable without first dying. Again the spirit of Icarus is evoked in the flight imagery, symbolizing the spiritual quest undertaken and the aspirations towards the eternal, while at the same time warning that this flight will inevitably lead to a fall.

Imitatio

The first edition of *L'Olive* was published under the same *privilège* as Du Bellay's theoretical text, *La Deffence et illustration de la langue françoyse*.[52] Du Bellay offered *La Deffence* not only as a doctrine of his poetic theory, but also as a manifesto for the Pléiade. In it he attacked many of the poetic practices of the time and suggested a new direction for French poetics.

The major tenets of *La Deffence* include the defense of the French language as a vehicle for poetic expression and assertions that the poet should enrich the poetic vocabulary of French to bring it up to par with the works of the Greek, Latin, and Italian masterpieces, that the direct translation of poetry is to the benefit of neither French literature nor the original text, and that French literature will only excel through the writing of original French poetry which creatively imitates the great classic models.[53]

L'Olive was meant to provide a model for the theory expounded in *La Deffence*. The work is full of classical, Italian, and, in particular, Petrarchan borrowings. There is a constant use not only of Petrarchan diction but also of mythic periphrasis and other poetic devices. However, the single most significant stylistic trait that Du Bellay imitates is the element of structural chaos. As in Petrarch's *Canzoniere*, each sonnet takes a different course and presents different aspects of love, yet the same themes intertwine throughout. The construction of *imitatio* as a labyrinthine poetic practice is not surprising given the preponderance of the image in churches as well as in the literature of the time.

Petrarch's metaphors for the structure of his *canzoniere* include "a labyrinth, a wood, [and] an unpeopled landscape crossed by no paths or by numberless ones."[54] Du Bellay, though reworking these same images, is not as explicit in providing metaphors. It is only in the combination of terminology, mythic allusions, and structural patterns that the image of the labyrinth can be perceived. Of particular note in understanding *L'Olive* as a labyrinthine text is Du Bellay's use of imitative deviation. The works of his predecessors serve as an Ariadne's thread for his writing, yet instead of following the thread directly, he often deviates from the path.

One would expect the sonnets of *L'Olive*, as a poetic model of the theories expounded in *La Deffence*, to imitate classical models but to be French in language, character, and originality.[55] Indeed, Du Bellay's French sonnets are modeled on his Latin and Italian predecessors, and there are consequently numerous classical and particularly Petrarchan devices in *L'Olive:*[56] antithesis, enumeration, cosmic and natural images applied to the personal beauty of the lady, neoplatonist themes of the unattainable mistress, and notions of ideal beauty. However, Du Bellay did not simply borrow style and imagery, he often translated lines or even whole sonnets from another source. Although a standard practice of the time, *imitatio* had its critics, and Du Bellay addressed this fact in his preface:

> Vrayment je confesse avoir imité Petrarque, & non lui seulement, mais aussi l'Arioste & d'autres modernes Italiens: pource qu'en l'argument que je traicte, je n'en ay point trouvé de meilleurs. Et si les anciens Romains, pour l'enrichissement de leur langue, n'ont fait le semblable en l'imitation des Grecz, je suis content n'avoir point d'excuse.[57]

Many of Du Bellay's poems are actually poetically rendered translations of Italian and classical sonnets, which contradicts one of the basic tenets of *La Deffence*. This discrepancy did not go unnoticed. Immediately after *L'Olive* was published, several of his contemporaries complained of a lack of originality in Du Bellay's writing. Guillaume des Autels states the case most succinctly in *Réplique aux furieuses défenses de Louis Meigret*. Guillaume argues that there is little difference between translating and the kind of "imitating" done by Du Bellay, where an entire sonnet of Petrarch, for example, is imitated, except that the imitator may omit the parts that he or she is unable to translate.[58] Another contemporary, Barthélemy Aneau, wrote a commentary on *La Deffence* entitled *Le Quintil horatian* in which he suggested retitling Du Bellay's work the "offense and denigration of the French language."[59]

In fact, out of the 115 sonnets in the 1550 augmented edition of *L'Olive*, only 40 are considered to be original, with most of these being from the new sonnets of the 1550 edition.[60] A majority of the sonnets are at least partly transliterated from Horace, Virgil, Petrarch, and a number of relatively obscure Italian poets. Out of the original collection, around a quarter of the poems are closely translated from *Rime diverse di molti eccellentissimi auttori nuovamente raccolte* collected by Gabriel Giolito de Ferrari. Furthermore, whole sections of *La Deffence* itself are translated into French from an Italian pamphlet, *Dialogo delle lingue* by Sperone Speroni (MNI 48). This is perhaps more shocking in the 1990's than it was in the sixteenth century. Many of Du Bellay's contemporaries were engaged in translating. Speroni himself said of Du Bellay's work that he was glad his book had been of use. What makes it surprising is that Du Bellay seems to argue against this very method.

There appears to be a fine line between creative imitation and translation. What these arguments ignore is that to a great extent Du Bellay does reach the goal he set out for the poet in *La Deffence*. The poet/imitator is one "qui donne foy aux choses douteuses, lumiere aux obscures, nouveauté aux antiques, usaige aux non accoutumées, & douceur aux apres & rudes" (DDI 140–41). French poets, Du Bellay asserts, should create a contemporary national literature. Part of doing this is in celebrating French heroes, cities, and landscapes. But just as important is the creation of new vocabulary and experimentation with language:

> Ne crains donques, Poëte futur, d'innover quelques termes, en un long poëme, principalement, avecques modestie toutesfois, analogie & jugement de l'oreille, & ne te soucie qui le treuve bon ou mauvais: esperant que la posterité l'approuvera. (139–40)

Old words which have fallen into disuse should be revived, new words should be invented, and numerous terms should be borrowed from the classical languages to enrich French.

In general, Du Bellay advises against using Latin and Greek proper names:

> chose vrayment absurde, que si tu appliquois une piece de velours verd à une robe de velours rouge. [. . .] Accommode donques telz noms propres, de quelque Langue que ce soit, à l'usaige de ton vulgaire [. . .] & dy *Hercule, Thesée, Achile, Ulysse, Virgile, Ciceron, Horace.* (141)

Words such as these can be adapted to the French language. Du Bellay also argues against the practice of translating Greek, Latin, and Italian poetry into French, a common practice at the time. Translation, he argues, is clumsy when applied to poetry and can never measure up to the original.[61] Yet the ancients and the Italians have excelled in poetry, and French writers have much to learn from them. Du Bellay offered classical poetry as a model of excellence and as the source of values and standards. So the path to the creation of great French literature lies in imitation of the best Latin, Greek, and Italian poets. Form, style, and symbolism should be imitated, but in French, with French imagery and originality. The poet must choose a model and through creative imitation write something of merit.

Other words can be invented or imitated. But in certain cases, it is necessary to borrow words for which there is no equivalent concept. This is especially true in the realm of poetry where "[il] sera necessaire emprunter beaucoup de choses non encor' traitées en nostre Langue" (DDI 138). The poet often has to use "de motz non acoutumés és choses non acoutumées" (139). Labyrinth is just such a term. Yet even when these terms are utilized, they will be "en notre Langue comme etrangers en une cité: aux quelz toutesfois les periphrazes serviront de truchementz" (59–60). This is at the heart of Du Bellay's conception of imitative translation. The secret of elocution, according to Du Bellay, lies in the use of "methaphores, alegories, comparaisons, similitudes, energies, & tant d'autres figures & ornemens, sans les quelz tout oraison & poëme sont nudz, manques & debiles" (35–36). Rather than attempting word for word translation, which degrades the original poem and accomplishes nothing of literary merit, the learned translator "fist plus tost l'office de paraphraste que de traducteur" (60). Therefore, translation effectively done is more imitation than translation, more reinterpretation than copy.

Du Bellay's understandings of translation and *imitatio* are not unique. The Roman critic, Quintilian, who was a major theoretical inspiration for Du Bellay, asserts: "[An imitator] can never hope to equal [his model] if he thinks it is his duty merely to tread in his footsteps: for the mere follower must always lag behind."[62] Petrarch expresses a similar notion:

> I am one who intends to follow our forebears' path but not always others' tracks; [. . .] I am one who delights in imitation and not in sameness [. . .] I do want a guide who leads me, not one who binds me to him, one who leaves me free use of my own sight, judgment, and freedom; I do not want him to forbid me to step where I wish, to go beyond him in some things, to attempt the inaccessible, to follow a shorter, or if I wish, an easier path, and to hasten or stop or even to part ways and to return.[63]

A poet cannot simply follow in the footsteps of the great writers, especially when these models are written in another language. The writer who attempts this will always be a pale reflection, a shadow. But the poet who, guided by these writings, finds new and interesting paths to explore has more chance of achieving brilliance.[64] Not only does Du Bellay acknowledge that he is guided by his predecessors, he hopes that he has traced a few new paths himself:

> et quasi comme applanir le chemin à ceux qui, excitez par mon petit labeur, voudroient enrichir nostre vulgaire de figures et locutions estrangeres, je mis en lumiere ma *Deffence et illustration de la langue françoise.*[65]

Du Bellay's "little labor" follows the traces left by Virgil and Petrarch, but he does not limit himself to the paths they have taken.

The imitative techniques employed by Du Bellay differ depending on whether he is using a major or a minor source.[66] When Du Bellay is imitating a Petrarchan sonnet, he will often loosely translate the first stanza and then deviate from the model. These imitations are not always easily discernible, as is the case for the first quatrain of Sonnet LXXXV:

> Parmy les fleurs ce faulx Amour tendit
> Une ré d'or legerement coulante,
> Soubs les rameaux d'une divine Plante,
> Ou de pié coy ce cruel m'atendit. (ll. 1–4)

> Amor fra l'erbe una leggiadra rete
> d'oro e di perle tese sott' un ramo
> dell'arbor sempre verde ch' i' tant' amo,
> ben che n'abbia ombre più triste che liete.
> (*Canzoniere* CLXXXI)[67]

Though there are distinct differences between this stanza and the lines by Petrarch which have inspired them, there are definite connections. The commonality of themes, word choice, and movement indicate that Du Bellay had Petrarch's sonnet in mind when he composed this poem, but this is not a mere translation of text. The rest of the sonnet "diverges from its Petrarchan intertext" (DV 133–38). Du Bellay has allowed his model to guide him to an extent, entering the poetic realm along the same route, evoking similar imagery and mood, but ultimately exploring its own paths.

Du Bellay often uses Petrarchan images, such as the laurel, for rhetorical effect. In some instances a single sonnet of *L'Olive* contains a mixture of images, themes, and phrases drawn from more than one Petrarchan sonnet. Another method of imitation utilized by Du Bellay involves combining selections from several quite distinct sources. In Sonnet V of *L'Olive*, the quatrains are inspired by the text of a sonnet from Petrarch's *Canzoniere*, while the tercets are an imitation of Ariosto.[68] Although the quatrains of Petrarch are not translated by Du Bellay, they are an undeniable intertext for the sonnet.

C'etoit la nuyt que la Divinité	Era il giorno ch' al sol si scoloraro
Du plus hault ciel en terre se rendit,	per la pietà del suo fattore i rai
Quand dessus moy Amour son arc tendit	quando i' fui preso, et non me ne
Et me fist serf de sa grand' deité.	guardai,
	ché i be' vostr' occhi, Donna, mi
	legaro.
Ny le sainct lieu de telle cruaulté,	Tempo non mi parea da far riparo
Ny le tens mesme assez me deffendit:	contr' a' colpi d'Amor; però m'andai
Le coup au coeur par les yeux descendit,	secur, senza sospetto, onde i miei guai
Trop ententifz à ceste grand' beauté.	nel commune dolor s'incominciaro.
(L'Olive V, ll. 1–8)	*(Canzoniere* III, ll. 1–8)[69]

Du Bellay laments that it was on Christmas night, the eve of Christ's birth, that love finding him defenseless shot him with her bow. For Petrarch, it was on Good Friday, the day of Christ's death, that love found him defenseless and bound him. Du Bellay is obviously echoing Petrarch in his pronouncement of the time of *inamoramento*, and at the same time he is altering, even reversing, the Petrarchan intertext.

With the minor sources, on the other hand, Du Bellay is more likely to imitate an entire sonnet, and the translations are generally much closer to the original text.[70] Still, even when Du Bellay chooses to translate an entire poem, he does so selectively, and despite what his critics maintain, even these imitations of minor poets are far from simple translations. Sonnet XXIV exemplifies the kind of imitation Du Bellay undertook with sonnets from the Giolito anthology.[71] The poem is a close translation of a sonnet by Batista Dalla Torre. The translation is not word for word, but it follows the original, until the final stanza. In the last verse Du Bellay deviates from Torre's sonnet in declaring that the beauty of Olive outshines that of Narcissus. By extension, Du Bellay implies that his sonnet is an improvement on the original poem which he is imitating. The poet imitates a model, but sheds new light on the object of contemplation.

Structuring Chaos

Within this seeming chaos there does appear to be a trajectory, albeit a rather roundabout one. Caldarini suggests that there is a distinct neoplatonic descent and return in *L'Olive*, a progression which he refers to as *circuitus spiritualis* (DOC 35). With all of the intertextual and intratextual references, the language and imagery of the sonnets twists and turns, doubling back in a pattern like a web or, indeed, a labyrinth. The themes, structures, and words are repeated over and over again but each time in new combinations. This repetition creates "structural patterns that unify the macrotext" (KO 29). Du Bellay's relationship with Olive is manifested in an ever-changing network of variations, with continually renewed patterns reaching beyond the text to intertexts which come both before and after *L'Olive*. The poet's opinions and concerns about love, the beloved, and the world are constantly changing, contradicting, repeating, and overlapping.

Katz has asserted that in *L'Olive* a repetition of terms and images combines with structural patternings to give the sequence an order and a unity (KO 25). He suggests that the first four sonnets serve as a matrix presenting all of the "rhetorical figures most common to the sequence" as well as "every dominant theme and motif of the entire collection" (KO 26). Indeed, the themes evoked in the introductory sonnets are found throughout the sequence, and they set the tone for the entire collection (KO 26). For instance, in the first sonnet there is an emphasis on periphrasis, metaphor, and antonomasia, the link between Olive and the tree,[72] the correlation between Olive and Laura, the search for immortality, praise for Olive, and the frustrations of love, all of which recur regularly in the sequence. At the same time, other significant themes, including the search for the ineffable, the Icarian flight, and death, are introduced later in the work. The repetition of words, motifs, and themes is undeniably significant in *L'Olive*; they form the threads which lead the reader through the text.

At the same time, nothing is static. There is a constantly shifting chain of signifiers. Even when the same concepts are rearticulated, it is the variations on structures and themes which are most significant. Immortality is a strong theme in the introductory matrix and indeed throughout the sequence. In Sonnet I, Du Bellay asserts that the work will immortalize Olive by singing her praises and making her more famous than Petrarch's Laura. The text becomes the avenue of Olive's immortality. When we look at those other sonnets which specifically relate the verses of the poetic *oeuvre* to Olive's immortality, an interesting structural pattern is discernible.

In the original collection Sonnet LIX was the concluding sonnet.[73] It is significant that this last sonnet of the first edition became part of the center in the revised edition, thus revealing the cyclical nature of the poetic quest. Sonnet LIX also asserts the aim of immortalizing Olive. However, Sonnet LIX does not stand on its own in the revised version of *L'Olive*. A related group of sonnets has been created in the center of the sequence, in which the idea of the poetic function of granting immortality again takes precedence. Katz calls attention to this "central, complex cluster" which begins with Sonnet LVIII and runs through Sonnet LXIV (31). There is a consistency of theme, a common explanation of the more literary aspects of Du Bellay's poetry, which binds these sonnets together.

In the revised edition, Sonnet LVIII was inserted before LIX, and this was not an arbitrary decision on Du Bellay's part. Sonnet LVIII holds the collection's first explicit treatment of neoplatonic concepts in *L'Olive*:[74] "De mon esprit les aesles sont guidées / Jusques au seing des plus haultes Idées / Idolatrant ta celeste beaulté."[75] Not only does Du Bellay indicate that his poetry consists of the highest ideas idolizing Olive's celestial beauty, he also lets the reader know that they have reached the center. One major difference between the introductory matrix and the center cluster is the theme of flight. Flight, which is intricately tied to death, is also the most direct path to the ineffable and immortality.

In Sonnet LXI, links between the verses of *L'Olive*, the beloved, and the quest for immortality are explicit:

> Allez, mes vers, portez dessus voz aeles
> Les sainctz rameaux de ma plante divine,
> Seul ornement de la terre Angevine,
> Et de mon coeur les vives etincelles.
>
> De vostre vol les bornes seront telles,
> Que des l'aurore, ou le Soleil decline,
> Je voy desja le monde qui s'incline
> A la beauté des beautez immortelles. (ll. 1–8)

Poetic immortality is directly tied to the beauty of the beloved. Sonnet LXI also hints at the success of the 1549 edition. This theme is extended in Sonnet CXV, which also connects poetic immortality to Laurel and Du Bellay's attempt to equal or surpass his Italian predecessor.[76]

The first, middle, and last sonnets all relate the poetry to Olive's qualities and thus afford her poetic immortality. The middle sonnets and the final sonnets both pursue poetic immortality through flight. The first sonnet and the last sonnet both seek to elevate Olive to a status equal to that of Petrarch's Laurel. Therefore, the sequence contains a consistency, a progression, and a return—a structure reflective of the trajectory of the labyrinth.

Du Bellay presents 115 variations on his love for Olive. Some of these passages are original, while others are imitations. But they all have in common the fact that they present a quest for an ideal. However, unlike Theseus, Du Bellay does not think that he will be able to reach the ineffable center of the labyrinth and escape unscathed. He implies that his fate will be more like that of Icarus. The image of Icarus is offered, not only as Du Bellay's personal assessment of his own situation as he aspires to the heavens, but also as a symbol of the ineffability of a poetic ideal. The poet's attempt to capture the ineffable in his writings cannot succeed. However, he employs the concept of *illustratio* in his struggle to articulate the inexpressible. In so doing, he creates images which reflect not only the physical world, but also an inner vision of the human predicament.

Chapter 2

The Contemplative Wanderings of Théophile de Viau and Saint-Amant

Labyrinths are common in the baroque aesthetic, which developed parallel to and intertwined with the continuation of the later Renaissance. They appear in art, in religious and alchemical theories, and in the architectural designs of churches and gardens. The Cretan maze also appears frequently in seventeenth-century literature. It was during the baroque period that the labyrinth became an established metaphor for the entanglements of love, building upon the imagery already utilized by the writers of the Pléiade. The confusing qualities of love were the primary theme in works such as Le Villain's *Labyrinthe de Récréation* (1602) and Fornier's *Le Labyrinthe d'Amour* (1610). However, the labyrinth in the baroque aesthetic reaches beyond the effects of love. The world itself is now perceived as maze-like and transitory.[1]

The baroque aesthetic is exemplified by *trompe-l'oeil, mise en abîme*, anamorphosis, illusion, and paradox. All of these diverse elements are connected by a concern with the manipulation of the conventions of linear perspective.[2] Movement in this baroque aesthetic involves reversals, reflections, and entanglements to such an extent that the labyrinth becomes a ready figure for the world. The ineffable, the sublime, and the grotesque are used imaginatively to interlace myth, science, music, and art into the intricate discourse of the text.

In the art of the classical Renaissance and the baroque, there is a proliferation of labyrinthine images.[3] The baroque poet tended to view the knowledge of art as essential to any understanding of the world and its representations; thus the era's artistic trends were extremely influential on the writer's craft. Saint-Amant, for example, asserts a strong relationship between poetry and art:

> Il est presqu'impossible de faire d'excellens vers, à cause de l'harmonie et de la représentation, sans avoir quelque particulière connoissance de la musique et de la peinture, tant il a de rapport entre la poésie et ces deux autres sciences qui sont comme des cousines germaines.[4]

The perspectives afforded by art and music contribute to Saint-Amant's conception of the harmonies and rapports he seeks in his poetry. The interconnectedness of the disparate elements of the world is revealed through the exploration of all of their attributes and serves to evoke strange and enticing worlds.

The symbol of the church labyrinth, "le chemin de Jérusalem," significant since the Middle Ages, is readily utilized in baroque literature. The connections which have developed between the labyrinth and spiritual progression are close ones.[5] Because the earth is understood to be home to the fallen—a place of deception and sin—the poet is often compelled to undertake a pilgrimage, seeking both to regain the freedom of Eden and to attain the celestial City of God.[6] The poet wanders through the labyrinth of the world in search of salvation.

Although the influence of the church labyrinth persists, the most striking visual labyrinths in the baroque period are those in the gardens of French aristocracy.[7] These maze gardens borrowed the figure of the church labyrinth but endowed it with new attributes and significations. Bartlett Giamatti has suggested that the garden in general serves as a master-image for "both the fallen and splendid order of creation."[8] Eden, the archetypal garden, exists at the center of the Cosmos. In baroque poetry, where landscapes are frequently utilized as literary symbols, the garden becomes both an abstract representation of the cosmos and a standard metaphor for the terrestrial Paradise. In the garden, one can escape from worldly problems and meditate or recuperate from the stresses of life. The garden in the baroque aesthetic is a piece of heaven on earth. The gardens designed by Bernard Palissy, André Mollet, Androuet du Cerceau, and André Le Nostre, to name but a few of the era's landscape architects, utilize shifting and multiple perspectives to "transform nature into a place of enchantment and marvelous visions."[9] While the garden as a whole was often seen as symbolic of paradise, two specific features are especially emphasized in this regard: grottoes, which serve as microcosms of the terrestrial paradise, and garden mazes, which represent the path towards celestial paradise.

The figures of the grotto and the labyrinth at first glance would seem to be quite distinct. On the mythopoeic level, however, there are many commonalities. Especially, in the context of the garden, the two images have connotations of paradise, and both are related to contemplation. The major symbolic distinction between the grotto and the labyrinth involves the concept of movement. While the grotto evokes the reflective meditation of rest, the labyrinthine imagination involves difficult movement.[10] In many ways the grotto is synonymous with the center of the labyrinth.

The use of grottoes in formal gardens reached France from Italy in the mid-sixteenth century. By the early seventeenth century, they had become fashionable. Charles VIII redesigned his gardens at Amboise to include a grotto reflecting the Earthly Paradise. François I, Richelieu, and the Duc de Guise were among the many who added grottoes to their gardens. These grottoes also held fountains, streams, waterfalls, and statuary.[11] Palissy's grottoes, including those at Tuileries and Ecouen, were typically decorated with "polychromatic ceramics"[12] depicting mythical beings, reptiles, fish, water-fowl and sea creatures.

Palissy, a reknowned designer of grottoes, conceived of the Renaissance garden and particularly its grotto as an imitation of "Earthly Paradise" (BM 54). The person who sits in the grotto is able, at least theoretically, to contemplate with the innocent freedom and abandon once experienced by the inhabitants of Eden. As a figure of the terrestrial paradise, the grotto represents a paradise lost (these grottoes were generally built on Roman ruins or simulated ruins). However, the creatures which inhabit this realm are not what one would expect to encounter in an Eden. The grotto is a place of beauty, but through illusion it is designed to thrill and to create a fearful pleasure.[13] The elaborate and ornate design of the grottoes served to bewilder and amaze the spectator. Ronsard, for example, describes the effect of the grotto of Meudon quite explicitly as causing visitors to stand in amazement.[14] The grotto and the grotesque create a site which is at once a place of rest and a place of marvels which cause the mind to wander.

While the image of the garden/grotto as paradise was expanding during the Renaissance, another mythic image, the labyrinth, was also being incorporated into the landscape of the garden.[15] The maze garden represented a different aspect of paradise. The labyrinth reflects the confusions of the world, yet at the center one finds the "ciel" or "Jérusalem." While Eden, the terrestrial paradise, is a bit of heaven on earth, the celestial paradise signified by the center is another earth in the heavens. According to biblical references, the Holy City, the New Jerusalem, will descend from the heavens at the end of time after the apocalypse. This celestial paradise is not a return to an ideal past but rather a projection into a future without precedent (DS). Thus the labyrinth is symbolic of worldly confusion, but at its center is the space where heaven and earth will meet.

The gardens of many French aristocrats in the Middle Ages included *dédales*. The labyrinth of the Hôtel Saint Paul in Paris (1360s) is the earliest mention of this feature in any French garden. Other early maze gardens include one at Rouvres (1372), one which was dismantled at the Hôtel des Tournelles in 1431, and one which was rebuilt at Baugé in 1477 (DIL 107; MM 165). By the late sixteenth century, landscape architects were creating mazes for many of the most renowned gardens of Europe. The popularity of maze gardens grew until, in the mid-seventeenth century, they had become so much the fashion that it is hard to find a garden listed in Du Cerceau's *Architecture* in which there is not some form of maze.[16] Some of these maze gardens are unicursal, whereas others have numerous intersections and crossroads. There are rounded mazes and those full of right angles. Du Cerceau's labyrinths generally include both circular and square features. The labyrinth at Chantilly had a pinwheel shape (see Figure 3); that at Choisy-le-Roi includes a spiral and several intertwining paths. Although some of these mazes are quite complex, others are only mildly puzzling. Many of the mazes featured statues, fountains, and ornaments. All share in common the need to wander through the twisting paths. Often the route will double back, and more than likely, the wanderer will become perplexed or lost. With its bewildering twists and turns, the labyrinth signifies the search for salvation through the confusions of the world. These maze gardens were actually often referred to as the "wilderness" (MML 127), not because they were untamed, but rather reflecting their bewildering attributes. In his contemplative wanderings the baroque poet was drawn to the garden with its grottoes and mazes.

"La Maison de Sylvie" and "Le Contemplateur": Movement and Confinement in the Baroque Labyrinth

Théophile de Viau's "La Maison de Sylvie" (1624) and Saint-Amant's "Le Contemplateur" (1627) both employ a poetic style and imagery reflective of the Renaissance garden. In particular, the two poets emphasize in their poems the importance of contemplative wandering, the resulting sense of wonder and amazement, and the shifting specular images of the self and other encountered in the maze.

Théophile de Viau was born in 1590 in Gascony to a Protestant family of the *petite noblesse*. In his youth, Théophile traveled with a troupe of wandering actors, writing plays for them. By 1616, he had settled in Paris, where he became a popular court poet and was especially favored by young noblemen. He enjoyed immense success, but this was not to last. His writings were considered too libertine by several powerful members of the court, and in 1619, he was exiled from Paris for a year. The Italian philosopher Vanini, whose work greatly influenced Théophile, had recently been executed in Toulouse, and Etienne Durand, a member of the same literary circles, was put to death for his political intrigues. If not for Théophile's popularity and his protectors in the court, he might have suffered a similar fate.

Banishment did nothing to lessen Théophile's popularity, and in fact when he returned to Paris in 1620, he was more popular than before.[17] However, Théophile had also gained strong critics, to whom he refers in "La Maison de Sylvie":

> Certains critiques curieux
> En trouvent les moeurs offensés
> Mais leurs soupçons injurieux
> Sont les crimes de leurs pensées. (IV: 31–34)[18]

Among his enemies was the Jesuit Priest Garasse, who was instrumental in eventually having Théophile tried in absentia and condemned to death.

Théophile was warned of his impending execution, and in 1623, he took refuge with Marie-Félice des Ursins and her husband the Duc de Montmorency at their estate in Chantilly. In "La Maison de Sylvie" Chantilly is referred to as the place:

> Où la vertu se réfugie,
> Et dont le port me fut ouvert
> Pour mettre ma tête à couvert
> Quand on brûla mon effigie. (I: 7–10)

While at Chantilly, Théophile resided in the Maison de Sylvie, a small house which had been constructed in 1604 to the east of the chateau. Théophile was under the protection of Marie-Félice, and it is to her that the Sylvie of the poem ostensibly refers.

As a medieval fortress, Chantilly had been built in a watery marsh area for added protection. During the early Renaissance, under a unified monarchy, the water was used instead for ornamental purposes.[19] Fountains, streams, and standing bodies of water became integral to the gardens. In the sixteenth century, Androuet du Cerceau transformed the old fortress of Chantilly for Guillaume de Montmorency.[20] Of course, the Renaissance gardens were often huge productions containing elements added and redesigned over the years so that, in effect, the gardens were never the work of one person or one group but instead reflect a medley of voices. Gardens were constantly being re-designed. The gardens for which Chantilly is most famous were designed by André Le Nostre, who was in charge of their reconstruction for the Grand Condé in 1670. Le Nostre's garden included a spiral course for the game of "goose" and a pinwheel labyrinth.[21]

> Au-delà de cette maison, encore, dans le "Parc de Sylvie," parmi les bosquets découpés établis par les soins de Le Nostre, l'on trouve les bosquets de Thésée et d'Ariane, le "carré de l'Arquebuse," "formé d'une croix de gazon avec des allées d'épicéas terminées par des portiques de maçonnerie" (pour le jeu), et le Labyrinthe, tracé par Desgots (1679).[22]

Whether La Nostre and Desgots were influenced by the connections between Théophile and the gardens cannot be ascertained. However, at the very least, when they designed the gardens to include a labyrinth and groves named after Theseus and Ariadne, these landscape architects were responding to the same aesthetic trends and the same paradigm.

The created whole of Théophile's text reflects the labyrinthine in its singular image of movement and intersecting passages. The speaker and the reader move constantly through the shifting world. At times the movement doubles back, retracing former paths: "Errant avec de faux plaisirs / Sur les traces des vieux désirs / Que conserve encore son âme" (III: 98–100). Always moving, but not necessarily moving forward, the reader passes through the "chemin des cieux" (II: 85), "allées vagabondes" (VI: 114), the "vertueux sentier" (X: 51), and "promenoirs" (X: 63) in his or her journey. Théophile presents the reader with a poetic world which is diverse and mobile. The name Théophile chooses for the voice of the narrator in the poem is Damon (IV: 100), an anagram for *nomad*, as well as *monad*. He is a man in exile, a wanderer seeking sanctuary, in the garden which is a microcosm of the world.

Théophile's writing has been referred to as kaleidoscopic or haphazard, but his own description of how a bee makes its honey or a bird its song best conveys his poetic aesthetic:

> Comme en la terre et par le ciel
> De petites mouches errantes
> Mêlent pour composer leur miel,
> Mille matières différentes,
> Formant ses airs qui sont ses fruits,
> L'oiseau digère mille bruits
> En une seule mélodie. (IX: 91–97)

Diverse materials, sounds, and movements flow in harmony, in a single melody—not simply in the images evoked, but also in the poetic elements. Alliteration and rhyme serve to reinforce the symbolism of the stanza, each section of which has a certain isolation like separate paths, yet the routes taken by these *mouches errantes* intersect in numerous ways.

The general rhyme scheme of the stanza is ABABCCDEED— *rime alternante*, couplet, *rime embrassée*. In the first three lines, there is an alliteration of the [p] sound: "par," "petites," "pour," and "composer," which also delineates the *rime alternante*. But there are other internal rhymes which both add to the movement and interweave the two major images of the bees making honey and the bird's song. The [m] sound runs through the entire sentence: "comme," "mouches," "mêlent," "miel," "mille," "matières," "mille," and "mélodie." Within this sequence there is an even richer alliteration which combines the [m] and the [l] sounds: "mêlent," "miel," "mille," "mille," and "mélodie." Then, there is an alliteration/assonance of the consonant vowel combination [ɛR]: "terre," "errantes," "matières," "airs," and "digère." There is also an alliteration of the [s] sound, which begins in the first line with "ciel" but becomes more significant in lines 95 through 97 (and carries over into the last three lines of this stanza). Finally, there is a visual alliteration in lines 91 ("comme [. . .] ciel"), 93 ("mêlent [. . .] miel") and 95 ("formant [. . .] fruit"). Separate ideas are connected through the repetition of the same structure. The rhythm itself wanders, intersects, reaches a momentary respite in the center, then moves on to new paths, creating a poetics of deviation. Both sound and visual qualities of the text contribute to the full effect of the stanza, weaving and structuring the disparate notions into a single melody.

Guido Saba suggests that Théophile has a "besoin d'exprimer avec sincérité tous les mouvements, sentiments et idées qui occupent son esprit."[23] Théophile does not so much imitate nature in his writing as he does freely express all that he sees and feels. Therefore, beauty is found not in a single image but in the total combination of images. The sentiments which are aroused within him cannot be limited any more than can his thoughts. For Théophile it is Sylvie who gives movement to the world: "Elle donne le mouvement / [. . .] à chaque élément" (VII: 25–26), and if he mixes so many diverse elements in the words that he addresses to Sylvie: "C'est que ma voix cherche des traits / Pour un chacun de vos attraits" (IX: 45–46).

Théophile has been thrust into his labyrinth out of necessity. He expresses the feeling of being trapped in a maze of love, friendship, imprisonment, and death. He reminisces over lost love, specifically that for Phaeton, the Icarian figure who plunged into the sea. Full of melancholy, Théophile retraces old desires, his mind wanders, and he errs, deceiving himself with false pleasures (III: 98–100). His poem has a serious tone, understandably so, as he has only barely escaped death himself.[24] He sees the beauty as well as the horror around him, and if Chantilly is his refuge, he realizes that it is also "ma prison" (VI: 13). Eventually, Théophile was captured and placed in a real prison. Although his allies in the court managed to stay the execution, Théophile spent two years (1624–25) in the Conciergerie. Some debate has occurred as to where Théophile de Viau actually was when he composed the ten odes entitled "La Maison de Sylvie." Whether he wrote the entire piece while in prison or had already commenced writing at Chantilly before his arrest, it is obvious that in the poem the two settings are used to compliment and contrast each other, and they are each reflected in the development of the imagery.

Various descriptions in the poem can be ascribed directly to the gardens of Chantilly. The first ode, for example, explores the "promenoirs merveilleux," the "fontaines," and the "arbres" (I: 85–90). Even when Théophile refers to the prison, he evokes visions of Chantilly:

> Encore dans ces lieux d'horreur
> Je ne sais quelle molle erreur
> Parmi tous ces objets funèbres
> Me tire toujours au plaisir,
> Et mon oeil qui suit mon désir
> Voit Chantilly dans ces ténèbres. (VIII: 95–100)

In the prison, the place of horror, his contemplative wanderings lead him back to Chantilly, back to the garden. Again, *erreur* is double-voiced, signifying both the wandering of thought and mistaking of the prison shadows for the sanctuary he desires. Likewise, though the verse constantly praises Marie-Félice and her gardens, much of the imagery utilized involves the theme of entrapment or imprisonment. The poetry explores the beauty of the gardens, intertwining myth with descriptions of the park, but this is constantly countered by the suffering and the imminent danger which hovers over the poet's head. In Chantilly, Théophile finds respite from the labyrinth of the world, but the center is for him still part of the maze. Following his imprisonment, Théophile was sentenced to ten years of banishment from Paris. The sentence was not rigidly enforced, but Théophile's health had been ruined while in prison, and he died a year later in Paris, on September 25, 1626, at the age of thirty-six.[25]

Saint-Amant was both a colleague and an admirer of Théophile. He had written of Théophile: "Ce grand et ce divin Oracle / Qui fait voir en tous ses propos / Les effets de quelque miracle."[26] Marc-Antoine de Gérard, sieur de Saint-Amant was born in Rouen in 1594 into a prosperous Protestant merchant family. He traveled extensively in his youth visiting the Canaries, West Africa, and the Caribbean aboard his family's merchant ships. He arrived on the Parisian scene around 1619, where he gained success due to both his

poetry and his skill on the lute.[27] Saint-Amant continued to travel
extensively during his lifetime—to Morocco, England, Rome, Corsica,
and Sweden.[28] One of Saint-Amant's patrons was the Duc de Retz.
Saint-Amant wrote many of his poems while staying on Retz' estates
in Brittany, especially the one on Belle-Isle off the southern coast.
"Le Contemplateur" specifically explores Saint-Amant's private
promenades on Belle-Isle: "Loin, dans une isle qu'à bon droit / On
honora du nom de Belle."[29]

Saint-Amant is in a less precarious situation than Théophile. The
scene for his contemplation is not a refuge but merely a beautiful
setting from which he can gaze out at the sea or at the land as his
pleasure leads him. Still the fate of his friend Théophile and the
politico-religious milieu encouraged Saint-Amant to convert from
Protestantism to Catholicism. Saint-Amant refers to Philippe
Cospeau, Bishop of Nantes, who oversaw the poet's conversion as the
"cause du salut de mon ame" (l. 4). The three dedicatory stanzas were
likely added for ulterior motives. They are full of praise for Cospeau
and do not really mesh with the tone and imagery of the rest of the
poem.

Saint-Amant's interest in grottoes and the grotto-esque was well
known. On Belle-Isle there was a certain grotto favored by Saint-
Amant, which as a result became known as "la grotte de Saint-Amant"
(BM 46). In 1634, Saint-Amant, who was a founding member of the
Académie Française, was asked to write the definitions for "les mots
grotesques" for the Académie's first dictionary. In his two most
famous works "La Solitude" and "Le Contemplateur," the figure of
the grotto is prominent.[30] But Saint-Amant does not limit himself to
the grotto; the labyrinth also figures in his promenade. In fact, an
analogy can be made between Belle-Isle and Crete, the *homme marin*
and the Minotaur, and Saint-Amant himself and Daedalus soaring on
wings above his creation.

The poetry of Saint-Amant reflects a world infinite in its
dynamic movement. The passages of "Le Contemplateur" move in a
circular fashion through a number of oddly connected images and a
torrent of words which Saint-Amant refers to as the "flus et reflus":

> Là, songeant au flus et reflus,
> Je m'abisme dans cette idée;
> Son mouvement me rend perclus,
> Et mon ame en est obsedée. (ll. 91–4)

The poet's search parallels his poem—it is perhaps eclectic, but it is not without direction. Saint-Amant's poems are full of movement in time as well as in space. He mixes different moods in close juxtaposition, from the serious to the grotesque, to the *précieux*, to the love of mystery and *trompe-l'oeil*.

The material world forms a base from which the poet's contemplative wanderings depart:

> Nature n'a point de secret
> Que d'un soin libre, mais discret,
> Ma curiosité ne sonde;
> Ses cabinets me sont ouvers,
> Et, dans ma recherche profonde,
> Je loge en moy tout l'univers. (ll. 85–90)

Every subject, no matter how trivial it may seem, is open to the poet's probing. A dove, a sea-shell, a glowworm. . . the small elements of nature can trigger a whole stream of consciousness. The sunrise, for example, can lead the poet to a memory of Michelangelo's "Judgement Day," which can in turn lead to the poet's apocalyptic vision. It may seem at first that there is no design in the poet's wanderings, that he is merely presenting a "sequence of striking and seemingly illogical visions, a flow of disparate fragments."[31] His thoughts wander down numerous paths, sometimes doubling back, other times branching off in another direction, like the maze-walker trying out the *fausses pistes* of the labyrinth. There does, however, seem to be a unity to the poem. When he lodges within himself all the universe, the speaker creates a unification of awareness.

The dialectic which develops between the structural unity of the cosmos and the image of indirection and chaos felt by the speaker reflects the figure of the labyrinth. When he plunges himself into the idea, Saint-Amant finds that its movement renders him paralyzed. He is overwhelmed but wishes more than ever to learn its secrets. He realizes all the while that he cannot know the first thing about it and "qu'on se pert à le chercher" (l. 100). In the very next stanza, he marvels at the use of the compass, the image of direction. This is, after all, the age of exploration, and Saint-Amant was a seafaring man. The complex patterns of this stanza demonstrate the labyrinthine links constructed in the poem:

> Là, mainte nef au gré du vent
> Sillonnant la plaine liquide
> Me fait repenser bien souvent
> A la boussole qui la guide;
> La miraculeuse vertu
> Dont ce cadran est revestu
> Foule ma raison subvertie,
> Et mes esprits, en ce discort,
> S'embrouillent dans la sympatie
> Du fer, de l'aymant et du nort. (ll. 101–10)

The rhyme scheme seems rather simple at first glance: ABABCCDEDE; *rime alternante*, couplet, *rime alternante*. But the linguistic patterns are quite intricate. First, there is a plethora of alliteration, especially of [s], [l], and [d]. Interestingly, the [l]'s are stressed in the first half of the stanza, while the [d] sound is prominent in the second half. Also of note is the fact that the [y] sound appears in the first line, as the end rhyme of the center couplet, reappears in the telling "subvertie," and finally, is stressed twice in the last line.

The rhyme scheme and the complex *réseau sonore* constitute the threads which intertwine and give a labyrinthine structure to the stanza. There are other instances of alliteration and assonance in this stanza: the [i] sound, the [ɑ̃], the [m], the [vɛ], the [ɔ̃], and the [z]— all of which serve to add flow and rhythm to the stanza. But perhaps the most intriguing patterning occurs at the end of each line. "Du vent" changes to "souvent," keeping the [vɑ̃] and slightly modifying the [y] sound to [u]. "Vertu" then mirrors the [y] and shifts from the [vã], sound to [vɛ]. Significantly, "revestu" inverts the "ver" of "vertu" while retaining the [ty]. It is in this center couplet that the paths of the poem intersect. A second path of the poem moves from "liquide" to "la guide." After the center couplet, the sound patterns are shifted for the remaining end-rhymes. "Subvertie" inverts the [y] and the [vɛ] sounds, combining them with the [i] sound from "liquide" and "la guide." "Sympatie" then retains both the alliteration of the [s] and the [ti]. The other post-center pathway reflects the [d] sound from the end of "guide" to become the initial sound and recovers the silent [t], and the alliterative [s] from "souvent." The [o] sound in "discort" seems at first to have appeared from nowhere, but looking more closely, there is a pattern here as well. The [y] taken in combination with the [i], [o], and [i] in lines 102, 103, and 104 has been dropped after the central couplet, so that in lines 107, 108, and 109, we have [i], [o], and [i] instead. Thus, there is symmetry, progression, and shifting which recur in the sound patterns of the stanza. Overall the effect of the patterning is to create a structured chaos and to emphasize the movement through the text. In the final line the pattern has gone almost full circle, and he is back where he started: "du vent" has become "du nort." A *logodaedalia* or labyrinth of words deflects the poet back to the beginning.

Saint-Amant is like Daedalus looking down on the Isle from the heights of the sky. His perspective is such that he must lower his gaze to see the bird's flight: "Où pour voir voler les oyseaux / Il faut que je baisse la veue" (ll. 43–44). From above he peers down on Thetis' prison. The ocean, a place of continual movement, is nevertheless confined to its place, and Thetis and his minions are confined to the ocean, but Saint-Amant reminds us of a time when this was not the case. During the deluge both the ocean and the creatures that dwell in it broke free from their prison (ll. 51–60). On this momentous occasion, humans were plunged "dans les abismes" (l. 59). Only Noah and his entourage were able to avoid the abyss, and they were also confined in a "logis flotant" (l. 63). Confinement and movement, ascent and descent—Saint-Amant plays with the "polyvalent connotations of these images."[32] Images of fall and descent are conveyed through terms such as "choir," "plonger," "descendre," "sonder," "s'abimer," and "tomber." Noah's ark floats above the mountains, descending finally to rest on the mountain summit. Saint-Amant himself, after soaring above the world, must take an indirect route, descending so that he may ascend again:

> Tantost, faisant agir mes sens
> Sur des sujets de moindre estofe,
> De marche en autre je descens
> Dans les termes du philosophe. (ll. 81–84)

He descends into a journey that is both Dantesque and reminiscent of the "descent into the darkness of the Platonic cave."[33] Unlike the humans plunged into the abyss, Saint-Amant writes: "je m'abime dans cette idée" (l. 92).

The world is presented through a torrent of imagery and ideas. Movement becomes the only constant in a transitory world. The poet's contemplative wanderings take as a point of departure the observation of nature, which arouses emotions, and the "stream of sensations becomes a stream of consciousness" (KL 13). Mobility is felt in the action of the poem; for instance, his account of fishing on Belle-Isle is "full of movement: the rowing of the boat, the trolling of the line in the water, the noisy swimming of the fish in pursuit."[34] This mobility is felt equally in the flow of the narration. One thought leads to another, each image linked to others both before and after it.

It is diversity and the flow of life which lead to the unification of awareness and the *moment privilégié*. Saint-Amant writes:

> Mon esprit changeant de projet,
> Saute de pensée en pensée.
> La diversité plaist aux yeux,
> Et la veue en fin est lassée
> De ne regarder que les cieux. (ll. 136–40)

In the movements of the heavens the patterns of unified diversity can be seen. Saint-Amant often refers to paths in the sky. Aside from the biblical connotations of the celestial paradise, Saint-Amant was well aware of the scientific aspects of astronomy. He is reputed to have had long conversations with Galileo in Siena. One of the greatest influences on Saint-Amant was Giambattista Marino, who also lived in Paris from 1615–1623. Marino's concept of *maraviglia*, which relates amazement to the movements of the heavens and the human effort to understand them, was especially influential on Saint-Amant's poetics. In the mythical, the biblical, and the scientific understandings of the movements of the planets and the stars, the labyrinth is an allegorical intertext for the interlacing routes followed by the heavenly bodies which Saint-Amant refers to as: "du ciel les glorieuses routes" (l. 374).

Saint-Amant and Théophile each undertake a contemplative quest through vividly depicted and wondrous worlds. Yet they take very indirect routes, for in a labyrinth nothing can be reached directly but only in a roundabout way. The language of the poems is maze-like with numerous twists and turns. In his profound search, the poet lodges within himself the entire universe. The poet wanders through the garden—the representation of paradise on earth—a reflection of the cosmos. At the center of the maze garden is the meeting place between celestial and terrestrial. Here myth meets reality. Théophile contemplates the garden of Chantilly and the world from a prison cell. Saint-Amant contemplates gardens and the world from the "wilderness" of Belle-Isle. In both poems the images of movement and confinement vacillate, each image reflecting the other, to create a complex and shifting figure of the world.

Amazement / Sense of Wonder

A strong etymological thread connects the concepts of amazement, maze, and labyrinth. The word "amaze" derives from the Old English *āmasian*, meaning to "confuse."[35] In the thirteenth century both a verb and noun form appeared which dropped the "a-." The verb form signified "to daze," and the noun form "delusion" or "delirium." Gradually by the late fourteenth century "maze" had come to mean a "structure of bewildering complexity."[36] Until this time, a "maze" was more a state of mind than a physical manifestation. But given that both signifiers were connected to bewilderment and confusion, the maze began to draw on the figure of the labyrinth for its substance, and the various forms of the word "maze" came to be associated with labyrinthine traits. The term "amazement" by the seventeenth century had come to signify that state of astonishment associated with being in a perplexing structure like a labyrinth. In the Baroque aesthetic the world itself reflects the bewildering complexities of a maze.

A sense of wonder is created in baroque poetry through the "interpenetration of the real and the mythical."[37] The gardens of Chantilly, where Théophile de Viau takes refuge, merge with the mythopoeic realm. Numerous mythological figures inhabit the spot which the poetic voice first advances as a place of solitude and tranquility.

Swans are not merely swans, and deer are not merely deer; nothing is limited to what it at first might appear to be. The most striking aspect of both "La Maison de Sylvie" and "Le Contemplateur" is the expression of amazement before the riches of nature. Baroque literature is often said to exhibit a love for exclamation, and this is certainly evident in Saint-Amant's poem:

> O bon Dieu! m'escriay-je alors,
> Que ta puissance est nonpareille
> D'avoir en un si petit corps
> Fait une si grande merveille! (ll. 221–30)

Even the smallest detail of nature, such as the glowworm which Saint-Amant contemplates, contains wonders which can bewitch our eyes. Saint-Amant "delights in the *merveilleux*."[38] Much of this wonder stems from paradox: that something so small can perform such a great marvel, that fire can burn without consuming.

Imbrie Buffum has stressed the importance of the theme of illusion in the poem. He gives the example of the fish that "thinks he is chasing prey, but is really about to be caught himself" (KL 17). The sea bream sees the string that has been laid for it and:

> Aussi tost nous suit à la trace.
> Son cours est leger et bruyant,
> Et la chose mesme qu'il chasse
> En fin l'attrape en le fuyant. (ll. 207–10)

In this inversion of the image of the guiding thread, the fish pursues the string which catches him by fleeing from him. The element of amazement or astonishment is extremely important to Saint-Amant's poetic style and appears throughout "Le Contemplateur."

Théophile de Viau is also amazed by what he finds in the gardens of Chantilly. Illusion, paradox, and wonder all serve to mirror the poet's enthrallment with nature, and nature in its turn expresses wonder in contemplating Sylvie:

> Elle fait qu'abordant la nuit
> Le jour plus bellement décline.
> Le Soleil craignait d'éclairer
> Et craignait de se retirer,
> Les étoiles n'osaient paraître,
> Les flots n'osaient s'entrepousser,
> Le zéphyre n'osait passer,
> L'herbe se retenait de croître. (II: 13–20)

Nature is so astounded by the beauty of Sylvie that even the most basic of phenomena curtail their natural functions out of amazement.

The baroque poets worked with perspective using metaphor and analogy to draw out the reflections between disparate items. Significantly, "mirror" [*miroir*], "marvel" [*merveille*], and "miracle" all arise from the same classical Latin root word *mirari*.[39] *Mirari* can itself be traced to the Indo-European term *smei-/smi-*, the same root for the English "smile," but which carried connotations of "being amazed."[40] The relationship between the labyrinth and the mirror extends beyond etymological connections, for "the minotaur [. . .]

will, if perceived carefully enough by Theseus, reveal itself as a fulfilling mirror, as the completion of the self in the other."[41] In both "Le Contemplateur" and "La Maison de Sylvie," the personae come face to face with other manifestations of self in encounters with the metamorphosed beings.

Saint-Amant writes of the *homme marin*: "Bref, à nous si fort il ressemble, / Que j'ay pensé parler à luy" (ll. 179–80). Saint-Amant's Thetis and Théophile's Tritons fulfill similar functions. In gazing upon them the poet actually reflects on whatever image of self he can see in them, which consequently "gives rise to a strange ambiguity: one sees a reflection that is simultaneously oneself and another."[42] In exploring his friendship with Tircis, Théophile remarks that:

> Nos influences enlacées
> S'étreignent d'un même lien,
> Et mes sentiments ne sont rien
> Que le miroir de ses pensées. (IV: 67–70)

The two friends see themselves in each other. Théophile uses interlacing alliteration to enhance the mirroring of the two men. The [m] and [s] sounds form an interesting pattern: s z s z / s m m / m s m s / m s s. The [n] sound and especially the assonance of the [ã] further interweave the elements of the passage. The stylistics create echoes and rhythms reinforcing the imagery of the mirror and the "influences enlacées."

The self-reflecting image is a major theme in the two poems. With kaleidoscopic mobility, poetic thought wanders through a labyrinth of shifting images of self and other. Animate and inanimate objects alike gaze at their reflections in these poems. Nature serves as a mirror in many ways, but water is the most common reflective surface—"ces miroirs flottants / Où l'objet change tant de place" (I: 101–2). The reflective properties of water are frequently utilized as metaphors for the inconstancy of the world in seventeenth-century French poetry.[43] Water, whose stability is one of constant movement, is the perfect image for such an aesthetic creation. Saint-Amant actually presents his world as a kind of convex mirror, *la plaine liquide.*[44] Each image reflects both that which precedes it and that which follows. The entire text mirrors reality, but in such a way that it is transparent, intangible. The concept of reflection constantly in motion complements well the perplexing movements within the labyrinth.

In "La Maison de Sylvie" the images used convey the idea not simply of a mirror but of a mirroring which is itself in transition and which will only reflect a fixed image for Sylvie herself:

> Je sais que ces miroirs flottants
> Où l'objet change tant de place,
> Pour elle devenus constants
> Auront une fidèle glace. (I: 100–10)

For anyone else the reflections are constantly shifting, but for Sylvie the mirror gazes back at her steadily.

The ultimate subject of self-reflection, Narcissus, is frequently utilized as an image in baroque poetry. In Ovid's retelling of the myth of Narcissus, there is an oscillation between "images of fluid insubstantiality and hard substance,"[45] between bodies and reflections. Narcissus, having rejected Echo (an auditory mirror) and everyone else who would love him, comes upon a clear pool of water. Worn-out by the heat and the hunt, he lies down to drink from the still body of water and becomes enthralled with the beauty that has enflamed everyone around him. In a peaceful, idyllic setting, he falls in love with his own image and drowns himself. The object becomes the subject, and though the two can never meet, they are trapped by their desire. A real union with the other would vanquish love, which thrives on the separateness of the beloved.

It is fitting that the mirror image is the ultimate reflection of Théophile's balancing of contraries. And water, which is in constant movement, is the perfect image for such an aesthetic creation. Théophile recalls the story of Narcissus and his obsession with the mirroring of his own image:

Le garçon qui se consuma
Dans les ondes qu'il alluma,
Voit là tous ses appas renaître,
Et ravi d'un objet si beau,
Il admire que son tombeau
Lui conserve encore son être. (VI: 45–50)

What is especially interesting about Théophile's echoes of the myth is the idea that the reflection becomes both his tomb and his place of rebirth, that which consumes him and that which guards his very being.

Center and Metamorphosis

In the Cretan myth, Theseus encounters the Minotaur, a monstrous reflection of self, at the center of the labyrinth. The idea of center is always integral to the labyrinth image. Georges Poulet suggests that the aim of all baroque poetry involves two contrary movements which cross over one another and find a meeting place, the "infinite center."[46] Chantilly gardens serve as a center of sorts, a sacred space created by the poet. The center is a place where all the contrary images meet. However, the center is still within the labyrinth—it is a trap as much as it is an escape. There is an interpenetration of the violent and the idyllic. Images of separation, loss, or violent conflict appear in virtually every stanza of the poem (CR 129), and they conflict with and at the same time enhance the images of love, friendship, and tranquility.

Rather than two contrary movements intersecting in the "infinite center," there appear to be numerous movements, some of them contrary, flowing through these poems. When the paths of two contraries cross, it creates intense imagery, but the movement, the flow of words, does not stop. An intersection is reached, but the infinite center is still elusive.[47] For Théophile, contrary emotions often go hand in hand. Wonder and horror, joy and sorrow, tranquility and movement co-exist in "La Maison de Sylvie." Forces which would generally be considered antagonistic are balanced. Harmony is not achieved in the poem, nor perhaps is it even desired, but rather a world is depicted where harmony and disharmony cannot be separated.

This phenomenon is evident in Saint-Amant's contemplations when his thoughts lead him to Michelangelo's "Last Judgement." He writes that the famous artist

> N'a rien tracé d'émerveillable
> Que ce penser de l'advenir,
> Plein d'une terreur agreable,
> Ne ramene en mon souvenir. (ll. 327–30)

The term "tracé" is significant here as it refers not merely to Michelangelo's painting but also to the traces which connect the various movements of the verse. Thoughts of the future spark memories of the past. Saint-Amant offers an apocalyptic moment, horrific yet wondrous—a moment remembered though it has not yet occurred.

The day of the Apocalypse will be the day Saint-Amant reaches the center of the labyrinth: "Et pense voir en appareil / Espouvantable et magnifique / JESUS au milieu du soleil" (ll. 338–40). The celestial paradise following the Apocalypse will transcend all tradition and replace the order of the world as we know it. Saint-Amant's *moment privilégié* is in part the result of a meeting of opposites. Numerous reversals will occur in that moment. The old will regain their youth, the crippled will be cured, but also the rich will lose their wealth. Paradox is an important concept in Saint-Amant's poetics, but even more significant is the meeting of two contraries in a single space: "S'escoute, à demy transporté, / Le bruit des ailes du Silence, / Qui vole dans l'obscurité" (ll. 248–50). The beautiful imagery in these lines exists largely because of the balancing of contraries.[48] Such a tendency is common in the baroque aesthetic, and in the writings of Saint-Amant and Théophile de Viau, this tendency becomes the norm.

The center of the baroque labyrinth is a place where all the contrary images meet. Intruders into this space will experience the ultimate movement, metamorphosis. Unlike *trompe-l'oeil*, where an event or object becomes confused or interchangeable with another, in metamorphosis the object actually changes (often into its opposite). Metamorphosis in the labyrinth relates specifically to the ritual rebirth of the wanderer who does not emerge from the maze unchanged. Images are not merely transitory and reflective—they are also transformed. Metamorphosis provides Théophile with "the trope par excellence to express change, transformation, and uncertainty of form."[49] The greatest sense of wonder in this poem stems from the combined beauty and horror of metamorphosis, which becomes an important metaphor for Théophile's poetic practice. The Tritons who wander too close to gaze upon Sylvie's beauty find themselves metamorphosed into stags:

> Chacun d'eux dans un corps de daim
> Cache sa forme dépouillée,
> S'etonne de se voir cornu,
> Et comment le poil est venu
> Dessus son écaille mouillée. (II: 36–40)

In their transformation they feel that they have been deceived and betrayed. The metamorphosis is a "cruel affront" (l. 41), yet the Tritons are torn between sadness and joy:

> Ils s'estiment heureux pourtant
> De prendre l'air qu'elle respire,
> Leur destin n'est que trop content
> De voir le jour sous son empire. (ll. 71–74)

Truly they have been changed, but the entire world has been transformed with them. The Tritons are faced with conflicting emotions, and when they are transformed into stags, they come to be trapped as much by their emotions as by their new shapes. Philomèle, who has been raped and whose tongue has been cut out, now is a nightingale and sings her lamentations. Cygnus mourns Phaeton's death so intensely that he is metamorphosed into a swan, and the

swans that swim peacefully on the water have as their origin Cygnus'
bereavement (RT 125). The tranquility of the scene is contrasted
with the sadness of past forms. Images of separation, loss or violent
conflict appear in virtually every stanza of the poem (CR 129). In
this realm of paradox and metamorphosis, the poetic voice discovers
that any boundaries between self and other are actually in flux. Like
Théophile's poetry, the swans come into being through a tragic
event.

Death and metamorphosis are directly related to the eternal
renewal of nature. This renewal holds some joy, but it also inevitably
retains its sorrow. The avian metaphor can be traced to Horace's
Odes as well as the metamorphosis into a swan. In the case of Horace,
metamorphosis is also linked to language and, therefore, to the
writing of the poem. Metamorphosis allowed Horace to "transcend
time and space: he will live on through his poetry, symbolized by the
swan who soars to every corner of the known world" (RT 124).

Théophile has adapted both the imagery and the poetic
implications, though he reminds himself of Icarus and his ill-fated
flight for freedom.[50] Like Icarus imprisoned in the labyrinth,
Théophile feels captive among the *promenoirs* of Chantilly gardens.
Death or imprisonment are certain for Théophile if he leaves his
sanctuary, yet he still holds some hope that by "suivant le vertueux
sentier" (X: 51) he may attain his goal:

> Implorons sa divine grace
> D'imprimer toujours devant nous
> Les marques d'une heureuse trace:
> C'est elle qui doit nous guider. (X: 102–5)

However, grace seems not to have guided him on the lucky path, for
Théophile died within a year of his release from prison.

In the baroque aesthetic, even death, which is sometimes seen as
the final labyrinth, does not halt the transitory nature of life. Death
imagery, funerary objects, and tombs are prevalent in both poems. In
Saint-Amant's apocalyptic vision: "Tout est destruit, et la Mort
mesme / Se voit contrainte de mourir" (ll. 439–40), yet the poem

defies the ability of the void of death to surpass the infinity of life. In Nature, as we have seen, there is eternal renewal. Saint-Amant suggests in the paradox above that when death dies, eternity will live on. He asks God to:

> Accorde-moy par ta bonté
> La gloire de l'éternité,
> Afin d'en couronner mon ame;
> Et fay qu'en ce terrible jour
> Je ne brusle point d'autre flame
> Que de celle de ton amour. (ll. 445–50)

Indeed nothing in the natural world offers a way out of the labyrinth of life and death. The only paths which afford such a liberty are the immortality attained through faith and the love of God, and the figurative immortality transmitted by the poem itself.

Théophile and Saint-Amant create verse which flows through a hundred seemingly disparate images, interlacing contraries in a singular labyrinthine image. Their poems mirror reality like the image reflected in water—intangible and transitory. Yet like the song of Théophile's bird, which "digère mille bruits / En une seule mélodie" (IX: 96–97), beauty exists in the total combination of images.

Chapter 3

Guidance and Error in Affairs of Love:
Ariane, *Bajazet*, and the Knotted Thread

Early in the year 1672, two tragedies premiered at the Hôtel de Bourgogne in Paris: Thomas Corneille's *Ariane*[1] and Jean Racine's *Bajazet*.[2] By the end of February, the two plays, each exploring the tragic entanglements of love, power, and deceit, were being performed in the theatre on alternating nights. According to Voltaire, although *Bajazet* was written in a higher caliber of verse, as dramas the two were highly complementary. He suggests that *Ariane* and *Bajazet* "expriment les mêmes sentiments et les mêmes pensées."[3] Indeed, although *Ariane* is simpler in style and metaphor, it was extremely popular and "balança beaucoup la réputation" of Racine's more complex play.[4]

One of the most significant parallels between *Ariane* and *Bajazet* is the conception of the knotted or ineffectual thread. In the myth of the Cretan labyrinth, it is the love and grace of Ariadne in the form of the thread that allows Theseus to find his way back out of the labyrinth. A shift occurred in the focus of the mythic intertext in the classical tragedy of the seventeenth century, and the amorous events which take place after the flight from Crete become more significant than the heroic feat. The guiding thread in these dramas tends to be severed rather than continuing to bind Thésée and Ariane together, or conversely, in the labyrinth of love, the thread proves to be faulty, even deadly.

The action in Corneille's *Ariane* is explicitly connected to the myth of the labyrinth, though the story is refigured with the focus on the affairs of the heart which occur after fleeing from Crete. Ariane, who has guided Thésée from the labyrinth, is subsequently abandoned and descends into an abyss from which there is no escape. Racine would deal explicitly with the Cretan myth in *Phèdre* (1677). However, it is *Bajazet* which proves to be the most labyrinthine of Racine's works. In *Bajazet* the characters live in a subterranean prison of confining walls and circuitous passageways that are both physical and psychological. Atalide attempts to provide the imprisoned hero with a thread which might lead him to freedom, but instead of guiding him, this thread becomes knotted around his throat and strangles him.

Abandoning Ariadne

During the seventeenth and eighteenth centuries, close to forty European operas centered on the story of Ariadne's abandonment. *Arianna a Nasso* (1608), set to music by Claudio Monteverdi, was the first of these productions. *Arianna* is largely credited with reviving interest in the Cretan myth.[5] It also signaled the refocusing of the action away from Theseus' defeat of the Minotaur to the subsequent affairs of love.

In retellings of the myth prior to the seventeenth century, Phaedra and Theseus meet many years after the ordeal in the labyrinth, and their love has nothing to do with Ariadne's abandonment. Alexandre Hardy's *Ariadne ravie* (1624) was one of the first texts to connect the two stories in print. In Hardy's retelling Phaedra flees Crete with her sister and Theseus and wins the hero's heart.[6] *Ariadne ravie* is one of the primary intertexts for *Ariane*, but other contemporary retellings also influenced Corneille's play. Donneau de Visé, a friend of Corneille's, had penned *Le Mariage de Bachus et d'Ariane*, a spectacular play which was performed at the theatre of the Marais a month prior to the first showing of *Ariane*. Corneille might also have been aware of Calderon's *Los tres mayores prodigios* (1636), the second "panel" of which retells the story of Ariadne.[7] In addition, Thomas Corneille was primarily influenced by his brother Pierre and by the classical tragedies of Jean Racine. Indeed, Corneille applies the rules of classical theatre to the popular new versions of the Ariadne story resulting in one of his greatest popular successes.

The plot of *Ariane* is simple, yet the events which precede the opening act and the character traits which make the plot possible are constituted by complex detours and reversals. Before the action commences, Ariane already has saved Thésée from the labyrinth—and for this he owes her everything. She has betrayed her father and her country to save the life of this man. Out of a sense of duty, Thésée has promised to marry her, but in the meantime his heart has wandered. Thésée and Phèdre in secret and against their wills have fallen in love. So Thésée, ostensibly awaiting the arrival of his friend Pirithous, has been stalling his marriage to Ariane.

Everyone in the drama expresses love in a roundabout way. Thésée speaks words to Ariane that are in his heart meant for her sister. Oenarus, the king of Naxos, pines for Ariane but cannot proclaim his love for her. He believes that he has no chance of winning her heart because Thésée and Ariane are thought to be so much enthralled with one another. So Oenarus only confides his love to Phèdre. Ironically, Thésée wishes that Oenarus would declare his love for Ariane so that breaking with her might be easier. Thésée cannot tell Ariane that he loves someone else; instead he attempts to guide her heart in other directions. When Pirithous reaches Naxos, Thésée convinces him to help manipulate Ariane's love in the direction of the king.

The signifier "labyrinth" is used in the verse to denote both the physical structure on Crete, from which Ariane delivered Thésée, and as a metaphor for the state of confusion and deceit which now surrounds the characters, especially Ariane. The sentiment expressed by Oenarus when he learns of Thésée's treachery recurs throughout the play. He exclaims: "Un si grand changement ne peut trop me surprendre, / J'en ai la certitude, & ne le puis comprendre" (IV:1). Ariane faces several great reversals in her fortune. All of the characters are amazed by the unforeseen detours which occur in the unfolding of the drama.

The state of confusion in which the characters operate is repeatedly evoked through the concept of erring. In the final scene of the play, Ariane plaintively asks herself: "Mais quelle est mon erreur?" (V:6). She has been threatening Thésée and suddenly realizes

that he is not in the room. So taken in context, her error might refer
to her seemingly delusional state. But on a larger scale, since betraying
her father, Ariane has become "errante, abandonnée" (III:3). She has
erred both in trusting her sister and in loving a man who does not love
her—"Ma rivale, & mon traître, aidés de mon erreur" (V:5). But her
overriding mistake, her "erreur fatale" (II:5) is that her passion has
blinded her to what is actually happening around her.

In the midst of this confused wandering, each character searches
for paths that suit his or her own passions and needs. In furthering
their "desseins," they also seek to guide others. Ariane has erred in
her choices, but she has also been misled. Indeed, the greatest
dichotomy in the drama exists between following and going astray,
between guidance and error. The theme of guidance is firmly
connected to Ariane and her famous thread. When she could have left
Thésée to perish in the labyrinth, instead she guided him out: "Par
moi, par mon amour, le labyrinthe ouvert" (III:4). As a result,
everyone believes that Thésée and Ariane are bound together by love
and obligation. This is accepted as a truth by everyone (except
Thésée and Phèdre, and even they are uncertain). As Arkas says to
Oenarus:

> Vous sûtes que Thésée avoit par son secours
> Du labyrinthe en Créte évité les détours,[8]
> Et que, pour reconnoître un amour si fidéle,
> Vainqueur du Minotaure, il fuyoit avec elle.
> Quel espoir vous laissoient des noeuds si bien formés? (I:1)

The same thread that guided Thésée out of the labyrinth is thought to
have metaphysically bound them together. Yet Arkas' words are as
full of polyvalent twists and turns as the labyrinth from which Thésée
escaped. Arkas uses "vainqueur du Minotaure" as a euphemism for
Thésée and "un amour si fidéle" refers to Ariane. But this periphrastic
signifier is not fixed. Thésée did meet a faithful love on his flight
from Crete. However, it was Phèdre rather than Ariane. And though
we can take Arkas' use of the metaphor of the intricate knots to
signify that Thésée and Ariane have been bound together by love, as

it turns out, another interpretation holds more validity. The thread that Ariane used to lead Thésée out of the labyrinth has become knotted by the complicated affairs of the heart.

Although Thésée had earlier stated that the heart cannot be guided, he attempts to influence Ariane to love Oenarus. When Pirithous questions the reasoning behind stalling the wedding, Thésée explains that he wanted to:

> Flatter l'espoir du roi, donner temps à sa flamme
> De pouvoir, malgré lui, tyranniser son ame,
> Gagner l'esprit de Phédre, & me débarrasser
> D'un hymen dont peut-être on m'aurait pû presser. (I:3)

He tries to guide the actions and the hearts of Oenarus, Phèdre, and Ariane. The one who was guided out of the labyrinth now attempts to be the guide. He has taken on the "Ariane" role, but ironically, to guide her away from him; thus he functions in effect as a labyrinthine detour. Pirithous, as he has reluctantly promised Thésée, also tries to guide Ariane, but she will not believe the implications of his words. Frustrated with his role as messenger and unwanted guide, he finally tells her: "Je me tais, c'est à vous à voir ce qu'il faut croire." (II:5). But Ariane, not liking the guidance she receives from Pirithous, seeks it elsewhere.

Ariane asks Phèdre to help lead Thésée back to her. She insists that if Phèdre had ever experienced love, she would know what Ariane was going through and could better convince Thésée to return:

> Hélas! Et plût au ciel que vous sûssiez aimer,
> Que vous pûssiez savoir par votre expérience
> Jusqu'où d'un fort amour s'étend la violence!
> Pour émouvoir l'ingrat, pour fléchir sa rigueur,
> Vous trouveriez bien mieux le chemin de son coeur,
> Vous auriez plus d'adresse à lui faire l'image
> De mes confus transports de douleur & de rage;

Tous les traits en seroient plus vivement tracés.

N'importe, essayez tout, parlez, priez, pressez. (II:7)[9]

Ariane unknowingly turns to her rival for aid. Phèdre does in fact know what Ariane is feeling, and she already knows the path to Thésée's heart. For her part, Phèdre is torn between duty to her sister, whom she has always followed faithfully, and her love for Thésée. She even attempts to talk Thésée into staying true to Ariane, albeit half-heartedly.

Near the end of the play, in desperation, Ariane turns to Thésée for guidance in her attempt to find out who her rival is:

Mais ce n'est pas pour vous que j'y puis prendre place,

Si l'infidélité ne vous peut étonner,

J'en veux avoir l'exemple, & non pas le donner.

C'est peu qu'aux yeux de tous vous brûliez pour une autre,

Tout ce que peut ma main, c'est d'imiter la vôtre,

Lorsque par votre hymen m'ayant rendu ma foi,

Vous m'aurez mise en droit de disposer de moi. (IV:4)

Ariane's plan for guidance is double-edged. She criticizes his actions by asking Thésée to lead her in infidelity and treachery, and though she does not necessarily intend to follow his example, she hopes that Thésée will guide her to her rival.

Thésée and Phèdre both feel remorse at having fallen in love. Thésée owes an obligation to Ariane for helping him kill the Minotaur and escape from the labyrinth:

Il est vrai, tout sans elle étoit désespéré.

Du succès attendu son adresse suivie,

Malgré le fort jaloux, m'a conservé la vie,

Je la dois à ses soins; mais par quelle rigueur

Vouloir que je la paye aux dépens de mon coeur? (I:2)

Thésée is torn between duty and passion. He owes Ariane his life, for when he was lost in the inextricable maze, she guided him out. But he has erred in both senses of the word. His heart has wandered, and morally he has chosen to go astray.

Thésée understands that Ariane now faces death, and he assumes enough responsibility to try to bind her to Oenarus who has the power to protect her:

> Sa fuite de Minos allume la colère,
> Pour se mettre à couvert elle a besoin d'appui,
> Le roi l'aime, faisons qu'elle s'attache à lui. (I:4)

But Thésée does not realize that in the labyrinth of love which Ariane has entered, he is the monster, and it is not physical protection alone that she needs. Abandoning her family and her country, she has entered this labyrinth to be with him:[10]

> Te suivre, c'étoit plus que me voir couronner?
> Fatigues, peines, maux, j'aimois tout par leur cause.
> Di-moi que non, ingrat, si ta lâcheté l'ose;
> Et, désavouant tout, éblouis-moi si bien,
> Que je puisse penser que tu ne me dois rien. (III:4)

She was content to be in exile as long as she could find a center and a place with Thésée. Again, Thésée has become her guide. But he is not leading her out of a maze, rather he is merely detouring her. As it becomes apparent that this center is no longer within her reach, Ariane vacillates between lucidity and madness (MA 66). She asks:

> Sur le gouffre des maux qui me vont abîmer,
> Pourquoi m'ouvrir les yeux quand je les veux fermer?
> Hélas! Il est donc vrai que mon ame abusée
> N'adoroit qu'un ingrat en adorant Thésée?
> [. . .] Mais quand elle s'égare,
> Pourquoi la regretter, cette raison barbare,
> Qui ne peut plus servir qu'à me faire mieux voir
> Le sujet de ma rage & de mon désespoir? (II:6)

She does not want to know the truth, nor even to be sane if the truth is that Thésée has abandoned her. Thésée has led her down the "détours si bas" into the abyss. She has put her life on the line and sacrificed everything for love only to find herself in "un revers si cruel" (II:6). Betrayed by both her lover and her sister, she now wanders around the palace "errante, interdite, abattue" (V:1).[11] In her vengeful insanity, she accepts the abyss, the labyrinth into which she has been thrust. She can even accept death:

> Ma mort n'est qu'un malheur qui ne vaut pas le craindre,
> Et ce parjure amant, qui se rit de ma foi,
> Quoiqu'il vive toujours, ne vivra plus pour moi? (V:1)

The one thing that could relieve her own suffering would be to see Thésée suffer as well, but it is too late—he is gone from her reach.

Phèdre's Labyrinth

Racine would later explore the mythic motif of the labyrinth in *Phèdre* (1677).[12] The labyrinthine aspects of this tragedy are explicit and have been covered by a number of critics. Maria Assad asserts that "La tragédie *Phèdre* est un labyrinthe textuel construit autour d'un monstre, Phèdre."[13] L. R. Muir examines the leitmotif of the monster in the labyrinth.[14] Nina da Vinci Nichols analyzes the transformation of the Ariadne myth in the play.[15] And Mathew Senior suggests that the labyrinth was originally the result of disordered desire.[16] In the Cretan myth, errant love (and its result—the Minotaur) was held in check by sacrifice until it could be destroyed by Thésée. Phèdre refigures this disorder, thereby creating a new metaphoric labyrinth.

The characters in *Phèdre* are lifted straight from the Cretan myth. Phèdre is daughter to Minos, sister to Ariane and the Minotaure, and wife to Thésée. Though the action takes place after the escape from the labyrinth, the myth is figuratively re-enacted in the course of the play. Phèdre attempts to recast the characters of this earlier episode, first by imagining Hippolyte as Thésée and herself as Ariane. She suggests that Hippolyte would easily have killed the Minotaure and found his way through the maze with the thread that she would have provided.[17] Then Phèdre recasts herself again in the role of the hero, who would not merely have provided Hippolyte/Thésée with thread, but rather would have rushed into the labyrinth and killed the Minotaure herself:

> C'est moi, prince, c'est moi dont l'utile secours
> Vous eût du labyrinthe enseigné les détours.
> Que de soins m'eût coûtés cette tête charmante!
> Un fil n'eût point assez rassuré votre amante:
> Compagne du péril qu'il vous fallait chercher,
> Moi-même devant vous j'aurais voulu marcher;
> Et Phèdre au labyrinthe avec vous descendue
> Se serait avec vous retrouvée ou perdue. (II:5, ll. 655–62)

Thereafter, even if they were forever lost in the labyrinth, Phèdre asserts, whatever happened would make no difference, for they would be together.

However, conscious that she is Hippolyte's stepmother, Phèdre shifts again and offers him a way out of the labyrinth by leading him to the Minotaure (for the hero cannot leave the labyrinth without first defeating the monster)—which in this case is Phèdre herself:

> Digne fils du héros qui t'a donné le jour,
> Délivre l'univers d'un monstre qui t'irrite.
> La veuve de Thésée ose aimer Hippolyte!
> Crois-moi, ce monstre affreux ne doit point t'échapper;
> Voilà mon coeur: c'est là que ta main doit frapper.
>
> (II:5, ll. 700–04)

She implores Hippolyte to kill her so that he can escape from the passionate labyrinth into which she has thrust him. Hippolyte, however, refuses to kill her and seeks another way out. In fact, in *Phèdre*, though both Thésée and Hippolyte are capable of dealing with a physical monster, neither is capable of combatting or even recognizing a metaphysical one (MM 7).

The dual themes of guidance and misguidance are quite abundant in *Phèdre*. In fact, Phèdre often attempts to do both at once: "Je t'en ai dit assez pour te tirer d'erreur" (ll. 670–71). This results in a prominence of the state of being lost. Variants of "perdre" alone appear seventeen times in the play.[18] *Phèdre* is Racine's best known treatment of the labyrinthine themes of guidance and error, yet years before, Racine had presented another piece of dramatic verse which explored the labyrinth as both metaphor and tragic site. In the seraglio of *Bajazet*, Racine developed a maze both internal and external of unparalleled proportions.

Amante éperdue

Bajazet is the sixth of Racine's eleven tragedies and unique for Racine in that it was inspired by stories of contemporary events. Racine sets all of his other tragedies in the mythic past. *Bajazet*, in contrast, is set in seventeenth-century Turkey. However, as he explains in his second preface: "Nous avons si peu de commerce avec les princes et les autres personnes qui vivent dans le sérail, que nous les considérons, pour ainsi dire, comme des gens qui vivent dans un autre siècle que le nôtre."[19] Because of its spatial and cultural distance from his audience, Racine believed that the Turkish setting could hold the mythic allure usually reserved for antiquity. The Turkish people, he suggests, are contemporary ancients. He implies that there are parallels between the lives of these people and those of the Greeks and Romans. There is nothing explicit in *Bajazet* that shows an authorial intent to present the seraglio as a Turkish equivalent to the labyrinth. The Cretan structure is never referred to by name, but the characters inhabit physical, linguistic, and psychological mazes. In a intricate subterranean prison, the characters plot intrigues, search for love, and attempt to avoid imminent death.

There are in essence five central characters in the play. The pivotal character, the Sultan Amurat, is entirely absent from the stage and the seraglio, yet his actions—and the rumors of his actions—largely determine the unfolding tragedy. Bajazet, the sultan's brother, has become a threat to the sultan's power and so has been imprisoned in the seraglio. Roxane is the sultan's mistress and rules the seraglio in his absence. Atalide, a cousin of the sultan, is also confidante to Roxane and secret lover of Bajazet. Acomat is the sultan's vizier, who has fallen into disfavor.

The intersecting interests of these characters create a complex web of intrigues or "network of conspiracies."[20] The action and interaction in *Bajazet* revolve predominantly around "les secrets des coeurs." This is not a mere love triangle; the elements of passion, power, language, and death add to the twisted and confusing plot. Acomat has determined that he can best regain power by promoting Bajazet as sultan, but in order to do so, he must arrange a union between Bajazet and Roxane. Roxane has received a message from Amurat commanding her to dispose of Bajazet, whom she has begun to love under the influence of Acomat and Atalide. Atalide loves Bajazet but believes that the only way to keep him alive is to facilitate a union between him and Roxane. Bajazet realizes that his life depends on convincing Roxane of his love, but he is not practiced at the art of deception. For the moment, Bajazet's freedom (or death) appears to be in Roxane's hands. But the situation is tenuous, for the state of unbalance and the possibility for change are contingent upon Amurat's absence.

L'Indigne Prison: The Labyrinthine Setting

All of the action takes place in the seraglio, a subterranean prison-maze, cut off from the outside world. In his youth Bajazet was a soldier respected by the armies; now he is confined to "l'indigne prison" (II:3, l. 611). Indeed, all of the characters are imprisoned in the palace, including those who imagine themselves to be free.[21] Even Roxane, who temporarily rules, is a captive of the seraglio.

The characters are confined within "ce lieu." The tragic site is closed. The vocabulary of enclosure is not overly abundant, yet the characters are constantly made aware of the oppressive walls which surround them. Even Acomat, who boasts: "Nourri dans le sérail, j'en connais les détours" (IV:7, l. 1424), has never seen parts of the passages and hidden chambers of the seraglio. When the play commences, Acomat has been led by a slave to a secret place to meet with Roxane:

> Où nos coeurs à nos yeux parlent en liberté.
> Par un chemin obscur un esclave me guide. (I:1, ll. 208–09)

There is much irony in the image of Acomat being guided by a slave to this secret place in the prison where he might speak freely. There is in fact no place in the seraglio where he is free to speak.

The doors to the seraglio are generally but not always closed. Amurat, Acomat, and Roxane all have, or claim to have, the power to open them. Roxane boasts to Bajazet:

> Songez-vous que je tiens les portes du palais;
> Que je puis vous l'ouvrir ou fermer pour jamais;
> Que j'ai sur votre vie un empire suprême. (II:1, ll. 507–09)

Roxane can have the gates to the palace opened, though it is unlikely that she can pass through them. In Amurat's absence, Roxane has been left in charge of the seraglio, but the question remains as to how much power she actually has. With a word she can bring death to Bajazet. Yet it seems the power that she exercises is limited to carrying out that which Amurat has already commanded. Roxane has gained and retains her power only in so far as she pleases the Sultan. For all her nominal authority, Roxane is confined to the seraglio. Bajazet offers a possible escape from her dilemma. If she marries Bajazet and they manage to usurp the empire, she will have assured for herself power on her own terms.

Acomat and Atalide are both persuasive—Acomat at convincing Roxane that she will gain more power in an alliance with Bajazet, and Atalide at assuring her of Bajazet's love. Yet Roxane realizes that if she follows this path, she will likely face death. Bajazet faces a similar predicament. Emprisoned in the harem, he has to attempt to please Roxane for his very life.[22] His only chance to escape from the seraglio is by marrying Roxane. In return for his love, Roxane will guide Bajazet safely out of his labyrinthine prison. On the other hand, if he refuses to marry her, she threatens: "J'abandonne l'ingrat et le laisse rentrer / Dans l'état malheureux d'où je l'ai su tirer" (I:3, ll. 324–25). The choice should be obvious, except that the situation is complicated by Bajazet's love for Atalide.

The labyrinth is more than the physical setting. In addition to the walls that separate the seraglio from the outside, there are numerous inner walls; the psychological and emotional barriers which exist between characters. When the characters speak of the "injustes détours" or the "détours si bas," they refer to the manipulations and forced intrigues of the emotional labyrinth in which they are confined.

Only Acomat actually manages to leave this labyrinthine prison. He is elderly, and love no longer interests him. He is concerned only with power and has gained enough to be able to manipulate and to escape when need be. Acomat merely has to escape from political intrigues and the confining walls of the seraglio. Bajazet, Roxane, and Atalide are confined in a physical prison, but more significantly, they are also trapped in a labyrinth of love.

Love and the Prison-House of Language

Bajazet is a prisoner in the seraglio; but he is also a prisoner of language. He finds himself constantly manipulated and constrained linguistically. The words of Atalide, Acomat, and Roxane determine Bajazet's course of action, often involving reversals. He seldom speaks for himself, and laments, "que ne puis-je parler!" (II:1, l. 561). In fact, Bajazet is "as unable to speak for himself as he is unable to liberate himself from the physical space that surrounds him."[23] He is on the verge of becoming a mute, like the eunuchs who guard the passages of the harem.

Bajazet is not alone in being subject to this combination of linguistic instability and confinement in the seraglio. Barthes asserts that "Le Sérail colle à Roxane à la fois comme condition, comme prison et comme labyrinthe, c'est-à-dire comme obscurité des signes" (BR 103). The complicated political intrigues are exacerbated by the chaos of language, and the seraglio becomes typified by the uncertainty of signs.[24] The inhabitants of the seraglio are privy to numerous rumors, messages, and codes, but they lack an authority who can tell them what is true. The only contact the characters have with Amurat are the rumors which arrive from the warfront. Even when Osmin brings news from the outside world, it is incomplete and distanced from the truth:

> Mais, comme vous savez, malgré ma diligence,
> Un long chemin sépare et le camp et Byzance;
> Mille obstacles divers m'ont même traversé:
> Et je puis ignorer tout ce qui s'est passé. (I:1, ll. 25–28)

By the time any news reaches the harem, it is old and certainly unreliable. The connection with the outside world is predicated upon rumors and partial truths. Though the knowledge which is created based on this discourse is tenuous at best, it tends to fuel itself, influencing the perspectives of those who live in the seraglio. Acomat recognizes this fact when he states:

> Peut-être il te souvient qu'un récit peu fidèle
> De la mort d'Amurat fit courir la nouvelle.
> La sultane, à ce bruit feignant de s'effrayer,
> Par ses cris douloureux eut soin de l'appuyer. (I:1, ll. 145–48)

Roxane validates the unsubstantiated rumor in her reaction to it (HS 112).

Speech in *Bajazet* is likely to lead the listener astray, as it is generally either based on rumors or miscomprehended. Furthermore, the seraglio is not a place where one can speak freely. Discourse is always risky in the harem where a "careless word can mean the difference between life and death."[25] There are strict rules in this realm, spies who lurk in the passages, and mutes who carry out swift retribution.

The lack of the ability to speak freely is exacerbated by the constant use of language to manipulate desire. Roxane's love for Bajazet grows from the words of Acomat and Atalide. Acomat uses his persuasive powers to bring the two together. He attempts to divert Roxane's love from Amurat and guide her heart towards Bajazet. Under his influence: "la sultane éperdue / N'eut plus d'autre désir que celui de sa vue" (I:1, ll. 141–42). Bajazet becomes an object of desire for her, though she has never up to now seen him.

Atalide especially understands that Bajazet's only chance of survival is an alliance with Roxane; so she uses her role as messenger to try to bring the two together. Atalide serves as an intermediary between Bajazet and Roxane: "Le voyait par mes yeux, lui parlait par ma bouche" (I:4, l. 350). In her efforts to save Bajazet, she has become a masterful deceiver, an expert at leading others into error. She has succeeded in fueling Roxane's passion, but when Bajazet speaks for himself, Roxanne remarks that "L'ingrat ne parle pas comme on le fait parler" (I:3, l. 276). Even Roxane notices that Atalide expresses Bajazet's love more convincingly than he does himself: "Vous parlez mieux pour lui qu'il ne parle lui-même" (III:6, l. 1058; HS 113). Yet partially because she too is blinded by desire and partially because she is also a prisoner of the labyrinth, Roxane does not realize that Atalide is manipulating her amorous and political aspirations.

In *Bajazet*, the thread of language is not used so much to guide as it is to misguide. Atalide knows that so long as Roxane does not realize her "erreur fatale" (I:4, l. 413) Bajazet is safe. Atalide feels that she has to lead the Sultana astray, for if she were to rectify Roxane's error she would lose her lover: "A l'erreur de Roxane ai-je dû m'opposer. Et perdre mon amant pour la désabuser?" (I:4, l. 355). In order to keep Bajazet from being lost, she must deceive Roxane.[26]

Bajazet allows himself to be guided by the words of Atalide and Acomat because it is his best, perhaps only, chance to escape. However, only the fact that Roxane is happy in the deception allows him to mislead her in this way; he asserts: "Je connus votre erreur; mais que pouvais-je faire? Je vis en même temps qu'elle vous était chère" (V:4, ll. 1501–2). Roxane is very fond of her error. She refers to her relationship with Bajazet as her "douce erreur si longtemps possédée" (II:1, l. 549). When Bajazet finally does tell Roxane how he truly feels, he condemns himself and destroys her dream.

Is any kind of communication possible in such circumstances? Truth in the seraglio is simply the power to enforce a perspective. With the Sultan away, no one can maintain stability, which in turn gives rise to intrigue. With the absence of truth, instability reigns. Yet even absent, Amurat is able to assert some control through the use of his messengers. It is Amurat's written order which deconstructs the illusions created by the other characters. Two messengers sent by Amurat bring word that Bajazet should be disposed of. A curious connection develops between language and death. The first messenger is killed before he can deliver the letter. Amurat's second messenger, Orcan, bears a similar letter with the added threat that Roxane herself will be executed if she does not carry out the order.

The letter from Amurat contains a straightforward "ordre souverain," but it is carried out in a labyrinthine manner. Roxane, who has allowed herself to be misguided, is now forced into action. She shows the letter to Atalide. When Atalide faints, Roxane discovers a hidden love letter from Bajazet. It is, therefore, the communications themselves which seal Bajazet's fate. The written word reveals hidden errors, but it also brings death.[27]

With a single word, "Sortez," Roxane sends Bajazet from her chambers to be strangled by the mutes. These mutes hold an interesting position as the guardians of this realm; they may not use spoken words, but the messages they deliver are deadly. Roxane is herself subsequently killed by Amurat's messenger, Orcan.

The Guiding Thread / The Fatal Knot

From the beginning, there are signs that the seraglio is not merely a "secret, subterranean chamber at the heart of a mysterious and dangerous maze,"[28] it is also a labyrinthine tomb. The Cretan labyinth was a prison for the Minotaur, but for all others, it was a house of death. The Athenians sent to the Minotaur's dwelling place were victims, sacrifices. The labyrinth served as a prison for them only as long as it took the Minotaur to hunt them down. Similarly, the seraglio is a house of death, and it is only a matter of time before Bajazet will be sacrificed to maintain order in the empire.

The theme of death is omnipresent and intrusive. Maya Slater has done a rigorous study of terminology relating to death in *Bajazet* and finds numerous instances of and variations on the theme. For instance, frequent synonyms for death include "mort," "supplice," "ruine," "trépas," "sacrifice," "meurtre," "chute," and "perte." Synonyms for to die include "mourir," "périr," "tomber," "expirer," "sacrifier," and "finir." Euphemisms for "to kill" include "assassiner," "trancher," "terminer," "achever," and "précipiter" (SB 145). And idioms such as "prendre cette victime" (V:10, l. 1670) are common.[29] Considering the limited vocabulary utilized in *Bajazet*, the preponderance of death imagery is overwhelming.

Racine creates a rhythm of death through the repetition and juxtaposition of various death terms: "Bajazet était *mort*. Nous l'avons rencontré / De *morts* et de *mourants* noblement entouré" (V:11, ll. 1699–1700, emphasis added). Furthermore, the idea of death is often presented in ways which generally would not carry such connotations. The word "vie" in the play tends to be employed in such a way that it actually signifies the fragility of life. "La vie" is used thirty-four times in *Bajazet*, and in all but three of these instances, it is used in the context of death (SB 145). Bajazet's life is far from secure. Amurat has designated Roxane the "arbitre" of Bajazet's life (V:4). She tells Bajazet that if he can prove his love to her, she will provide a way out of the labyrinth of the seraglio: "Le chemin est encore ouvert au repentir" (II:1, l. 540). But if he does not, she can and will have him killed. If Bajazet's words fail to please Roxane, "Il se perdra" (I:4, l. 402). Bajazet lives under the constant threat of death.

Acomat reminds Bajazet: "Dites un mot, et vous nous sauvez tous" (II:3, l. 620). Atalide urges him to speak kindly to receive

Roxane's pardon: "Allez, Seigneur: sauvez votre vie et la mienne" (II:5, l. 785).[30] Under the manipulation by Atalide and Acomat, Bajazet vacillates between duty and desire, life and death. His choices are based on both his internal conflicts and the external circumstances.[31]

Bajazet does not see death as the worst fate. He has faced death as a soldier and has even become accustomed to death in the tomb-like seraglio. As he tells Acomat:

> La mort n'est point pour moi le comble des disgrâces;
> J'osai, tout jeune encor, la chercher sur vos traces;
> Et l'indigne prison où je suis renfermé
> A la voir de plus près m'a même accoutumé. (II:3, ll. 609–12)

In his youth, Bajazet had followed Acomat on paths which might easily have led to death, and he lives amidst the macabre which is omnipresent in the prison of the seraglio. Bajazet chooses death over the compromises he would have to make in order to live.

Atalide provides a *fil* which she hopes will save Bajazet's life, but in the process, she actually creates threads which are as twisted as the labyrinth from which she hopes to lead her lover. Atalide has bound Bajazet to Roxane with a defective thread, and they become entangled because of her own relationship with Bajazet. The resulting knots serve as a metaphor for the unstable relationships and discursive spaces which are created within the text.[32] Atalide is originally bound to Bajazet by blood, as they are cousins, but "L'Amour serra les noeuds par le sang commencés" [I:4, l. 360]).[33] When Roxane realizes that Bajazet's heart will not be hers, she twists the threads even further: "Loin de vous séparer, je prétends aujourd'hui / Par des noeuds éternels vous unir avec lui" (V:6, ll. 1623–24). Though Atalide naively takes these words to mean that Roxane will allow them to be married, Roxane intends instead to tighten the knots around both of their necks, uniting them in death (SB 144).

Although it is the mute servants who strangle Bajazet, Atalide blames herself for having created the threads which are tightened around his throat:

Oui, c'est moi, cher amant, qui t'arrache la vie;
Roxane, ou le sultan, ne te l'ont point ravie:
Moi seule, j'ai tissu le lien malheureux
Dont tu viens d'éprouver les détestables noeuds.
(V:12, ll. 1729–32)

Atalide does not understand that while she has been able to create discourse, she has never had the power to turn her words into action. The seraglio, the labyrinth to which all of these characters have been consigned, is a place where love, power, and language are all inextricably intertwined. Language is supposed to allow one to traverse the twisted walls of perception, but in *Bajazet* the thread of communication becomes knotted. The characters are guided by their own passions and misled by the manipulations, deceits, and rumors.

The tone of the drama is set early in the play when Acomat questions Osmin about the "secret des coeurs" (I:1, l. 31). Acomat bases the actions he will take on Osmin's account of events outside the seraglio:

Instruis-moi des secrets que peut t'avoir appris
Un voyage si long pour moi seul entrepris,
De ce qu'ont vu tes yeux parle en témoin sincère;
Songe que du récit, Osmin, que tu vas faire,
Dépendent les destins de l'empire ottoman. (I:1, ll. 11–15)

Everything that follows is therefore based on the secondhand perceptions of the messenger.

Indeed, each character in *Bajazet* has his or her own *dessein*, suspicions, and perspectives. In Act II there are four distinct interpretations of the encounter between Bajazet and Roxane which has occurred off-stage.[34] Each character's perception is guided by desires, ambitions, and emotions. So from one event their perspectives deviate along four separate paths. Acomat who saw but could not hear the exchange believes that he has witnessed true love, which will result in Bajazet becoming the new sultan (and Acomat regaining the power which has been denied him).

Atalide, who neither saw nor heard the exchange, bases her account solely on what Acomat has told her. Despite what she knows of Bajazet, and despite the fact that she has persuaded him to take this course of action, she believes that Bajazet has actually given his love to the sultana:

> Ah! peut-être, après tout, que sans trop se forcer,
> Tout ce qu'il a pu dire, il a pu le penser.
> Peut-être en la voyant, plus sensible pour elle,
> Il a vu dans ses yeux quelque grâce nouvelle;
> Elle aura devant lui fait parler ses douleurs;
> Elle l'aime; un empire autorise ses pleurs:
> Tant d'amour touche enfin une âme généreuse.
> Hélas! que de raisons contre une malheureuse! (III:3, ll. 915–22)

Atalide knows that Bajazet is inexperienced in the art of deception. She therefore assumes that he could never have found the eloquence to sway Roxane unless he truly loved her. For Atalide, this signifies that Bajazet has betrayed her and will marry Roxane.

In Bajazet's own version of the encounter, he asserts that he barely had to speak for Roxane to forget all of her doubts. Roxane has convinced herself that they are destined for a "hymen infaillible" (III:4, l. 990). Although he had to do little to convince Roxane of his devotion to her, Bajazet still feels guilty for his deceptions, calling himself barbarous, unjust, and criminal.

Roxane's version of the encounter is the last to be told, and she herself recognizes that it is a sudden reversal ("un si prompt retour") of her earlier mistrust of Bajazet:

> A peine cependant Bajazet m'a parlé;
> L'amour fit le serment, l'amour l'a violé.
> J'ai cru dans son désordre entrevoir sa tendresse:
> J'ai prononcé sa grâce, et je crois sa promesse.
>   (III:5, ll. 1023–26)[35]

Roxane's account ironically echoes Bajazet's own assertion that she was convinced of his love with little effort on his part. Though she finally seems to be sure of Bajazet's love, a trace of doubt remains. When she says "j'ai cru" and "je crois," she is trying to convince herself that her words are true.

Bajazet, Roxane, and Atalide are all guided by semantic indirection, the labyrinthine discourse of deception. The characters are easily swayed, even when the words spoken to them are untrustworthy and contradict what they already know. Because they are surrounded by false and partial messages, like dead-end corridors of the labyrinth, the texts these characters seek to create have no chance of leading them to truth. There is frequently a disjunction between intended and perceived meanings when the characters in *Bajazet* attempt to communicate, resulting in a "disparity between expectation and event, appearance and reality, longing and realization" (JI 51). Thus, despite her situation, Roxane has faith in her own power, and can convince herself that Bajazet loves her. Bajazet confined in the seraglio can proclaim, "Je suis libre" (III:4, l. 948). From within the labyrinth, he can see only the passages open before and behind him. He can ignore the fact that if seen from above, it would be evident that the entire network of detours and deviations is enclosed, confining him in a limited space. And Atalide can believe that Bajazet has betrayed her one minute and the next argue that his death is all her fault. Each of these misconceptions influences the action that the characters will take, but each can be deconstructed by someone who can see the overall "dessein."

Unfortunately for the characters in *Bajazet*, only viewers of the drama, like Daedalus, have the privilege of seeing the "dessein" from above. The characters can only see from within the passages to which they are relegated. As was the case in Corneille's *Ariane*, there exist both physical and pyschological labyrinths. In *Ariane*, Thésée is led out of the Cretan labyrinth, but Ariane is abandoned in an emotional maze that is all too real for her. The thread that bound Thésée to Ariane is severed, and she is lost. In the seraglio of *Bajazet,* the physical and psychological labyrinths co-exist and the thread that is meant to guide Bajazet becomes knotted around his throat. In both cases, it is the intangible labyrinths which prove to be the more formidible prisons for the characters of tragic verse.

Chapter 4

Absence and Poetic Creation: Refiguring the Labyrinth in Mallarmé's *Mythe Moderne*

In 1863, Stéphane Mallarmé was assigned to work in a lycée in Tournon. During the next three years, exiled from Paris, Mallarmé endured a mental crisis which he compared to death. Yet during his "nuits de Tournon," he descended into himself and discovered there the impetus for a *Grand Oeuvre*. This dream would shape his literary endeavors throughout his life though still barely scratch the surface of what he had hoped to achieve.

Of utmost importance in the creation of the *Grand Oeuvre* is the development of a modern myth, which would embody the archetypal figures of mythology but bear relevance to the drama of contemporary life. One of the more significant manifestations of archetypal setting refigured by Mallarmé into his new myth is that of the labyrinth which is evoked directly at times but is more often revealed in his language of webs, paths, constellations, and infinite conjunctions.

In the center of the Mallarméan maze resides a place of purity which is at the same time the realm of absence. During his *crise*, absence, already part of Mallarmé's symbolism, became integral to his poetic theory. Two of Mallarmé's poems are explored in this chapter: *Igitur*, which was conceived by Mallarmé during his crisis and was viewed by him as a curative work reflecting his own rebirth from impotency, and "Toast funèbre," which was written in honor of Théophile Gautier after his death. Both of these poems explore the relationship between creativity and absence in the dual labyrinth of tomb and text.

Myth, Alchemy, and the Thread of Language
in the *Grand Oeuvre*

In *Les Dieux antiques* Mallarmé poses the question: "Qu'est-ce que ce labyrinthe?"[1] The labyrinth is presented as another manifestation of the nuptial chamber built by Odysseus for Penelope, which is itself a variant of the archetypal meandering garden "que le Soleil dispose pour sa fiancée, l'Aurore" (DA 1233). Mallarmé's answer reveals the inherent circuitous nature of the mythic symbol, which is defined not by material referents, but by its resemblances to other mythic symbols. A chain of mythical significations inevitably detours any literal meaning the reader might hope to find in the text.

Mallarmé ultimately views all myth and legend as inspired by "quelque phénomène naturel." What he has identified as "le grand et perpétuel sujet" is found in the natural solar cycles and "la lutte de la lumière et de l'ombre" (DA 1169). The Cretan labyrinth is one of the mythic symbols signifying the eternal solar drama. The heroes *Persée*, *Oedipe*, and *Thésée* are all presented in his collection as variants of the archetypal "seigneur de la lumière" (DA 1228). Theseus and his solar counterparts wander along a circuitous path in search of an initiatory death and rebirth (the setting of the sun and the new dawn). The myths involving these heroes "*ne sont jamais* 'QU'UNE DES NOMBREUSES NARRATIONS DU GRAND DRAME SOLAIRE ACCOMPLI SOUS NOS YEUX CHAQUE JOUR ET CHAQUE ANNÉE'" (DA 1257). Because the labyrinth exists at the conjunction of light and darkness, presence and absence, and life and death, it is a symbol in which multiple contraries are united in a single monument.

Mallarmé's ideas in *Les Dieux antiques* were not unique; in fact, the book is by and large a translation of George Cox's *A Manual of Mythology in the Form of Question and Answer* (1867). The idea of the archetypal solar myth had many proponents in nineteenth-century Europe, including George Cox, Max Müller, and Louis Ménard. Ménard, in particular, conceived of myth as the synthesis of contraries, the resolution of oppositions. The role of the archetypal solar drama and the tetralogical *tragédie de la nature* in Mallarmé's writings has been well documented in two critical works, Gardner Davies' *Mallarmé et le drame solaire*[2] and Lawrence Watson's *Mallarmé's Mythic Language*.[3] Davies attributes Mallarmé's interest in the solar myth primarily to the influence of Cox, whereas Watson sees in Mallarmé the general influence of philology, which includes "not just the scientific study of languages particularly through historical linguistics and comparative grammar, but also scientific investigation of social organization, religion, and above all, mythology, especially in the context of ancient civilizations" (WL 4–5). Certainly Cox's study was also defined by the zeitgeist and the general intellectual atmosphere, and Mallarmé's translation was only part of a broader investigation undertaken to prepare for his *Livre*.

Mallarmé wrote to his friend Cazalis that he was embarking on a study of the religions and rituals of mankind from their earliest manifestations: "Pour susciter l'activité, j'associerai à ces années d'études un but pratique qui sera mon 'Egyptologie.'"[4] He also wrote to his friend Eugène Lefébure, a renowned Eygptologist, that he intended to explore the nuances of Sanskrit, Greek, and Latin, after which he would undertake "une étude plus extérieure des langues sémitiques."[5] More and more Mallarmé's poetry evolved its own cult, drawing on many myths and religions but limited to none.

Significantly, Mallarmé is not simply reflecting on mythic symbols in his poetry, rather he seeks to create "a new myth and rite for mankind." He advocated a new cult with the *Livre*, or *Grand Oeuvre*, as its missal (WL 16). This *Grand Oeuvre* would contain original "mythes modernes," drawn syncretically from theater, music, religion, the occult, science, and linguistics, but it would find its form in poetry. In *Les Dieux antiques* what Mallarmé added to Cox's book was the idea of modern poetry founded on myth. He included an anthology of "Poèmes mythologiques modernes"[6] and asserted that myth was not a thing of the past.

Indeed, for Mallarmé, the classic heroes of myth are not alone in walking through the labyrinth. The great drama of the modern hero is also a reflection of the battle between light and shadow. One such modern hero who affected Mallarmé's thought was Shakespeare's Hamlet, of whom Mallarmé writes:

> mais avance *le seigneur latent qui ne peut devenir*, juvénile ombre
> de tous, ainsi tenant du mythe. Son solitaire drame! et qui, parfois,
> tant ce promeneur d'un labyrinthe de trouble et de griefs en
> prolonge les circuits avec le suspens d'un acte inachevé. . .[7]

Hamlet the maze-walker extends the circuits of his own labyrinth with
every action he takes. Furthermore, *Hamlet* is not simply good
drama, it is the "seul théâtre de notre esprit, prototype du reste" (CT
300). The character of Hamlet represents everyman. He is the
shadow of us all, but as signified by the terms "juvénile" and "latent,"
he is incapable of exiting his labyrinth to reach adulthood.

In the *Grand Oeuvre*, much of the imagery would be drawn from
the more mystic or occult religions, particularly alchemy and the
Kabbalah. As in *Les Dieux antiques*, the labyrinth holds a strong
symbolic position in alchemical traditions. The labyrinth fulfilled a
magical function and was one of the secrets attributed to Solomon.[8]
Several labyrinthine figures, including some of those found in
cathedrals, are referred to alternately as "The Labyrinth of Solomon"
or *Prison de Salomon*.[9] For the alchemists:

> l'image du labyrinthe s'offre [. . .] comme emblématique du travail
> entier de l'OEuvre, avec ses deux difficultés majeures: celle de la
> voie qu'il convient de suivre pour atteindre le centre,—où se livre
> le rude combat des deux natures,—l'autre, du chemin que l'artiste
> doit tenir pour en sortir. C'est ici que le *fil d'Ariane* lui devient
> nécessaire, s'il ne veut errer parmi les méandres de l'ouvrage sans
> parvenir à en découvrir l'issue. [. . .] le *fil d'Ariane* [. . .] permit à
> Thésée d'accomplir son dessein.[10]

The labyrinth was used symbolically to represent the *Grand Oeuvre*
itself and the initiation into the secrets of alchemy. The adept
searches for the right path to the center and understanding. This is
not to say that Mallarmé practiced any of the occult arts but that he
saw a place for the language and images of magic in his symbolism.
Mallarmé was also engaged in a search for meaning in his own life and
art.

Several critics have discussed Mallarmé's relationship to alchemy and reached quite different conclusions. Huckle, for example, sees alchemical imagery as a significant part of Mallarmé's work.[11] Fowlie raises the possibility of an alchemical connection but asserts that "Ritualist" better describes Mallarmé.[12] Cohn assures the reader that Mallarmé kept his distance from the "pauvres kabbalistes," yet he notes several striking similarities in metaphor between *Igitur* and Eliphas Lévi's *Nuctemeron of Appolonius of Tyana*.[13] In 1867, Villiers de l'Isle-Adam recommended to Mallarmé Lévi's *Dogme et rituel de la haute magie* (1860) in response to Mallarmé's request for help in researching precious stones, a topic on which he hoped to write a book. In the same letter, Villiers mentions that he has more faith in Mallarmé's alchemy than he does even in that of Auriol Théophraste Bombaste, "ce divin Paracelse."[14] Another acquaintance Louis Ménard had researched the writings of the alchemist Hermes Trismegistes from 1863–1864 (WL 74). Furthermore, Mallarmé's young colleague J.-K. Huysmans was quite knowledgeable about the contemporary occult scene, as evidenced by *Là-Bas*,[15] in which discussion of the history of the occult is woven throughout and a Parisian Black Mass is described in detail.[16]

No evidence exists to indicate that Mallarmé ever read any of the vast collection of alchemical and occult *grimoires* available in the nineteenth century, nor is there evidence that he ever experimented in such practices himself. But whether from his own reading or from discussion with Villiers and Huysmans, it is evident that he was quite familiar with the terminology and symbols of the occult.

In an essay entitled "Magie," Mallarmé compares the work of the poet to that of the *enchanteur*:

Je dis qu'existe entre les vieux procédés et le sortilège, que restera la poésie, une parité secrète; [. . .] Evoquer, dans une ombre exprès, l'objet tu, par des mots allusifs, jamais directs, se réduisant à du silence égal, comporte tentative proche de créer: vraisemblable dans la limite de l'idée uniquement mise en jeu par l'enchanteur de lettres jusqu'à ce que, certes, scintille, quelque illusion égale au regard. Le vers, trait incantatoire! et, on ne déniera au cercle que perpétuellement ferme, ouvre la rime une similitude avec les ronds, parmi l'herbe, de la fée ou du magicien.[17]

Mallarmé sees many similarities between poetry and magic, or the pursuit of gold-making. Both use language to reach their inner creative potential. He even compares the stylistic use of rhyme to the magic circles in which the *enchanteur* stands when performing an incantation. The greatest indication of this correlation is that Mallarmé borrows the alchemical term *Grand Oeuvre* in reference to his own Masterwork. In his autobiographical essay Mallarmé writes: "J'ai toujours rêvé et tenté autre chose, avec une patience d'alchimiste [. . .] comme on brûlait jadis son mobilier et les poutres de son toit, pour alimenter le fourneau du Grand OEuvre" (OC 662). He even implies in a letter to Henri Cazalis that he has inherited the term from "les alchimistes, nos ancêtres" (CI 242).

However, as with his mythological and religious imagery, Mallarmé has taken whatever symbols best fit into his own ideas of poetry and the mysteries of the cosmos. Mallarmé was likely drawn to the occult for the metaphorical potential of its symbols. Peter Dayan has suggested that "taken metaphorically, rather than literally, many of the occult and alchemical ambitions appear to Mallarmé instructive and exemplary: particularly the search for the absolute, and the substitution of a hidden logic for the rationale of the bourgeois."[18]

The tradition of Solomon's labyrinth/prison can be traced to the great temple he is said to have built in Jerusalem.[19] In his commentary on Ezekiel's vision of the Temple of Jerusalem, Jerome compares this structure to the labyrinth as described in the *Aeneid*:

> So also I, entering the ocean of those scriptures and, so to speak, the labyrinth of the mysteries of God [. . .] do not claim perfect knowledge of truth, but dare offer some indications of doctrine to those who wish to know, not by my own powers, but through the mercy of Christ, who himself resolves the tricks and doubtful turns (ambages) for us in our wanderings, guiding our blind footsteps by

the Holy Spirit. Following him, we will be able to reach the haven, an explanation of the prophet Ezekiel.[20]

Likewise, the Alchemic Citadel is described as a labyrinthine structure: "difficult and narrow is the way, and many are those who stray in treading it into wrong paths, where they are to find only deceit, error, and falsehood."[21] The citadel is surrounded by twenty-one rooms, only one of which has an entrance to the citadel. These twenty rooms with no exit signify the "twenty roads in which seekers after the alchemic doctrine can go astray" (GW 348). The twenty-first room represents the true path, but in order to reach the center, the adept must pass "a warden who bars him from the sill of a light drawbridge spanning the broad moat filled with water which isolates the citadel" (GW 348). And this is only the beginning of the trials and tribulations the adept must pass through to reach the center where the Philosopher's Stone resides. Most crucial to reaching the center is knowledge of the *Grand Oeuvre*.

In *Les Dieux antiques*, Mallarmé speaks of "les mythes mêlés intimement à la parole." In Mallarméan discourse, myth and poetry are both situated in the metaphorical dimension of language.[22] When Mallarmé draws upon the vast array of mythic and occult symbols and recombines them in his poetry, he fully exploits the infinitely reflexive capacity of metaphor, creating "une théologie des lettres."[23] In the realm of metaphor, language becomes a fluid thread which is woven through the text. Mallarmé in his writing conveys a "pensée symbolique pluri-dimensionnelle,"[24] or what Leroi-Gourhan terms mythographic language.[25] He uses words to construct verbal constellations on the page. Rather than searching for linear truths, his words create intricately woven images.

The spacing of words establishes an architecture in which the dissemination of the whites "produces a tropological structure that circulates infinitely around itself through the incessant supplement of an extra turn."[26] This linguistic blueprint of the *Livre* parallels the Kabbalistic labyrinth of the *Sefirot* created by the sacred letters, in which the first letter of each of the ten Serifah emanates outwards from the first (see Figure 4).

Peter Dayan, in *Mallarmé's Divine Transposition*, notes that Blanchot, Barthes, Kristeva, and Derrida all distinguish Mallarmé's language from linear discursive classical literature (DT 120). Linear language has a two-dimensional movement and attempts to tell a truth. Written language is phoneticized and linear in space, whereas spoken language is phonetic and linear in time (LGG 270). Mallarmé defies this dichotomy and does not confine his written language to the line between words and truth. The thread of language in the Mallarméan text bends and refracts and at times doubles back on itself. For example, there is running through *Igitur* a series of interwoven terms. In the paragraph that begins "A peu près ce qui suit," variants of the two words absolute and infinity criss-cross until for a moment the two intersect in a single passage: "'absolu' . . . L'infini . . . Infini . . . l'absolu . . . l'Infini vis-à-vis de l'Absolu" (OC 434). The words repeat with a difference each time they occur. Other words enter the linguistic play. The roll of the dice is repeated in *le hasard*—the etymology of which stems from the Arabic word *al-zahr*, "jeu de dés."[27] As these words interact, a semantic network is created.

If we consider mythology to be a multidimensional construct based upon the verbal, and mythography a multidimensional construct based upon the visual, as Leroi-Gourhan suggests (LGG 272), then Mallarmé's writings would fall somewhere in between these two poles. In mythographic language, "la nature des associations mentales qu'il suscite est d'un ordre parallèle à celui du mythe verbal, étranger à une spécification rigoureuse des coordonnées spatio-temporelles" (DG 128). In this conception, Mallarmé's mythographic sign will suggest mental images which can point in several divergent directions.[28]

Igitur By Any Other Name or *La presque disparition d'Igitur*

Igitur, written between 1867 and 1870, was published posthumously, and Mallarmé had only shared it with a few friends. Still, Paul Claudel considered *Igitur* the matrix out of which all of Mallarmé's art emerged,[29] and Mallarmé might have intended for it to be part of his *Grand Oeuvre*. The title of the work has received much analysis. "Igitur" signifies "therefore" or "as a consequence" in Latin, and Roland de Renéville contends that in this instance it invokes a passage from the Vulgate *igitur perfecti sunt coeli et terra et omnis ornata eorum* ["Therefore the heavens and the earth were finished"] (CM 20). This endows Igitur with connotations of creation and consequence, the significance of which is immediately thrown into question by the madness of Elbehnon. As the end of his race, a name reflecting "consequence," especially with its biblical connotations, seems appropriate.

At the same time, there are many parallels between the characters of Igitur and Hamlet. Hamlet's castle was Elsinor, which may have influenced the naming of Elbehnon, the full title of the poem being *Igitur ou la Folie d'Elbehnon* (CM 24). Like Theseus, or Hamlet, Igitur is the "suprême incarnation de cette race," the shadow of us all. Igitur descends "les escaliers, de l'esprit humain, va au fond des choses"[30] and explores the labyrinthine corridors of his mind. One could even conjecture that as the project was conceived while Mallarmé lived in Tournon, this could have influenced the title— Ig**itur** / Elbeh**non**. Mallarmé referred to his crisis years as "les nuits de Tournon."

Renéville has also asserted that Elbehnon might be read as *el behnon*, meaning "the sons of Elohim" (CM 20). Alternately, Jeffrey Perl suggests that *El behnon* could be Mallarmé's version of the Hebrew for a mystical term connoting the creative attribute of divinity.[31] It should be noted that Elohim and El are names used for God (or aspects of God) in many Hebrew, Kabbalistic, and alchemical texts. Both of these names, as well as a few others, are often found on the magic circles of alchemists, the most renowned of which is Solomon's seal. The *grimoire* repeatedly evoked in *Igitur* is also frequently attributed to Solomon.[32] Though it seems that the *Ur-Livre* no longer exists intact, there are numerous contenders, including *La Clavicule de Salomon*, *Le Livre de Salomon*, and *Le Secret des secrets, autrement la Clavicule de Salomon ou le véritable Grimoire* (GW 96). Solomon's palace was known as *Iahar-Halibanon*, "Forest of Lebanon" (GW 96).

Ci-gît is another possible connotation; the hero is after all going down in the tomb to die. "Ci-gît Igitur" would be a fitting epitaph.[33] The "ur" of "Ci-gît ur" could be borrowed from the German term for "original," as in the *Ur-Hamlet*. Ur is also the birthplace of Abraham, another biblical figure who, like Solomon, is associated by the alchemists with their *Grand Oeuvre*.[34] Ur, the Mesopotamian kingdom of the ziggurats, had been rediscovered in the 1850's by British archaeologists. All of these possible significations combine, not to establish a fixed character and setting, but to create a new polyvalent myth. Mallarmé achieves a hero, a setting, and a drama which are archetypal yet still reflect his contemporary dilemma.

In his correspondance with Cazalis, Mallarmé asserts that he is writing *Igitur* to combat his *ennui*: "c'est un conte, par lequel je veux terrasser le vieux monstre de l'Impuissance, son sujet du reste, afin de me cloîtrer dans mon grand labeur déjà réétudié. S'il est fait (le conte), je suis guéri. *Simila similibus*."[35] Mallarmé views his writing as a metaphysical exploration of his own personal *crise*, mirrored in the internal journey of Igitur. While engaged in his great labor he is confronted with a personal Minotaur—depression and an inability to write. He saw *Igitur* as a cure, an exorcism (the *Simila similibus* at the end seems to imply an incantation, or ritual) to rid himself of the monster of *ennui*. He states further: "Malheureusement, en creusant le vers à ce point, j'ai rencontré deux abîmes qui me désespèrent. L'un est le Néant. . . L'autre vide que j'ai trouvé est celui de ma poitrine."[36] In a letter to Théodore Aubanel, Mallarmé had written of his crisis: "Je suis mort, et ressuscité."[37] Like Igitur, Mallarmé seems to have descended into the maze and into his own mind.

The poem has many parallels with the archetypal spiritual adventure described by Joseph Campbell in his *Hero with a Thousand Faces*, and the journey of the protagonist clearly follows the initiatory pattern of the descent into the tomb.[38] Cohn describes *Igitur* as the archetypal spiritual adventure, "a descent into the dark womb of the unconscious, eternal night, and reemergence, rebirth to a vision of undying light and truth" (CM 2). According to Eliade, the labyrinthine initiation involves a symbolic death and descent into Hell where personal monsters are confronted. After having overcome the

Minotaur, there is a symbolic rebirth.[39] Like Theseus' tracing of the labyrinth, Igitur's adventure is reflective of a ritual of initiation.

During the period when Mallarmé was working on *Igitur*, he informed several colleagues that he had reached the center of self. For instance, in a letter to Théodore Aubanel on July 28, 1866, Mallarmé writes:

> J'ai voulu te dire simplement que je venais de jeter le plan de mon oeuvre entier, après avoir trouvé la clef de moi-même, clef de voûte, ou centre si tu veux, pour ne pas nous brouiller de métaphores,—centre de moi-même, où je me tiens comme une araignée sacrée, sur les principaux fils déjà sortis de mon esprit, et à l'aide desquels je tisserai *aux points de rencontre* de merveilleuses dentelles, que je devine, et qui existent déjà dans le sein de la Beauté. (CI 224–25)

The text in this conception is likened to a spider web with its "entrelacs perpétuel,"[40] and Mallarmé figures as the weaver of words. The metaphor of the web reflects the text and its meandering prose, echoes, and alliterations; the threads tracing the passages of the text. Between being and nothingness are the words of the poem.

Signifiers used to denote the persona and its mirrorings include: "il," "Igitur," "enfant," "moi projeté absolu," "je," "l'absolu," "l'hôte," "mon personnage," "vision de moi," "le personnage d'horreur," "le fantôme de l'horreur," "un personnage," "suprême incarnation de cette race," and "le pauvre personnage." There is a constant procession of signification. The persona of the poem is always already in motion. The Mallarméan "jeu" is at once the weave and infinitely self-supporting, self-distancing reflection.

Often the movement will return to an already used signifier, but each time it is seen from a new vantage in the "cercles vibratoires de notre pensée."[41] Therefore, these terms are not the same each time Mallarmé uses them, nor are they the same from reader to reader. Mallarmé refers to this phenomenon as "le hasard infini des conjonctions" (I 435). With each new signification, the previous Igitur is simultaneously absent and present.

One of the recurrent images in *Igitur* is that of the mirror. Igitur is constantly gazing into the mirror where he sees each reflection in a different light. In "the endless becoming-procession of phenomena" (CM 138), he can easily forget himself and enter a free-fall, as Mallarmé claims was the case in Tournon:

> je tombai, victorieux, éperdument et infiniment—jusqu'à ce qu'enfin je me sois revu un jour devant ma glace de Venise, tel que je m'étais oublié plusieurs mois auparavant [. . .] j'ai encore besoin [. . .] de me regarder dans cette glace pour penser et [. . .] si elle n'était pas devant la table où je t'écris cette lettre, je redeviendrais le Néant.[42]

However, the mirroring of obscurity is not merely a notion of the dialectic between absence and presence. Midnight exists in both the light and the shadows around it. Everything is connected in that all objects have reflections or shadows of one kind or another. Even the shadows cast shadows. Mallarmé's "l'architecture des ténèbres" is created by "ces ombres, des deux côtés multipliées à l'infini."[43] Similarly, the ancient book on the table contains words spoken long ago. Sounds in the labyrinth do not end; like the *escalier*, they spiral on and on. In between being and nothingness, there are traces. The closing of the tomb doors merges with the ticking of the clock which becomes the beating of wings, the *halètement*, his own heartbeat, an echo.

The concept of interwoven meanings is reinforced by the image of the "fil arachnéen" which Igitur notices as he enters the dark spiraling stairs. The thread, which is described in one long meandering sentence, interlaces all the objects in a web. In alchemical symbolism, the web is linked to the labyrinth, and Ariane is paralleled with the spider in the center of her web. Batsdorff made this relationship explicit in the seventeenth-century manuscript *Le Filet d'Ariadne*.[44] This symbolism is still in use in the twentieth century, when Fulcanelli writes that: "Ariane, l'araignée mystique, échappée d'Amiens, a seulement laissé sur le pavé du choeur la trace de sa toile" (FC 62–63). The thread spun by Ariadne is meant to lead the adept through the labyrinth of the *Grand Oeuvre*. For Mallarmé the image of the web becomes a text within a text, with the metaphor of the thread mirroring both the labyrinthine journey and the *conte* itself.

The image of the web appears again in the "fraise arachnéen" which separates Igitur's face from his body.[45] Rather than a mere chain of substitutions, Igitur is confronted with a web of significations which effectively severs his identity from his being. Mallarmé suggests in "Crise de vers" that "l'oeuvre pure implique la disparition élocutoire du poëte, qui cède l'initiative aux mots."[46] Each signification of self is exposed and left behind until the self is "dénué de toute signification que de présence" (I 435).

Jean-Pierre Richard presents the movement of *Igitur* as a combination of zigzag and spiral. Actually it begins as a linear progression. Then Igitur loses his way on the stairs—moving through the darkness. The descent of the stairway is likened to a spiraling fall:

> se présente une vision de la chute interrompue de panneaux,
> comme si c'était soi-même qui, doué du mouvement suspendu, le
> retournât sur soi en la spirale vertigineuse conséquente. (I 437)

The movement becomes circuitous though still retains linearity. However, at this point, Igitur's trajectory is interwoven with other movements, what Cohn has labelled "circular regress" or "tetrapolarity."

Blanchot in *L'Espace littéraire* argues that the trajectory in *Igitur* revolves around three interconnected movements. First, there is the decision to act and the accompanying symbolic deed. Then there are the vibratory circles of thinking or dreaming by means of which the mind advances outside of itself. Finally, there is the rhythm of Night, which is manifest in the ticking of the clock, the beating of the heart, and the fluttering of wings (BEL 111–12). The vibratory circles of thought and the rhythms of the Night are both linked to Mallarmé's notion of the mirroring of obscurity. Blanchot contends that all three movements are necessary for Igitur to reach death (BEL 111).

In the end, Igitur lies in the ashes of his ancestors, drinks "la goutte de néant," and is absorbed by the poem.[47] The tomb, which is also the poem, becomes a sign of the poet's absence. Igitur has reached the center, but all that resides there is nothingness. Like the "Corne de licorne," the tomb is another object filled with a mysterious absence. Mallarmé stresses in his discourse on language that words have "l'aptitude à rendre les choses absentes, à les susciter en cette absence, puis à rester fidèle à cette valeur de l'absence, à l'accomplir jusqu'au bout dans une suprême et silencieuse disparition" (BEL 109–110). One of the underlying ideas of Mallarmé's theories of poetic creation is that of the transposition of material objects into the "presque disparition vibratoire" of the "notion pure" (CV 368). Sometimes Mallarmé refers to this primordial state as "L'Azur" or "Le Néant"; other times he speaks of a cosmic poem "Le Livre," of which all poetry is a reflection. L'être, le néant, l'absolu, and l'infini, while not exactly synonymous, all denote the pure understanding which would exist in the center of the labyrinth. The journey through the labyrinth of self in Igitur passes the point of substitutions to reach the "château de la pureté" at the center, where self dissolves into nothingness, but nothingness is itself aborted. The poem temporarily absorbs the roll of the dice.

The center of the self has no direct physical manifestation; it cannot be located in the body, nor is it subject to the perpetual substitution of thought and language. Therefore, indirectly, the soul/center guarantees the presence of self because it is outside the play of différance. The center is the space where there are no more substitutions. "Le Néant parti" and all that remains is "le chateau de la pureté." The negation of shifting significations resides at the ever-elusive center of all the twisting, circuitous passages.

In reaching the depths of his unconscious, Igitur "puts an end to his duality and wholly reenters the world of pure material presence, which is also a world of metaphysical nothingness—that is, one where the opposition between presence and absence does not exist."[48] The functioning of nothingness in the process of creation is not as unusual as it might at first sound. In fact, the concept of nothingness holds an integral position in a number of metaphysical traditions. For example, in Kabbalistic thought, there is a realm which cannot be comprehended by any created being and is therefore defined as "nothingness"—*ayin*.[49] Some mystics have taken *creato ex nihilo* to mean that all things have been created from the nothingness of God.[50] (This gives another possible significance for the title: *El be non* [God is nothing]). Emanation in Kabbalistic theory denotes the emergence of all things from within God. These emanations are called *Sefirot*. Sometimes they are represented as ten concentric spheres, or an outward gyration of circles. In the beginning, God encompassed all things. So in order to make room for creation, it was necessary for God to contract, fold or enter into himself; this act is called *zimzum*. Elohim descends into himself in order to make room for the creative process. Mallarmé offers a new mythic figure of the fold which is quite similar to the *zimzum*. "La figure mallarméenne du *pli* par exemple nous permettra de rejoindre l'érotique au sensible, puis au réflexif, au métaphysique, au littéraire: le pli étant à la fois sexe, feuillage, miroir, livre, tombeau, toutes réalités qu'il rassemble en un certain rêve très spécial d'intimité" (RU 28). In *Igitur*, the "seigneur latent" is constantly engaged in several figurations of *pli*. The ancient book, the mirror, and the tomb all reflect Igitur's own sexuality which is suspended until he can reach the center. Finally, deep inside himself he can cast the dice from the formerly empty unicorn's horn.

Mallarmé also descends into himself in his effort to regain his creative impulse. Of his crisis in Tournon, Mallarmé wrote that he was only able to escape from his own descent after his "Pensée s'est pensée, et est arrivée à une conception pure."[51] It is with thought and language that Mallarmé hopes to reach the notion pure. In Mallarmé's poetry the object is dissolved, leaving only the idea of the vanished object:

A quoi bon la merveille de transposer un fait de nature en sa presque disparition vibratoire selon le jeu de la parole, cependant; si ce n'est pour qu'en émane, sans la gêne d'un proche ou concret rappel, la notion pure. (CV 368)

Through language one comes closest to attaining the absolute essence of things.

Everything is connected, mirrored, or shadowed, but it is especially the chain of words which leads the hero to the center. Poetry takes the place of the ancestor's book, the alchemical *Livre*. Mallarmé writes in a revealing letter to Cazalis: "mais j'avoue que la Science que j'ai acquise, ou retrouvée au fond de l'homme que je fus, ne me suffirait pas, et que ce ne serait pas sans un serrement de coeur réel que j'entrerais dans la Disparition suprême, si je n'avais pas fini mon oeuvre, qui est *L'OEuvre*, le Grand'Oeuvre, comme disaient les alchimistes, nos ancêtres."[52] In this letter he refers to his crisis, his major new project which he wishes to finish before he dies (as opposed to an initiatory disappearance). Igitur's ancestors are the alchemists, but they are also "les enchanteurs des lettres" who have preceded Mallarmé in his quest.

"Toast funèbre": Gautier's *Disparition suprême*

"Toast funèbre" (1873), the first of a number of *tombeaux* poems written by Mallarmé to celebrate the memory of poets who had influenced his own works, was written on the occasion of Théophile Gautier's death. A group of poets, including Mallarmé, joined forces to write *Le Tombeau de Théophile Gautier* to mark the occasion and to honor the poet. Mallarmé laments the death of a Master poet, but his funerary poem has relevance far beyond this. The poem not only celebrates the absent voice of Gautier, it also serves as a reflection of Mallarmé's ideas on death, absence, and most significantly, on the poetic endeavor. Though "Toast funèbre" shares some imagery and themes with *Igitur*, a major distinction between the two poems is that in *Igitur* the death of self is a fictional "initiatory" death. In "Toast funèbre" Mallarmé is addressing the actual tomb of a fellow poet. Mallarmé distinguishes quite clearly between the "presque disparition" and the "disparition suprême."

The editor Alphonse Lemerre writes in the introduction to *Le Tombeau*, "Nous avons eu la pensée de consacrer à la Mémoire de ce

Maître un monument littéraire renouvelé de ces Tombeaux que les Poëtes du XVI siècle élevaient à leurs morts illustres."[53] So these nineteenth-century poets were writing their "Tombeaux" in the tradition of the Renaissance funerary poem. This fact gains more significance when one realizes that Renaissance funerary poems were themselves consciously modeled after Greek anthologies.[54] Given this literary connection, it is not surprising that Mallarmé's imagery carries echoes of a Greek funerary torch, a minotaur, and the labyrinth.

As it is typically interpreted, the "toast funèbre" of the poem is a toast to the dead poet: "Salut de la démence et libation blême, / Ne crois pas qu'au magique espoir du corridor / J'offre ma coupe vide où souffre un monstre d'or!" (TF, ll. 2–4). The term "salut," however, does contain multiple valences. It is a farewell to the deceased, yet "salut" also denotes salvation, and *la coupe de salut* is the sacramental cup of the eucharist which contains the body and blood of Christ, through the agency of which the Christian hopes to attain eternal life. The "monstre d'or," when coupled with the "coupe," brings to mind the monstrance—the golden receptacle which contains the sacred host, the body of Christ. The toast is also reminiscent of Faust's summoning of Mephistopheles by drinking a secret potion (FM 172–73). But Mallarmé cannot magically call forth Gautier's apparition. The cup is empty, and Gautier has merged with nothingness.

Another intriguing signification exists for the "coupe vide." Mallarmé often employs images of empty containers as a sign of impotency: the unicorn horn of *Igitur*, the empty tomb, an empty cup. Gautier's body is said to have been placed in "un lieu de porphyre" (l. 6). Porphyry, a stone in which gems are conceived and embedded, is metaphorically related to the womb.[55] It should be noted that Mallarmé saw his own crisis in terms of impotency, and that in *Igitur* the dice cast from the unicorn's horn are absorbed into the "chateau de la pureté," imagery that is full of sexual innuendo. The masculine dice holder and the feminine horn unite in the androgynous unicorn—"Le Cornet est la Corne de licorne—d'unicorne. Mais l'Acte s'accomplit" (I 441). But as soon as the die is cast, the act is finished, and the unity is no more. The interlacing of womb, tomb, sex, death and the poetic act are apparent in both *Igitur* and "Toast funèbre."

The first line of "Toast funèbre" is isolated from the rest of the poem:

O de notre bonheur, toi, le fatal emblème![56]

The significance of this isolation is reinforced by the image of the solitary hero in the second stanza. The "toi" of the poem is separated, isolated—an emblem which, though it may be physical in its manifestation, is unreachable in death. The second person pronoun suggests that the poet addresses Gautier and that he is the emblem. In the Greek, *emblema* meant an insertion (from *em*—in, and *ballein*—to throw, or put) (WD). This is appropriate for Gautier, whose body has been inserted into the tomb. Yet an emblem is also a representative object, a signifier with connotations of truth. The tomb and the labyrinth are already emblems of philosophical and moral significance. Gautier in "Toast funèbre" becomes an emblem denoting the poet in general and the poet's venture.

As in *Igitur*, the funerary monument with its corridors and walkways recalls the maze; in fact, labyrinthine structures recur throughout the poem: "corridor," "portes," "murs," "allée." The images of the corridor and the "monstre d'or" evoke the intertext of the Cretan labyrinth constructed by Daedalus to hold the Minotaur.[57] Gautier is inserted into the tomb, but for the sake of the poem, he is inserted into the labyrinth, where his image takes the place of the Minotaur, the "monstre d'or," at the center. This *monstre d'or* combines several images: the monstrance, the alchemist's gold (which can only be reached by attaining the center of Solomon's labyrinth), and the Minotaur. The Minotaur is golden due to both his royal heritage, and his tortuous beauty (an idea later explored by the surrealists, especially in the journal *Minotaure* and in Picasso's *Minotauromachy*).[58] In Mallarmé's mythology, the Minotaur is a creature conceived at midnight, when the bull which pulls the chariot of the sun meets Pasiphaé, who is symbolic of the morning (DA

1233). The Minotaur is born of the unity of light and shadow, presence and absence. This is where the concept of the gaze, which Mallarmé refers to in the poem as a "regard diaphane," becomes crucial. Both the Minotaur in the Cretan myth and Gautier in "Toast funèbre" serve in the capacity of the Other. The reader who enters the labyrinth of the poem must face the entombed image of Gautier, just as Theseus faced the Minotaur. The image of Gautier actually becomes a specular image of the reader in his or her journey through the poem.

Gautier's body also is presented as an object both present in and absent from the poem. The body is Gautier, and yet Gautier's essence is absent. Yet as an emblem, an apparition against which the poetic voice takes measure of itself, Gautier's spectre encounters reflections of self in the tomb. Now instead of a figure of duality, there is a chain of signification. He is alternately—"vierge héros," "le Maître," "le splendide génie éternel"—in contrast to his appearance as the "fatal emblème," "le monstre d'or," and "l'absence."

"Toast funèbre" is first and foremost an evocation of the void and the poet's relationship to it. "Vaste gouffre," "l'amas de la brume," and "le néant" clearly bring the void to mind. In "Toast funèbre," death is the ending of life; it leads to nothingness:

> Ton apparition ne va pas me suffire:
> Car je t'ai mis moi-même, en un lieu de porphyre.

Although the ancient Greeks had their own ideas on the afterlife, Mallarmé uses the Greek ritual to negate the Christian idea of resurrection.

> Le rite est pour les mains d'éteindre le flambeau
> Contre le fer épais des portes du tombeau. (ll. 7–8)

The extinguishing of the torch on the tomb symbolizes the cessation of life.[59] Mathieu Giraldo's *Histoire curieuse et pittoresque des sorciers* (Paris, 1846), a popular book through the end of the nineteenth century, contains a frontispiece which depicts Dr. John

Dee, the astrologer of Queen Elisabeth, and Edward Kelly, a medium, evoking the spirit of a dead person at an English cemetery. Dee holds a torch aloft in his hand. The effort to communicate with the dead involved the extinguishing of a torch. These necromancers are discussed in *Le Satanisme et la magie*, a book for which Mallarmé's colleague Huysmans wrote the preface.[60] The torch represents both the farewell to the dead and the effort to communicate with the spirit world.

No matter how heroic he may be in life, Gautier in death cannot be a spiritual guide through the labyrinth because "le splendide génie éternel n'a pas d'ombre" (l. 38). The poem, however, does live on, and the dead poet is placed within the labyrinth of the poetic text, in which he is sealed, like the pharoahs entombed in the Egyptian labyrinth. For Mallarmé, the "magique espoir du corridor" is indeed an empty hope. There is no communicating with the dead, and Gautier is not to be resurrected, yet at the same time, his poetry is present. The rite is not merely the symbolic gesture of extinguishing the torch against the iron gate of the tomb; it also appears to represent the actual writing of the poem. With this in mind, it becomes apparent that the golden monster which Mallarmé offers in his toast also refers to the poem. Both the tomb and the poem will hold Gautier, or at least his absence: "Très-simple de chanter l'absence du poète, / Que ce beau monument l'enferme tout entier" (ll. 9–11). The beautiful monument has multiple significations. First it represents the tomb—a symbol of Gautier's absence. It is also the *tombeau* into which Mallarmé places the dead poet and so is synonymous with the poem. Finally, Gautier has left behind the monument of his own *oeuvre*, which contradicts his absence. The extinguishing of the torch and the writing of the "tombeau," both by his own hands, deny the idea of the resurrection. As Fowlie has asserted, all that is left of Gautier is contained in the monuments erected for him, the tomb and the poem (FM 174). As suggested in the first line of the poem which is isolated from all the other lines, the image that has been created of Gautier is set apart and unattainable.

As the adjective "fatal" implies, it is the poet in death, inserted in the tomb, which becomes emblematic. On one level, this emblem can stand for Gautier, or a figure of death, but this emblem is not a fixed sign. It also, and more importantly, represents the subject as perceived in the Other. The object of the poem "toi, le fatal emblème" is actually a constantly shifting chain of signs: "monstre d'or," "apparition," "l'absence du poète," "vierge héros," "Homme aboli," "le Maître," "le splendide génie éternel," "poète pur," and "Gautier." Gautier is mentioned by name only at the end of the poem as the last in the chain.

The term "blason" (l. 17) in the poem refers to emblems of heraldry, but it also signifies a pompous display of words (WD), and the poems are themselves "des deuils épars" for the loss of Gautier. The poet is identified as a hero who had sought to acquire knowledge and immortality, which can be gained through tracing the labyrinth and defeating the minotaur.

Knowledge of the ideal can never be attained. In death a person passes into pure form, becoming one with the labyrinth, but once death is reached, the ideal can no longer be conceived nor can it be communicated. Gautier cannot say the words of knowledge because he has become part of "le néant." In the final stanza of "Toast funèbre" Mallarmé again affirms that life is "déjà tout le séjour." Gautier has merged with the Nothingness. The closest the poet can come to immortality is in his poetry. However, the poem is not simply an image of absence. What is left of Gautier is embedded in the labyrinth of the "Tombeaux" poems. He is both present and absent, like the gems that are generally embedded in *porphyre*. It is the dead poet who is the emblem of the poem, the tributary ornament of which Mallarmé writes. Just as Igitur appears as the Mallarméan mythic hero, "le suprême incarnation de [sa] race," Gautier is depicted as the poet figure inscribed in his own textual labyrinth. He is emblematic both as the Master poet in death and, as the first line of the poem implies, as a representative figure for all poets. The poet seeks to reach the ineffable through creative endeavor, but at best can only attain a hybrid. Like the Minotaur ("un monstre d'or"), the poet's creation is half ideal and half a perverted distortion of reality. The Minotaur is also symbolic of death, and it is with the absence of life that the poet finally merges with the ideal to be present thereafter only in the "Tombeaux."

The language of the poem is itself a multicursal maze with numerous twists and turns interlaced with labyrinthine imagery. The words of the poet, like the wanderer in the labyrinth, are constantly progressing, but even for a poet like Gautier, so full of words, the answer remains the same, "Je ne sais pas!" (l. 31). Perhaps if the poet cannot be a Hero, he or she can be viewed as a spiritual guide. The third stanza begins with "Le Maître, par un oeil profond" (l. 32). As a Master poet, Gautier serves as a guide through life's mysteries. With his "regard diaphane" the way through the labyrinth of the physical world becomes transparent. Gautier is both the hero of silence and the master of speech (FM 178). Like Adam, he gives "le mystère d'un nom" to the different objects in his garden. However, not all mysteries are solved. The reader who manages to unravel the maze of Mallarmé's poem will at best find an approximate rendering of "what the living author has imperfectly understood" (FM 182). Unlike the virginal, unchanging dream of the passerby, the world is restless, changing ("l'inquiète merveille") and beyond human comprehension.

Mallarmé does envision at least a metaphoric resolution to the chain of deferral in the form of the poem itself. Poetry, Mallarmé writes, is the *unique source* for dealing with complex intellectual problems.[61] The poem is always a place of transformation, and its absolute meaning is never attainable. In Mallarmé the "notion pure" is negatively defined by its absence in material reality. However, it is revealed in poetry itself as a result of poetry's "immanent reflexivity and self-sufficiency" (RM 73), by the search for the best possible equilibrium. In the words of Mallarmé:

> la Poésie est l'expression, par le langage humain ramené à son rythme essentiel, du sens mystérieux des aspects de l'existence: elle doue ainsi d'authenticité notre séjour et constitue la seule tâche spirituelle.[62]

The poem is an unsolvable mystery, but at least the poet has the capacity to put the dream into words.

Chapter 5

Deviations of the Heart
in the Labyrinth of the World
in Marguerite Yourcenar's *Feux*

Marguerite Yourcenar displays an intense interest in mythology even in her earliest writings. The explicitness of mythic intertexts is so prevalent that myth is generally regarded as the primary locus of her *oeuvre*.[1] Yourcenar herself has asserted that myth "a été pour l'artiste et le poète européen une tentative de langage universel."[2] The Cretan myth of the labyrinth and its associated characters, in particular, have influenced her thought and recur as themes in her works.

Part of Yourcenar's fascination with the labyrinth can be traced to her father, Michel de Crayencour, who translated into French *Le Labyrinthe du Monde et le Paradis du Coeur*, a seventeenth-century text by Jan Amos Comenius.[3] In Comenius' allegorical work, a pilgrim explores the world only to find that fulfillment is to be gained not in the external realm but in the inner recesses of his own heart. Yourcenar later would borrow the title of this book for her autobiographical work *Le Labyrinthe du Monde*.[4]

Yourcenar's first book of poetry *Le Jardin des chimères*,[5] written when she was just sixteen, is a retelling of the story of Icarus. In her poetic rendition, Icarus is not the headstrong youth who mistakenly flies too close to the sun, rather he seeks escape from the labyrinth of the world through a "fusion volontaire dans l'absolu."[6] She also wrote a drama based on the Cretan myth, *Qui n'a pas son Minotaure?* (1963).[7] In this theatrical piece the labyrinth is presented as every person's inner darkness.[8] Yourcenar has asserted of her play that it contains "la vision du monde qui sous-tend tous mes livres."[9] The theme of the labyrinth recurs throughout her works, not merely those where the motif is explicit. Her dramatic reinterpretation of the myth was conceived during a literary game in the 1930's:

> A Paris, vers 1932, à moins que ce ne fût en 1933 ou même en 1934, deux jeunes hommes et une femme se proposèrent un beau jour le petit jeu littéraire qui consiste à se distribuer réciproquement les rôles de Thésée, d'Ariane et du Minotaure, à charge d'écrire chacun de son côté un sketch ou un conte présentant son point de vue sur cette aventure.[10]

The young woman was Yourcenar, and her story, originally published as *Ariane et l'aventurier*, deconstructs Theseus' role as hero and positions Ariadne as the central character.[11] Yourcenar had a special affinity with Ariane who appeared earlier in *Les Dieux ne sont pas morts*, in a poem entitled "Paroles d'Ariane."[12]

Feux was first written in 1935 when the author was 32. This lyric text, an *entrelacement* of poetic prose and personal thoughts, incorporates numerous aspects of the labyrinthine aesthetic, including labyrinths of love and death, descent into the self, and Icarian flight. As in her other works, Yourcenar consciously uses elements from traditional myths, transforming these myths to express the contemporary cultural consciousness. Significantly, the first story of *Feux*, "Phèdre ou le désespoir," includes a refiguration of the labyrinth. The daedalian structure is metamorphosed into the corridors of the subway system, and in this story, it is Phèdre rather than Thésée who must descend into its depths:

> Poussée par la cohue de ses ancêtres, elle glisse le long de ces corridors de métro, pleins d'une odeur de bête, où les rames fendent l'eau grasse du Styx, où les rails luisants ne proposent que le suicide ou le départ.[13]

The corridors of this modern labyrinth still reek with the odor of her monstrous brother, whatever form he might now take, and the options available to Phèdre are ultimately the same faced by anyone who enters the Minotaur's lair: death or escape.

Many of the characters and motifs of mythology are retained in Yourcenar's text, but modified to suit the new context. Yet "Phèdre ou le désespoir" is not merely a myth of antiquity viewed through a modern lens. The labyrinth itself has a polysemic character,[14] and Yourcenar makes ample use of the intertextual significations. The mythical, historical, and legendary figures of *Feux* echo previous incarnations. Most directly, Yourcenar's retelling of "Phèdre" is a distorted reflection of the Racinian tragedy *Phèdre*. As Yourcenar explains in her preface:

> A des degrés divers, tous ces récits modernisent le passé; certains, de plus, s'inspirent de stages intermédiaires que ces mythes ou ces légendes ont franchis avant d'arriver jusqu'à nous, de sorte que "l'antique" proprement dit n'est souvent dans *Feux* qu'une première couche peu visible. Phèdre n'est nullement la Phèdre athénienne; c'est l'ardent coupable que nous tenons de Racine. (10)

Racine's Phèdre herself remolds the myth, creating new metaphoric labyrinths and refiguring the misdirections of the maze. She attempts to reenact the events of the myth, by casting herself and Hippolyte in various roles.[15] Yourcenar's Phèdre endeavors to achieve the same ends; blinded by her passion, she has constructed a realm of misdirection around her.

Among the layers of meaning and echoes of previous incarnations, Phèdre inhabits a mythical world with a distinctly modern atmosphere. Similarly, Yourcenar's drama *Qui n'a pas son Minotaure?*, the first version of which was written just a few years prior to *Feux*, establishes correlations between the mythical past and modern realities:

> Le Minotaure et son antre, les victimes courant d'elles-mêmes à la mort, les Thésées velléitaires et les Minos clignant de l'oeil au crime, éclairés par le jet des projecteurs de 1944, acquéraient tout à coup une terrible réalité de symboles.[16]

In the description of the victims being carted away to their deaths in the labyrinth, there are numerous allusions to the German death camps. Thésée refers to one of the victims as a "jeune Hébreu" (Scène III, 193), the Minotaure's fits are described as "holocaustes," and the Athenians are called "les élus" (Scène II, 187) (HV 21–22).

In all of her works, Yourcenar interweaves mythical and modern voices. In *Feux* these polyphonic vignettes alternate with a number of *pensées* of a deeply personal nature. *Feux* was published at the end of a relationship, and for Yourcenar the work is an attempt to reconcile her own affairs of the heart. Most of the *pensées* are taken directly from her diary, and in the preface, Yourcenar refers to *Feux* as "produit d'une crise passionnelle" (9). Her personal reflections on love are mirrored in the protagonists of the lyrical prose pieces, each of whom experiences an all-encompassing love. She describes the book as "une série de proses lyriques reliées entre elles par une certaine notion de l'amour" (9). The stories can be viewed as variations on the theme of love, and the *pensées* serve as personal threads of thought which tie the text together. The interweaving of these primarily mythical explorations of love with the meditations from her diary allows the personal experience to merge with the divine and thus "ne rien perdre de la complexité d'une émotion ou de la ferveur de celle-ci" (20).

Deviations in the Textual Labyrinth

The textual labyrinth by definition contains a general trajectory involving a descent into the text, the reaching of a center, and a reascension, but if it is a multicursal labyrinth, it is also a space full of deviations.[17] Although there are numerous detours and deviations in *Feux*, they may be categorized as essentially threefold. First, the myths deviate from the fixed frameworks commonly associated with them. Secondly, there are structural and metaphorical deviations created in the multiple voices and shifting significations. And finally, there are the deviations from societal norms and expectations regarding affairs of the heart.

Yourcenar's rearticulations of myth invariably stray from their intertextual sources. This is in part due to their modernization, but it also results from Yourcenar's deconstruction or demythification of the symbolic content associated with the figures she employs. Rather than extol their heroic virtues, Yourcenar aims

> to dismantle their symbolic hypostasis, to reinvest the myths with the ductility lost, and to project against their fixed structural framework conceptions that undermine their semiotic fixity, revealing them to be fraught with the very contradictions they have ostensibly served to resolve. (HV 5)

The contradictions involved in the Cretan myth have always been part of the symbolic repertoire, but they are often buried under the adventures of the hero; the sacrificed victims are saved, the Minotaur is defeated . . . but at the same time, Ariadne is deserted, and Theseus' oversight leads to the death of his father. Of course, Theseus did not singlehandedly escape from the labyrinth; he could not have found his way out again without Ariadne's guiding thread. These contradictions demand attention in Yourcenar's retellings of the tale. In *Qui n'a pas son Minotaure?*, Theseus does not even succeed in defeating the Minotaur, finding only past and future selves in the labyrinth, which he can neither defeat nor understand. Tellingly, Ariadne and Autolycos, who are listening to the confrontation in the labyrinth, discover that Theseus and the Minotaur have indistinguishable voices.

The dialogue actually becomes polyphonic in some instances, the most explicit of which occurs in Scene II of *Qui n'a pas son Minotaure?*. This scene takes place in the ship's hold and unfolds entirely in the dark. The voices of the sacrificial victims, identified only by number, discuss their predicament *en route* to the Minotaure's labyrinth. These voices represent a wide range of existential thought, each displaying some degree of validity, yet each defining self in reaction to *le monde extérieur*.

In *Feux* this polyphonic effect is achieved in part through the use of the *pensées*. The *pensées*, according to Yourcenar's preface, serve both to clarify and obscure the stories. As she explains in the

"Avertissement" to the original edition of *Feux*: "L'auteur a entremêlé des pensées, qui furent pour lui les théorèmes de la passion, de récits qui les illustrent, les expliquent, et souvent les masquent."[18] The interlocutor's voice of the *pensées* engages in a dialogue with the voices of the stories. These *pensées* have been reordered from their positions in the original publication of *Feux*[19] to complement the prose poems. The alternating structure gives additional meaning to the parts and to the whole.

Each prose poem is one long meandering paragraph, what Harry Rutledge refers to as a "surrealist stream of consciousness."[20] Both within stories and throughout the text, the same symbols are repeated in different combinations creating a "kaleidoscope" of dizzying proportions. Image patterns "constantly shift and form new designs. The elements in the compositions thus formed may be identical or similar words whose repetition forms a bond among two or more stories, or with the *pensées*" (FFF 26). Chains of signification interweave and recur with subtle deviations. This patterning adds a labyrinthine quality to the text.[21]

The stories each give a different perspective on love utilizing a voice distinct from the others. Despite the fact that there is no explicit dialogue in the narrative, the various voices of the text constantly interact. The *pensées* are all told in the first person, though the perspectives vary constantly. In the first half of *Feux*, all of the stories are told in the third person. Starting with "Marie-Madeleine ou le salut," the narrative switches to the first person. In the final story, "Sappho ou le suicide," the first person pronoun is used only once, as the first word: "Je viens de voir au fond des miroirs d'une loge une femme qui s'appelle Sappho" (193). After this sentence, there is a return to the use of the third person: "Elle est pâle comme la neige, la mort, ou le visage clair des lépreuses." Yet this is a return with a difference. The "je" in the end is able to see itself reflected in the Other, similar to Ariane's merger with the cosmic in the end of *Qui n'a pas son Minotaure?*.

The images of love enjoyed by the characters in *Feux* also deviate from the norms of society. This contributes to Yourcenar's emphasis on the need to cleanse self by entering the corridors of the mind. In her preface, Yourcenar describes the expressionism of her writing as "une forme d'aveu naturel et nécessaire" (YF 20). The confessional nature of the text endows her chosen pen name *Yourcenar* with possible symbolism as well: the text conceived of as a letter to the reader, signed "your sinner." Yourcenar writes: "Je ne crois pas comme ils croient, je ne vis pas comme ils vivent, je n'aime pas comme ils aiment" (30). But even if her thoughts and her loves are unacceptable to the public, they are not without precedent in myth, and in the end, what is deviant for Yourcenar is not defined by societal norms but rather by self.

In *Qui n'a pas son Minotaure?*, as Thésée and Phèdre sail away, Phèdre, foreshadowing her future passionate obsession, innocently says: "J'espère, Thésée, que je me ferai aimer d'Hippolyte" (Scène X, 231). In *Feux*, this passion has already come to fruition. Phèdre's love for Hippolyte is not truly biologically incestuous, though love for a stepson would likely be regarded as such in most societies. In Hippolyte, Phèdre searches for what she lacks: youth, masculinity, virginity, and purity. At the same time, she constructs an Hippolyte who personifies the very qualities she seeks: "Elle fabrique sa beauté, sa chasteté, ses faiblesses; elle les extrait du fond d'elle-même; elle isole de lui cette pureté détestable pour pouvoir la haïr sous la figure d'une fade vierge" (YF 33). She takes qualities buried in herself and uses them to construct Hippolyte; for her, he reflects aspects of the self that have been submerged in her own persona. She externalizes her own needs and inadequacies and then becomes dependent upon this externalization.

Phèdre not only creates an Hippolyte to suit her needs, she also turns the surroundings into a labyrinth: "Dans cette forêt vierge qui est le lieu d'Hippolyte, elle plante malgré soi les poteaux indicateurs du palais de Minos: elle trace à travers ces broussailles le chemin à sens unique de la Fatalité" (33). Phèdre is so familiar with the passages of the labyrinth, her "palais familial," that she insists: "Je ne puis m'y perdre." For this reason, she asserts: "La mort, pour me tuer, aura besoin de ma complicité" (39). Without some complicity on her part, Phèdre will not be destroyed by the labyrinth.

In the first group of *pensées*, the persona asserts: "Il y a entre nous mieux qu'un amour: une complicité" (29). This complicity is exactly what is necessary for a love relationship to exist between Phèdre and Hippolyte. Phèdre's love is based on a deceptive mirroring of self that she looks for in her stepson. But in order for the deception to work, Hippolyte would have to comply with Phèdre's vision of him.[22] When he does not, this throws Phèdre into despair.

The reader encounters a constantly shifting image of the subject in the passages of *Feux*. At the same time, there are shifting images of gender roles and relationships, to such an extent that Yourcenar employs the image of the "bal masqué" to refer to her book. The cross-dressing which occurs in "Achille ou le mensonge" and "Clytemnestre ou le crime" is indicative of the fluidity of identity which occurs in *Feux*. When Sappho embarks on a quest for her female lover Attys, she finds Phaon, a male lover instead. Phaon is a mirror image of Attys, despite the obvious gender difference—so much so that for a time Sappho attempts to deny her own sexuality and her own self-identity.

The Descent into Self

Farrell and Farrell have suggested that the basic theme of *Feux* is "a journey, a quest, a descent into the self (or into Hell) and the return" (50). More specifically, it is the journey of the maze-walker. In her preface to *Qui n'a pas son Minotaure?*, Yourcenar writes:

> La promenade de Thésée dans les détours du Labyrinthe, bâclée en quelques lignes dans l'ancienne *Ariane*, s'intériorisait en quelque sorte, me donnait envie de décrire la grotesque démarche d'un homme égaré dans les replis de soi-même.[23]

This is precisely what occurs in *Feux*. The structure of the labyrinth is internalized in the text and in Yourcenar's own reflections on love. Starting with "Phèdre ou le désespoir" and ending with "Sappho ou le suicide," *Feux* mirrors the descent and reascension, or the entering and exiting, of the labyrinth of self.

The figure of the daedalian maze recurs throughout *Feux*, though it is most recognizable in the first story. The subway system, "les corridors souterrains de nos villes" (23), through which Phèdre searches, are referred to as "sa Crète souterraine" (36). The reader does not have to stretch the imagination to find the labyrinth in the story of Phédon whose "sang coulait en mille détours comme ces fleuves souterrains" (144), or in "Sappho ou le suicide," as she searches for her lover through the most rundown sections of the cities she visits.

In fact, the structure of the text itself reflects the figure of the labyrinth. There are nine stories: the first four emphasizing the descent into the labyrinth, a center story in which the persona has reached the lowest point, and the final four stories which involve the reascension out of the labyrinth. Farrell and Farrell have noted that "the author has carefully structured the book, distributing and balancing its components so that the second half echoes and mirrors the first half" (FFF 27). At the same time, within each story and among stories, there are interconnections and repetitions. Furthermore, the *pensées* serve to interweave all of the elements of the text, and reinforce the notion that *Feux* is a personal journey into the labyrinth.

Born Marguerite Antoinette Jeanne Marie Ghislaine Cleenewerke de Crayencour, she chose her pen name, later to become her legal name, as an anagram. She dropped the second "c" in Crayencour so that what remains is four letters, a center, and four more letters: "Your c enar." Viewed again in this light, the anagram may also be understood as a reference to "your inner c(enter)." Her name and her "self" thus serve as an emblem for the structure of the text.

This descent into self represents the experience of a "vertiginous disorientation" (HV 28–29) countered by an attempt to define self internally. The personal voice of the *pensées* serves as a guiding thread. In the first three stories, the voices are given a third person pronoun (two of them are also masculine) because they are viewed as voices external to Yourcenar's self. When the voices are recognized as being internal, the narrative begins a reascension. Finally, at the return to the exit/entrance, the voices are recognized as being aspects of self, and the he, she, and I all merge.

The theme of the descent into self recurs in *Feux*. Phèdre's labyrinth grows out of her impossible love for her stepson Hippolyte. This unrequited love causes withdrawal, which is plainly symbolized first in Phèdre's abandoning of Crete and then in her desertion of Thésée's well-ordered world, "where passions like hers did not exist" (FFF 30–31). Phèdre's desire for the unattainable Other is so great that it seems inevitable that she will yield to her passion. Confronted with the coldness of Hippolyte, she descends into the labyrinth, "son propre enfer" (34). As Yourcenar states, "elle reconstruit au fond de soi-même un Labyrinthe où elle ne peut que se retrouver" (34). Phèdre, like Daedalus and like the poet, constructs the labyrinth herself, yet the guiding thread becomes ineffectual for her, and instead of leading her, it only constricts her heart: "le fil d'Ariane ne lui permet plus d'en sortir, puisqu'elle se l'embobine au coeur" (34). When Hippolyte disappears from her life, "aspirée par ce vide, elle s'engouffre dans la mort" (35). She kills herself because she is unable to cope with the image of self she discovers.

Both the second and the third story involve Achilles. In "Achille ou le mensonge," the legendary hero is in hiding disguised as a woman. He suffers both from his virtual imprisonment and from his undisguised desire to become Déidamie, "cette femme qu'il avait essayé, non seulement de posséder, mais d'être" (50). In a blind passion, he strangles Déidamie and escapes from his prison aided by a "masculine" woman, Misandre. Significantly, in committing his murder, Achille throws down his sword and "se ser[t] pour serrer le cou de Déidamie de ses mains de fille" (49). After symbolically killing his feminine self, Achille turns to a more "masculine" form of murder on the battlefield.[24] In "Patrocle ou le destin," Achille fights with a sword as a "man." He kills Penthésilée a "masculine" woman who was worthy of being a friend and "le seul être au monde qui ressemblait à Patrocle" (69). The battle scene is compared to a Russian ballet, or dance, which Achille ends with a throw of the sword. The deviations here are at least twofold. In the implicit homosexuality or bisexuality there is a deviance from societal norms. But there is another form of deviation at play. Achille kills twice. The first time, dressed as a woman, he symbolically strangles his feminine self. The second time, on the battlefield, he kills a female reflection of his beloved Patrocle. Achille is bewildered and directionless, and as a result, he searches for mirrorings in the world external to self. His deviations lead Achille to kill both a lover who is a reflection of himself, and a female Patrocles who, he realizes too late, could easily have been his lover.

The dual deviations continue in story four "Antigone ou le choix." Antigone is both a daughter of and a sister to Oedipe. She is born of deviance, and in order to escape from the labyrinth of the world, she seeks the absolute. The man who would be her lover, Hémon, "se précipite sur ses pas dans les corridors noirs" (83). Although she loves several men in her life, she does so with "l'affreuse virginité qui consiste à n'être pas de ce monde" (80). Like an Ariadne figure, Antigone guides her blind father/brother through battlefields and maze-like cities. Yet rather than accept love, for herself, she only seeks separation from this world. The only exit from her labyrinth is that of death.

Léna's story, "Léna ou le secret," the most elaborate of the prose poems, lies at the center. The *pensées* following "Léna" render explicit the idea that this is the lowest point of the descent described in *Feux*. Yourcenar writes: "Je ne tomberai pas. J'ai atteint le centre" (112). In Léna, the reader sees a total emasculation of the protagonist's self. Léna would do anything for the love of Aristogiton. So when he begins a relationship with his co-conspirator, Harmodios, Léna does not protest. She becomes the servant of her lover, and worst of all, she no longer takes any control over the events in her life. She plays no part in constructing herself or her lover, and there is no complicity in their love—only in her degradation. When the plot to overthrow the dictator fails, Léna's great embarrassment is that "elle n'était qu'une servante et nullement une complice" (109). Rather than making this humiliating confession, Léna cuts off her tongue. To keep from revealing secrets which she does not even have, she gives up her ability to talk—though at this point, the loss is only symbolic, as she had lost her voice long before.

It is in the center of the text that the persona rediscovers "le vrai sens des métaphores de poètes" (100). Particularly, she refers to the line from Racine, "Brûlé de plus de feux que je n'en allumai."[25] All she has received from love is adoration or pity, and she now realizes that "l'amour fou" can be at the center of the type of emasculation represented in Léna.

In the sixth story "Marie-Madeleine ou le salut," the reascension begins. The protagonist mirrors Antigone in her search for an absolute. The differences are, however, distinct. Whereas Antigone seeks escape from this world (YF 80), Marie-Madeleine is very much a worldly woman. Another distinction is that Marie-Madeleine is led in her ascension by Jésus, who significantly holds a ball of thread when he rises from the tomb. It is this guidance that allows Marie-Madeleine to learn to see the value in her experiences.

In the seventh story "Phédon ou le vertige," Phédon, taken into slavery as a youth, also needs guidance to ascend from the depths. Phédon, for whom the straight road seems circular (143), is guided by the wisdom of Socrate, who is "idéal comme une caricature, qui se suffisait au point d'être devenu son propre créateur" (153). Despite the wisdom they have witnessed, after his death, Socrate's disciples reveal that they are only "les membres épars du Philosophe éteint" (164). They are guided by his wisdom but unable to internalize it. Only Phédon continues to dance "sur la sagesse" (165). Phédon comes to the realization that:

> Il n'y a ni vertu, ni pitié, ni amour, ni pudeur, ni leurs puissants contraires, mais rien qu'une coquille vide dansant au haut d'une joie qui est aussi la Douleur, un éclair de beauté dans un orage de formes. (166)

Phédon moves beyond time and space, beyond dialectics.[26] The story of "Phédon ou le vertige" does not utilize explicit images of the labyrinth, but it adds to the overall labyrinthine structure of the text. The protagonist tells the story in the first person, and he rises above the walls of the worldly maze. Phédon has found his freedom; still his contentment is gained in disengaging from the world.

In "Clytemnestre ou le crime," there is an inversion of the second story. Just as Achille kills Déidamie, his female reflection, Clytemnestre, in killing Agamemnon, with whom she identifies, kills a male reflection of herself. Over the years, during his absence, "Je me substituais peu à peu à l'homme qui me manquait et dont j'étais hantée" (178–79). And when she kills him, she does so with "une hache," the weapon of the Minotaur. Whereas Achille's murder was the product of passion, Clytemnestre's victory is forty years in the making, and it is an action which will affirm self.

Several themes come to fruition in "Sappho ou le suicide." Sappho is no longer able to look at herself in the mirror. She turns away "pour ne pas voir ses seins tristes" (194). Unlike Narcissus, who certainly loves who he is, "Sappho dans ses compagnes adore amèrement ce qu'elle n'a pas été" (198). Just as Phèdre seeks what is missing in herself in her relationship with Hippolyte, Sappho at first looks to Attys for a completion of self. This is why as she faces the wardrobe mirrors, "elle pleure le linge disparu de la jeune fille aimée" (204). Attys has left her, and Sappho embarks on a quest to reclaim her lost love. She searches for Attys in the labyrinth of the world. When she finds a man who resembles Attys, she stops the search. But "ce Phaon à l'aise dans le travesti n'est plus qu'un substitut de la belle nymphe absente" (211). When Phaon eventually dresses in Attys' negligee, Sappho comes to the realization that "elle ne peut où qu'elle aille que retrouver Attys" (212). In all of her lovers, she will relive the happiness and the despair of her affair only to be abandoned again and again by a series of Attyses. Sappho has realized that her story too will repeat itself because anyone she loves will be Attys: "Ce visage démesuré lui bouche toutes les issues qui ne donnent pas sur la mort" (212). In order to escape this cycle, she decides to kill herself. The theme of the first story, suicide, returns, and the narrative arrives back where it started.

The Greek poetess-turned-acrobat decides to fall to her death from her trapeze. She climbs to an impossible height:

> la barre du trapèze balancée en plein vide change en oiseau cet être
> fatigué de n'être qu'à demi femme. [. . .] Sappho plonge, les bras

ouverts comme pour embrasser la moitié de l'infini, ne laissant
derrière soi que le balancement d'une corde pour preuve de son
départ du ciel. (213, 215)

Fortunately, her skill, experience, and artistry do not allow her to die.
She cannot miss the trapeze, and when she jumps, she lands in a net.
Sappho is pulled from the net "ruisselant de sueur comme une noyée
d'eau de mer" (129). A parallel is made with Icarus, who lands in the
sea and drowns, but the image of birth supersedes the Icarian
symbolism. Not only does she survive, but she ascends out of the
depths of the labyrinth, and the final image is one of rebirth.

Icarus, Ariadne, and the Rebirth of the Acrobat

In *Le Jardin des chimères*, Yourcenar created a dramatic retelling
of Icarus' flight. The adventurer in this tale defeats the Chimera and
dons its wings. Using these, he attempts to reach the sun, and the
supreme liberation.[27] Impressed with his youth, his courage, and his
dream, the people offer to make Icarus a leader. The winds tell him of
the lands he could visit with his wings, and the Sirens profess to love
him. But he forsakes all this, preferring instead to reach for the sun.
The voice of Hélios asserts at the end of the poem that Icarus'
inability to reach the absolute and his death when he falls from such
heights should not be considered failure since his glory is in "having
dreamed and tried, regardless of his ultimate end."[28] Yourcenar writes:

> Gloire à celui qui veut s'évader du mensonge!
> Gloire à celui qui tente, en un suprême élan,
> De monter . . .
> Vers le rayonnement des clartés immortelles!
> Le sacrifice obscur n'est jamais infertile . . . (YJ 117)

Echoes of this Icarus can be perceived throughout *Feux*. Images of
vertigo, falling, and death appear constantly, contrasting with the
image of flight, birds, airplanes, and angels.

The drama between flight and fall is most apparent in "Sappho ou le suicide." Sappho, the Icarian figure of the text, is "trop ailée pour le sol, trop charnelle pour le ciel, ses pieds frottés de cire ont rompu le pacte qui nous joint à la terre" (195). Sappho, the poet turned acrobat, is given symbolic wings: "Elle a l'air d'un athlète qui refuserait d'être ange pour ne pas enlever tout prix à ses sauts périlleux; de près, drapée de longs peignoirs qui lui restituent ses ailes, on lui trouve l'air d'être déguisée en femme" (195). She climbs the ladder higher and higher, ascending to impossible heights. The description of her ascension denotes a transcendence of the human condition (FFF 26). Like Ariadne, she metamorphoses:

> la barre du trapèze balancée en plein vide change en oiseau cet être
> fatigué de n'être qu'à demi femme; elle flotte, alcyon de son propre
> gouffre, suspendue par un pied sous les yeux du public qui ne croit
> pas au malheur. (YF 213–14)

The question remains as to why Sappho does not perish, and an answer can be found through the exploration of another mythic intertext from the Cretan myth.

In *Qui n'a pas son Minotaure?*, Ariane offers Thésée the opportunity to redeem himself. Thésée's companions were taken while he was being seduced by Phèdre, but now by using Ariane's thread, he has the possibility of entering the labyrinth and saving them. Thésée, who hopes to defeat the Minotaure, welcomes Ariane's offer and connects himself to this thread "comme le nouveau-né à sa mère" (Scène V, 205). Ariane has allowed herself to believe that Thésée is a heroic figure with whom she might find fulfillment, and so she attempts to save him from her sister and from himself. But Thésée cannot defeat his Minotaure; he cannot even locate the monster:

> Je m'y perds. . . Il fait noir comme dans un antre. Rien de plus
> exténuant que de se battre avec la nuit. Elle supprime le monde
> extérieur. J'ai l'impression de plonger dans mes ténèbres internes,
> et les circonvolutions du Labyrinthe me fait penser à mes

entrailles. Trouverai-je le Minotaure au fond? S'il n'existe pas, je vais me couvrir de ridicule. (Scène VI, 207)

Thésée never does fight the monster; all he finds in the labyrinth are images of future and past selves which he refuses to recognize. His failure lies partially in the fact that even in his internal adventure Thésée focuses on physical aspects. He makes the connection between the labyrinth and his entrails but sees no correlation to his psyche.

Ariane comes to the realization that if she cannot find fulfillment in a "hero" like Thésée, she will never find it with anyone outside of herself. In order to gain the love of Thésée, she would have to enter into a complicity with him which would necessitate acting more like her sister, and Ariane is well aware that she will never triumph over Phèdre by becoming Phèdre (YQ 222). She would rather keep control of her own life. She therefore rejects the "dynamics of mimesis" in which everyone around her is intimately involved (HV 30).

There is a clear distinction between the other characters who base their construction of self on external factors and Ariane, who learns to follow a thread within herself. The Athenian victims sent to appease the Minotaure and the law of Minos allow their understandings of events to be directed by forces external to themselves. Phèdre likewise dreams of participating in her brother's hunts and hopes to find herself through being carried away by a hero. The Racinian Phèdre, whose intrigues create labyrinths, is echoed by young Phèdre and her desires. That Phèdre is leaving the island only to enter a new labyrinth of passion is indicated by her double-voiced final words as she sails off with Thésée, worried that her new stepson might not love her.

Ariane almost falls into this same trap, but when she discovers that Thésée is unable to find impetus and direction within himself, she finally accepts that there is no chance he could provide guidance for her life. Ariane recognizes that "seule, l'inquiétude de l'homme invente la Crète et fabrique Athènes" (Scène VIII, 220). She refuses to allow her actions to be dictated by "human misdirection" (HV 39).

Ariane turns away from the violence of her family and Thésée, but she will not accept becoming a passive bystander like the sacrificial victims. Instead she seeks to define her own consciousness. In the end, Ariane is the only one who actually has an encounter with the Minotaure. Everyone else looks for some external thread to guide them—only Ariane finds an internal thread which can lead her to the center of herself where the Minotaure resides. After Thésée leaves the island of Naxos with Phèdre, Ariane is approached by Bacchus and discovers that the Minotaure is one of his manifestations. Though Ariane has followed her own path, she now receives guidance from Bacchus. He offers her immortality. Still, she is sceptical of anything that is outside of herself. As she ponders the possibilities, Bacchus begins to change right before her eyes:

> Quoi? Cette chevelure n'est plus faite que de myrte, de muguet sauvage. . . Ces muscles gonflés sont des rocs où serpentent des veines de sardoine. . . Que tu es beau, rocher des âges! Tu t'étires, tu changes; de rocher tu deviens cristal, banquise, grand nuage blanc. . . Ni homme ni bête, peut-être pas même Dieu. . . Sorti des noms. . . Sorti des règnes. (YQ 228)

He assumes the form of the shifting interconnected cosmos which is both internal and external to her search for self. Her island rises up "to become a constellation,"[29] and gradually a mythic marriage occurs which allows Ariane to merge with the fabric of the universe.

The theme of Ariadne's thread first appears in *Feux* in the story of Phèdre, who has recreated a labyrinth inside herself. Ariadne's thread cannot guide her, "puisqu'elle se l'embobine au coeur" (34). Other characters, especially Marie-Madeleine and Phédon, also receive external guidance as they attempt to make their way out of their labyrinths. As for Sappho, in the end, rather than an external thread, she finds a guiding thread inside herself, one of skill and artistry which pulls her to the net despite her protests.[30]

Sappho, among her numerous resonances, has within her echoes of the two figures about whom Yourcenar has written with enthusiasm: Icarus and Ariadne. Like Icarus, she reaches impossible heights, but as an acrobat, she swings on a *fil*. Even when she is attempting to commit suicide, she cannot bring herself to let go of her lifeline. And when she does fall, she is caught by a net of threads. Farrell and Farrell see the acrobat as an image of inversion which "involves the exchange of masculine and feminine characteristics."[30] Even more to the point, as the final story is the only one which equates the "je" with the other, Sappho can be said to represent a merger of male and female. She is a bisexual, possibly even hermaphroditic figure. Sappho is truly a cross between Icarus and Ariadne. The merger of the mythical and the personal at the end of Sappho's story can be likened to Ariadne's merger with Bacchus. Fluidity of self and sexuality are no longer deviations but instead represent polyphonic unity.

Yourcenar does not make use of myth merely for literary purposes; this labyrinthine journey involves self-discovery and healing.[31] As Yourcenar states in the final group of *pensées*: "On ne bâtit un bonheur que sur un fondement de désespoir. Je crois que je vais pouvoir me mettre à construire" (217). The *pensées* close with a resolve not to be limited, but to enter into the depths of the heart and transcend despair.

Afterword

As a religious image, the labyrinth reflects the sacred truths of birth, initiation, death, and rebirth. In its ritual manifestations, the labyrinth prepares initiates for both a sacred life on earth and for rebirth into the afterlife. These mythic significations of the labyrinth have been retained to varying degrees in the corridors of the sign. In addition, the labyrinth has come to represent the quest for truth, self-knowledge, or love as well as the general condition of the world we live in.

The figure of the labyrinth represents both the search and the goal. But the goal is often constructed as being ineffable because it is outside the play of signification in the text. The center of the daedalian maze has connotations of both original presence and future possibilities. Numerous dualities reside in the labyrinth because the mythic signifier has always already acted as a linguistic sign, and these former and present aspects of the signifier exist simultaneously. In each new signification, the previous sign is both absent and present. The labyrinth embodies both the dialectically opposing significations and their synthesis. The text therefore can be conceived as a partial manifestation of the labyrinthine play of language, but it is not a totality, as it is extended by each interaction of author, text, and reader. The labyrinth is similar to a spider web in conception and design with its network of interlacing threads and its fusion of linear and circular dimensions.

The poetic texts discussed within have shaped the present-day conception of the labyrinth, and contemporary literature is replete with labyrinthine imagery. In fact, the twentieth century has been called the "age of the labyrinth" (PL 685). The suitability of this metaphor stems in part from the deconstruction of the notion that the center is an attainable goal.

The same words are always rearticulated to express new ideas, with the old meanings obscured. Thoughts, for all their diversity, return again and again to the same idea. The labyrinth is expressive of the underlying elements of the human condition as well as being a self-reflective metaphor for poetics. Michel Foucault asserts that:

> Peut-être cet espace des mythes sans âge est-il celui de tout langage—du langage qui s'avance à l'infini dans le labyrinthe des choses, mais que son essentielle et merveilleuse pauvreté ramène à lui-même en lui donnant son pouvoir de métamorphose: dire autre chose avec les mêmes mots, donner aux mêmes mots un autre sens.[1]

Each use of the labyrinth serves to reaccentuate the mythical signifier. This single emblem signifies the synthesis of life and death, the material and the spiritual, and absence and presence. The shifting connotations of the labyrinth amplify the polyvalence of the figure. In the maze of signification, everything has shadows, echoes, and traces.

There is an undeniably labyrinthine quality to the kind of unrestricted semantic play suggested in Jacques Derrida's concept of dissemination, with its constant dispersal and reformation of meaning. Derrida asserts that language is not merely a system of differences, but a system of differences perpetually deferred. Language is an endless process of *différance* and absence, a linguistic chain *ad infinitum.* There is necessarily a signifying network of signs, and it is only within this network that meaning is produced. For Derrida, all signifieds, not merely the mythic ones, always already function as signifiers. From the moment they enter the linguistic game, "there is not a single signified that escapes, even if recaptured, the play of signifying references that constitute language."[2] The search for signification is therefore infinite, "multiplication sans fin."[3] For this reason, Jacques Derrida has asserted that any discourse on myth "must itself be mythomorphic."[4]

Derrida argues that myth is always an acentric structure which has no absolute center (DSS 487). To search for center or truth within a discursive formation is an exhaustive and never-ending effort because it involves pealing back layer upon layer of historical meaning. Such is the quest for center that the search only leads back upon itself—there is nothing at the center except yet another quest. The labyrinthine center is not a fixed sign; it can be an initiatory experience for the subject or it can mean death of the self. The minotaur who resides in the center is a creature dual in form, and the circuitous path which leads to the center is often unnavigable. Yet the desire for a center persists. This desire for a center is what Derrida has called "logocentrism," and he sees no resolution to this search.

Derrida's theory of deconstruction can easily be construed in labyrinthine terms, and though he never chose to explicitly use the metaphor, his American disciple J. Hillis Miller has employed labyrinthine imagery with gusto. In Miller's conception, Ariadne's thread is manifest in the words of the poem strung together in the passages of the text. This thread of words may lead the reader through the textual labyrinth, but it is these very same words which create the labyrinth. Criticism is viewed as extending the labyrinth by creating more language about the poem's language. Miller writes,

> far from providing a benign escape from the maze, Ariadne's thread makes the labyrinth, is the labyrinth. The interpretation or solving of the puzzles of the textual web only adds more filaments to the web. One can never escape from the labyrinth because the activity of escaping makes more labyrinth, the thread of a linear narrative or story. Criticism is the production of more thread to embroider the texture or textile already there.[5]

The deconstructive critic enters the textual labyrinth and looks for the loose thread which will unravel it, but the very process of deconstruction also extends the labyrinth of signification.

In the postmodern world, where the self is in constant flux and there are multiple choices to be made for every event, life can easily be depicted as a series of labyrinths, or alternately, as one never-ending labyrinth. However, as Michel Foucault suggests:

> au moment le plus énigmatique, dans la rupture de tout chemin, quand on accède à la perte ou à l'origine absolue, quand on est au seuil de l'autre, le labyrinthe offre soudain le Même: son dernier

enchevêtrement, la ruse qu'il cache en son centre, c'est un miroir
de l'autre côté duquel on trouve l'identique. (FR 120)

When one reaches the middle and thinks he or she has solved the
maze, the surprise is that one is simply confronted with another
labyrinth, or the same labyrinth again. In a sense, fiction compensates
for the absence of an original truth or presence because in the literary
text, the reader has a privileged view of the labyrinth from both
within and above.

Appendix

Figure 1
Unicursal Labyrinth at Chartres Cathedral, adapted from Jules Gailhabaud,
L'Architecture du Vme au XVIIme siècle et les Arts qui en dépendent,
Paris 1858

Figure 2
Multicursal labyrinth, adapted from a maze design by André Mollet,
Le Jardin de plaisir, Sweden 1651

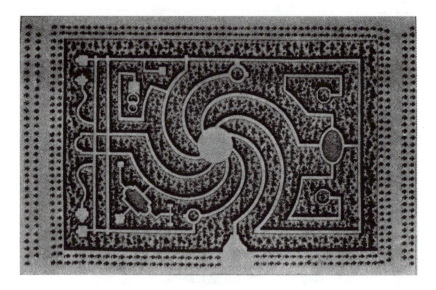

Figure 3
Pinwheel labyrinth at Chantilly Gardens (seventeenth century)
from Jacques François Blondel, *Cours d'architecture civile ou Traité de la
decoration, Distribution et construction des bâtiments contenant les leçons
données en 1750, et les années suivantes*, ed. M. Patte, Paris 1771–1777

Figure 4
Sefirot emanating from the first *sefirah*,
adapted from Moses Cordovero, *Pardes Rimmonim*, Cracow, 1592

Notes

Introduction

1. For a general account of the myth, see Edith Hamilton, *Mythology* (New York: Mentor, 1969).
2. Virgil, *The Aeneid*, trans. Patric Dickinson (New York: Mentor Books, 1961), Book 6, 121.
3. Ovid, *Metamorphoses*, trans. Frank Justus Miller (Cambridge: Harvard University Press, Loeb Classical Library, 1956), Book 8, 168.
4. "Emprisonné dans le labyrinthe avec son père qui avait aidé Ariane et Thésée à tuer le Minotaure, [Icare] réussit à s'évader de sa prison avec l'aide de Pasiphaé et grâce aux ailes que Dédale lui a faites et qu'il a fixées avec de la cire sur ses épaules" ("Icare," *Dictionnaire des symboles*, ed. Jean Chevalier and Alain Gheerbrant [Paris: Laffont, 1969] 417). Edith Hamilton writes that King Minos knew that Theseus could only have escaped with Daedalus' help: "Accordingly [King Minos] imprisoned [Daedalus] and his son Icarus in the Labyrinth, certainly a proof that it was excellently devised since not even the maker of it could discover the exit without a clue" (139).
5. Penelope Reed Doob, *The Idea of the Labyrinth from Classical Antiquity through the Middle Ages* (Ithaca: Cornell University Press, 1990) 175–78.
6. John Ruskin, *Works*, vol. 27, ed. E. T. Cook Alexander Wedderburn (London: George Allen, 1907) 407–8.
7. W. H. Mathews, *Mazes and Labyrinths: Their History and Development* (New York: Dover, 1970) 176.
8. I refer to both labyrinths and mazes rather interchangeably in this study, though there is an important distinction. A labyrinth is a type of maze, but a maze is not always a labyrinth.
9. Pliny, *Natural History*, trans. D. E. Eichholz, LCL, vol. 10 (London: Heinemann, 1962) 68–69; DIL 21.
10. Jacques François Blondel, *Cours d'architecture civile ou Traité de la decoration, Distribution et construction des bâtiments contenant les leçons données en 1750, et les années suivantes*, ed. M. Patte (Paris, 1771-7); W. H. Mathews, *Mazes and Labyrinths: Their History and Development* (New York: Dover, 1970) 121.
11. For an indepth look at the literary manifestations of the spiral and other vortices, see Charles D. Minahen's *Vortex/t: The Poetics of Turbulence* (University Park: Pennsylvania State University Press, 1992).

12. "Le labyrinthe serait une combinaison de deux motifs de la spirale et de la tresse et exprimerait une volonté très évidente de *figurer l'infini*" ("Labyrinthe," DS, 447).

13. Martin Heidegger, *What is a Thing?*, trans. W. B. Barton, Jr. (Chicago: Regnery, 1967) 242.

14. Not all of the works I have chosen to examine are poems in the strictest sense of the word. They are all poetic texts, but Racine's *Bajazet* (*OEuvres complètes* [Paris: Seuil, 1962] 183–203) is a poetic drama, and Yourcenar's *Feux* (Paris: Gallimard, 1974) is a combination of lyric prose and poetic *pensées*.

15. Dante, *The Divine Comedy, Inferno*, trans. Mark Musa (New York: Penguin, 1984).

16. Petrarch, *Canzoniere, Canzoniere, trionfi, rime varie* (Torino: Giulio Einaudi, 1958); *Petrarch's Lyric Poems: The* Rime sparse *and Other Lyrics*, trans. and ed. Robert M. Durling (Cambridge: Harvard University Press, 1976).

17. Paolo Santarcangeli, *Le Livre des labyrinthes. Histoire d'un mythe et d'un symbole*, trans. Monique Lacau (Paris: Gallimard, 1974).

18. Hermann Kern, *Labirinti: Forme e interputazioni. 5000 anni di prenzenza di un archetipo*, trans. Libero Sosio (Milan: Feltirinelli, 1981).

19. For writers such as Jorge Luis Borges, Mircea Eliade, Raymond Roussel, Michel Butor, James Joyce, Franz Kafka, Marguerite Yourcenar, and Umberto Eco, to name only a few, the labyrinth serves as a central motif.

20. Wendy Faris, *Labyrinths of Language* (Baltimore: Johns Hopkins University Press, 1988).

21. Donald Gutierrez, *The Maze in the Mind and the World: Labyrinths in Modern Literature* (Troy, New York: Whitston, 1985).

22. There are numerous articles dealing with the labyrinth as a mythic symbol and with the rites and dances connected to the myth. Those articles which are significant to the work at hand are mentioned in the following section on the Cretan myth.

23. Northrop Frye, *Anatomy of Criticism: Four Essays* (Princeton: Princeton University Press, 1957).

24. Kern examines this relationship in chapter 2 of *Labirinti*.

25. Boccaccio, *Il Comento alla Divina Commedia*, ed. Domenico Guerri, 3 vols. (Bari: Laterza, 1918) 2, 108. See also note 28.

26. "La caverne, chez Platon, comme l'antre chez Empédocle, signifie, me-sembe-t-il, notre monde, où la marche vers l'intelligence est pour l'âme la délivrance de ses liens et l'ascension hors de la caverne" (Plotinus, *The Fourth Ennead*, Eighth Tractate: "The Soul's Descent into the Body," *The Enneads*; *Dictionnaire des symboles*, ed. Jean Chevalier and Alain Gheerbrant [Paris: Laffont, 1969]).

27. Mircea Eliade, *Myths, Dreams, and Mysteries. The Encounter Between Contemporary Faiths and Archaic Realities*, trans. Philip Mairet (London: Harvill Press, 1960) 23.

28. Henri Jeanmaire, *Couroï et Courètes. Essai sur l'éducation spartiate et sur les rites d'adolescence dans l'antiquité hellénique* (Lille, 1939).

29. For example, Hermann Güntert (*Labyrinth; eine sprach-wissentschaftliche Untersuchung* [Heidelberg, 1932]) explores the relationship between the labyrinth and megalithic tombs; C. N. Deedes ("The Labyrinth," *The Labyrinth*, ed. S. H. Hooke [London, 1935]) looks at the use of labyrinthine seals and rituals surrounding Egyptian and Mesopotamian tombs; and A. Bernard Deacon (*Journal of the Royal Anthropological Institute 64* [1934]) examines the labyrinthine images in rituals of the Malekula of New Hebrides.

30. Mircea Eliade, *Rites and Symbols of Initiation. The Mysteries of Birth and Rebirth*, trans. Willard R. Trask (New York: Harper & Row, 1965) xii.

31. Among the Malekula upon dying the dead person's soul meets a female monster named Temes who awaits the soul by the mouth of a cave. Temes has drawn a labyrinthine design on the ground beside her, and when the soul approaches, she erases half of the design. Those who have been initiated know the path and can find their way to the place of the dead, but the uninitiated are devoured by Temes (ER 62).

32. *Liber sine nomine (Petrarch's Book Without A Name)*, trans. Norman P. Zacour (Toronto: Pontifical Institute of Mediaeval Studies, 1973) 118. This is an echo of what Sibyl, who lives in a labyrinthine cave herself, tells Aeneas of the road to Hades in the *Aeneid*: "easy is the descent to Avernus: night and day the door of gloomy Dis stands open; but to recall thy steps and pass out to the upper air, this is the task, this is the toil!" (6: 122–23).

33. Boccaccio, *Comento*, 2, 108; Francesco da Buti, *Commento sopra la Divina Comedia*, 3 vols., ed. Crescentino Giannini (Pisa: Fratelli Nistri, 1858–1862), 1, 323–24; and Benvenuto, *Comentum super Dantis Aldigherij Comoediam*, 5 vols., ed. J. P. Lacaita (Florence, 1887), 1, 385.

34. See, for example, Edith Schnapper, "Labyrinths and Labyrinthine Dances in Christian Churches," *Festchrift Otto Erich Deutsch*, ed. Walter Gerstenberg, Jan LaRue, and Wolfgang Rehm (Kassel: Bärenveiter, 1963) 352–60; and Penelope Reed Doob, "The Auxerre Labyrinth Dance," *Proceedings of the Society of Dance History Scholars* (1985): 132–41.

35. Marius Victorinus, *Ars grammatica*, vol. 6, *Grammatici latini*, ed. Heinrich Keil (Hildesheim: Georg Olms, 1961) 60; DIL 68.

36. Robert Graves, *The Greek Myths*, vol. 1 (New York: Braziller, 1957) 342–43.

37. Plutarch, "Theseus," *Plutarch's Lives of Illustrious Men*, vol. 1, trans. J. Langhorne and W. Langhorne (London: Bohn, 1853) 9–10.

38. DIL 68; see also Penelope Reed Doob, "The Auxerre Labyrinth Dance," 132–41.

39. Claude Paradin, *Devises héroïques et emblèmes* (1621), as quoted in MML, 96.

40. All of the following churches have or have had labyrinths: Amiens Cathedral (1288 to 1825), the parish church of St. Quentin, Rheims Cathedral (1240 to 1779), the chapter house of the Bayeux Cathedral, the Sens Cathedral (destroyed in 1769), the Auxerre Cathedral (destroyed in 1690), the pavement of the Abbey of St. Bertin (destroyed around 1780), the Poitiers Cathedral, the Abbaye de Pont l'Abbé, the Abbey of St. Stephen at Caen (destroyed in 1802), Arras, and Chartres (MML 60). The labyrinth at Chartres was known as the "league of Jerusalem" (Germain Bazin, *Paradeisos: The Art of the Garden* [Boston: Little, Brown, and Company, 1990] 52).

41. *Ovide moralisé*, a fourteenth-century poem of unknown authorship (ed. C. de Boer, M. G. de Boer, and J. Van't Sant [Amsterdam 1931]), is a good example of this phenomenon.

42. Joseph Campbell, *The Hero With a Thousand Faces* (Princeton: Princeton University Press, Bollingen Series, 1968) 19.

43. Richard Chase writes in this regard, "A myth is a tale, a narrative, or a poem; myth is literature and must be considered as an aesthetic creation of human imagination" ("Notes on the Study of Myth," *Myth and Literature. Contemporary Theory and Practice*, ed. John B. Vickery [Lincoln: University of Nebraska Press, 1966] 73).

44. Joachim Du Bellay, *L'Olive, Oeuvres poétiques*, vol. 1, ed. Yvonne Bellenger (Paris: Nizet, 1989).

45. Racine uses the Cretan intertext explicitly in another drama, *Phèdre, OEuvres complètes*, 246–64.

46. Haskell M. Block, "The Myth of the Artist," *Literary Criticism and Myth*, ed. Joseph P. Strelka (University Park: Pennsylvania State University Press, 1980) 3–4.

47. For example, Ernst Cassirer, *Language and Myth*, trans. Susanne Langer (New York: Harper, 1946).

48. Kurt Weinberg, "Language as Mythopoesis: Mallarmé's Self-referential Sonnet," *Literary Criticism and Myth*, ed. Joseph P. Strelka (University Park: Pennsylvania State University Press, 1980) 142.

49. As already noted, in numerous versions, Daedalus is imprisoned for providing Ariadne with the thread (HM 139). However, there are accounts in which Daedalus is imprisoned for making the artificial bull, which allowed Pasiphaë to mate with the bull from the sea (GMI 312).

50. Jacques Lacan, "Le Stade du miroir comme formateur de la fonction du Je," *Ecrits* (Paris: Seuil, 1966) 93–100.

51. Stéphane Mallarmé, *Igitur*, *OEuvres complètes*, ed. Henri Mondor and G. Jean-Aubry (Paris: Gallimard-Pléiade, 1945) 421–51.

52. Saint-Amant, "Le Contemplateur," *Poésies baroques* (Paris: Vialetay, 1968) 51–66.

53. Théophile de Viau, "La Maison de Sylvie," *OEuvres poétiques*, ed. Guido Saba (Paris: Bordas, 1990) 298–338.

54. Saint-Amant, "Le Contemplateur," l. 102, 54.

55. Edward P. Nolan, "*The Forbidden Forest*: Eliade as Artist and Shaman," *Mircea Eliade in Perspective*, ed. David Carrasco and Jane Swanberg (Boulder: Westview Press, 1985) 115–16.

56. André Peyronie,"The Labyrinth," *Companion to Literary Myths, Heroes and Archetypes*, ed. Pierre Brunel, trans. Wendy Allatson, Judith Hayward, and Trista Selous (New York: Routledge, 1992) 685.

57. Doob, "The Labyrinth as Significant Form: Two Paradigms," DIL, 39–63.

58. Barthes, *Mythologies*, trans. Annette Lavers (New York: Noonday, 1972) 115.

59. Barthes, *Le Plaisir du texte* (Paris: Seuil, 1973) 101. Interestingly, Mallarmé uses the metaphor of the spider web to a similar effect in *Igitur*.

60. As quoted by Pierre Rosenstiehl in "The *Dodécadédale*, or In Praise of Heuristics," *October* 26 (Fall 1983): 19.

61. The term "text" derives from the Latin *textus*, meaning "woven."

Chapter 1

1. André Peyronie, "The Labyrinth," *Companion to Literary Myths, Heroes and Archetypes*, ed. Pierre Brunel, trans. Wendy Allatson, Judith Hayward, and Trista Selous (New York: Routledge, 1992) 694–95.

2. Du Bellay uses the term explicitly four times in his poetic *oeuvre*: "Les cueurs humains un labyrinthe sont," XXIII: 17, and "Qui, par le labyrinth' d'un chemin tortueux," XL: 46 *Divers jeux rustiques* (1558) (ed. Verdun L. Saulnier [Geneva: Droz, 1947]); "Et son vieux labyrinth' la Crete n'oublira," II: 8, *Les Antiquités de Rome* (1558), *Oeuvres poétiques*, vol. 2 (ed. D. Aris and F. Joukovsky [Paris: Classiques Garnier, 1996]); and "Du labyrinth' de tes vertus," XVIII: 156, *Poésies diverses* (ed. Henri Chamard, vol. 5).

3. In both French and English the term "labyrinth" is actually used as an anatomical term for a section of "the inner ear or its bony or membrous

part;—so called from its complex shape" (*Webster's New International Dictionary*, 2nd ed. Unabridged [Merriam & Webster 1934]).

4. Joachim Du Bellay, *L'Olive, Oeuvres poétiques*, vol. 1, ed. Yvonne Bellenger (Paris: Nizet, 1989).

5. In fact, in the entire sonnet sequence Olive herself is only named twice, and only once without reference to the plant of the same name.

6. Sara Sturm-Maddox, *Petrarch's Laurels* (University Park: Pennsylvania State University Press, 1992).

7. Jean-Claude Carron, *Discours de l'errance amoureuse* (Paris: Vrin, 1986) 11.

8. Pontus de Tyard, *Les Erreurs amoureuses*, ed. John A. McClelland (Geneva: Droz, 1967).

9. The theme of poetic immortality, employed by all of the Pléiade poets, is generally accepted as Platonic in origin (R. V. Merrill and R. J. Clements, "*Vertu* and Immortality," *Platonism in French Renaissance Poetry* [New York: University Press, 1957] 59).

10. Part of Sonnet LVIII is translated from the first quatrain of Petrarch's Sonnet CCV (Bellenger, DO, 180 n.).

11. Ovid, Book VIII, *The Metamorphoses of Ovid*, trans. Mary M. Innis (New York: Penguin, 1955) 103–235.

12. Francesco Petrarch, *Petrarch's Lyric Poems: The* Rime sparse *and Other Lyrics*, trans. and ed. Robert M. Durling (Cambridge: Harvard University Press, 1976) Sonnet 307: ll. 1–8, 486.

13. Doranne Fenoaltea has noted the relationship between the image of flight and the writer's pen in "Establishing Contrasts: An Aspect of Scève's Use of Petrarch's Poetry in the *Délie*," *Studi francesi* 19 (1975): 17–33. (JoAnn DellaNeva, "Du Bellay: Reader of Scève, Reader of Petrarch," *Romanic Review* 79.3 [May 1988]: 407)

14. See J. Eymard, "Du Bellay, Icare et le Cygne," *Annales de l'Université de Toulouse-Le Mirail*, NS 14, Special Edition, *Littératures* (1979): 305–13; Marc Eigeldinger, "Le Mythe d'Icare dans la poésie française du 16e siècle," *Cahiers de l'Association Internationale des Etudes françaises* 25 (1973): 261–80; Peter Sharratt, "Du Bellay and the Icarus Complex," *Myth and Legend in French Literature*, ed. Keith Aspley, David Bellos, and Peter Sharratt (London: Humanities Research Association, 1982) 73–92; Niall Rudd, "Daedalus and Icarus (ii) From the Renaissance to the present day," *Ovid Renewed*, ed. Charles Martindale (Cambridge: Cambridge University Press, 1988) 37–53.

15. Rudd, "Daedalus and Icarus (ii)," 41.

16. Pierre de Ronsard, *OEuvres completes de Pierre de Ronsard*, vol. II, ed. Paul Laumonier (Paris: Lemerre, 1914–1919) 152.

17. Sonnet VI, *OEuvres complètes de Pierre de Ronsard*, vol. XVIII, 180. (Bellenger, DO, 181–82 n.)

18. Scève borrowed and rearticulated the feather image from Petrarch (DD 407).

19. Imitated from a sonnet by Bentivoglio (*Rime diverse di molti eccellentissmi auttori nuovamente raccolte*, ed. Gabriel Giolito de Ferrari [Venice, 1545] II, 78). (Bellenger, DO, 198–99 n.)

20. Du Bellay imitates this scene in his *De l'immortalité des poëtes* (*Recueil de poésie, OEuvres poétiques*, vol. 3, ed. Henri Chamard [Paris: Société des Textes français modernes, 1961] 52–53).

21. Niall Rudd, "Daedalus and Icarus (i) From Rome to the End of the Middle Ages," *Ovid Renewed*, ed. Charles Martindale (Cambridge: Cambridge University Press, 1988) 22.

22. Inspired by Ariosto's Sonnet XX (Bellenger, DO, 180 n.).

23. Thomas Thomson (ed.), *L'Olive: A Selection with Notes* (Blairgowrie, Scotland: Lochee, 1986) 56.

24. Inspired by P. Barbati (Giolito). (Bellenger, DO, 205 n.)

25. George Hugo Tucker, *The Poet's Odyssey. Joachim Du Bellay and the Antiquitez de Rome* (Oxford: Clarendon Press, 1990) 36.

26. Jerry C. Nash, "Cette 'beauté nompareille': Du Bellay et l'écriture de l'impossible," *Du Bellay: Actes du Colloque International d'Angers du 26 au 29 mai 1989*, vol. 1. (Angers: Presses de l'Université d'Angers, 1990) 18.

27. The tercets of this sonnet are translated from Ariosto, *Orlando furioso*. XXXII, xxi, ll. 9–14. Ariosto's sonnet is translated thus by La Boetie:
    > Mais, pauvre, helas, de qui me dois-je plaindre,
    > Que de mon fol et insensé desir,
    > Qui vole au ciel et si hault veut attaindre,
    > Qu'un feu bruslant ses aeles vient saisir?
    > Du ciel il tombe, et pour cela n'est moindre
    > Mon dur tourment, mon aigre desplaisir.
    > Il monte encor et au feu s'abandonne,
    > Et jamais fin à mes cheutes ne donne.

    (*Poètes du XVIe siècle*, ed. A.-M. Schmidt [Paris: Bibliothèque de la Pléiade, 1964] 673; Bellenger, DO, 174–75 n.)

28. Joachim Du Bellay, *OEuvres de l'Invention de l'Autheur, OEuvres poétiques*, vol. 4, ed. Henri Chamard (Paris: Hachette, 1908) 90.

29. Gaetano Cipolla argues that the labyrinth constitutes the nucleus of Petrarchan imagery (*Labyrinth: Studies on an Archetype* [New York: Legas, 1987]). Doob also sees the labyrinth as a major image in Petrarch's writings (*The Idea of the Labyrinth*, 158–62).

30. Petrarch, *Liber sine nomine (Petrarch's Book Without A Name)*, trans. Norman P. Zacour (Toronto: Pontifical Institute of Mediaeval Studies, 1973) 72–73.

31. Gaetano Cipolla, "Labyrinthine Imagery in Petrarch," *Italica* 54 (1977): 267.

32. Although Scève had in 1544 published the first French *canzoniere*, *Délie*, he wrote it in dizains. It was Du Bellay and later Ronsard (*Amours*) who produced the first French *canzoniere* in sonnets.

33. Sonnet XII of Ariosto, *Quel arboscel che'n le solinghe rive*, ll. 12–14. (Bellenger, DO, 160 n.)

34. Crowns of ivy were also symbolic of poetic glory, especially during the classical period.

35. The olive tree was sacred to Minerva and to Athena, who gave the tree to the Athenians (TOS 47).

36. Sonnets I, l. 14; XXXIV, l. 13; CIV, l. 14; CV, l. 10; CXV, l. 14.

37. Sonnet XXXIII of *L'Olive* imitates Ariosto XIII and Petrarch's Sonnet LXI. The second quatrain is a rather close imitation of Petrarch's sonnet (Bellenger, DO, 173 n.):

    Blessed be the day and the month and the year
    and the season and the time and the hour and the instant
    and the beautiful countryside and the place where I was struck
    by the two lovely eyes that have bound me. (61: 1–4; PDR 138)

38. A similar process takes place in Pontus de Tyard's *Les Erreurs amoureuses* where desire is "fondée sur l'inaccessibilité de l'objet dont la possession est indéfiniment différée" (CEA 145).

39. Nash writes that in Du Bellay's thought "the poet should not write an already existing ordinary kind of meaning but rather use language and imagery to *constitute* a bright, unique presence and meaning" (Jerry C. Nash, "The Poetics of Seeing and Showing: Du Bellay's Love Lyrics," *Lapidary Inscriptions. Renaissance Essays for Donald A. Stone, Jr.*, ed. Barbara C. Bowen and Jerry C. Nash [Lexington, Kentucky: French Forum, 1991] 52).

40. Translated from Sonnet VII of Ariosto (Bellenger, DO, 33 n.).

41. Du Bellay's Sonnet XIX is a loose imitation of Vincenzo Martelli's Sonnet XX in the Giolito anthology; only 3 verses are closely echoed (JoAnn DellaNeva, "Variations in a Minor Key: Du Bellay's Imitations of the Giolito Anthology Poets," *French Forum* 14.2 [May 1989]: 134–35). The poem unfolds in *vers rapportés*, a process in which different images (in this case, 3) are systematically sustained and explored in parallel.

42. Sonnet XXX is a translation of Ariosto's Sonnet VIII, "Ben che'l martir sin periglioso e grave," which Ronsard imitated as well in *Amours* (1552) (Bellenger, DO, 171–72 n.).

43. Richard Katz, *The Ordered Text. The Sonnet Sequences of Du Bellay* (New York: Peter Lang, 1985) 30.
44. Keith Cameron, *La Concordance des Oeuvres poétiques de Joachim Du Bellay* (Geneva: Droz, 1988).
45. Ernesta Caldarini notes that sonnet XLIII is a rearticulation of a sonnet by the Italian poet Francesco Coccio (Giolito). The first quatrain and the second tercet are faithful imitations, and Du Bellay has retained the rhyme of the quatrains (Caldarini, ed., *L'Olive* [Geneva: Droz, 1974] 98).
46. A translation of a sonnet by Claudio Tolomei (Bellenger, DO, 110 n.), but also imitates the rhetoric of Petrarch's Sonnet CCCXII, ll. 1–9, and Sonnet CCLXXI.
47. Alice Cameron, *The Influence of Ariosto's Epic and Lyric Poetry on Ronsard and His Group* (Baltimore: Johns Hopkins, 1930) 96.
48. Inspired by Petrarch's Sonnet CLXII (Bellenger, DO, 187 n.).
49. Robert Griffin, *Coronation of the Poet: Joachim Du Bellay's Debt to the Trivium* (Berkeley: University of California Press, 1969) 100.
50. Sonnet XLVIII, l. 1. This is a liberal translation of a sonnet by Giulio Camillo (Giolito) (Bellenger, DO, 67 n.).
51. Sonnet LXXX is a loose translation of a sonnet by Pietro Barignano (Bellenger, DO, 95 n.).
52. In 1550, *L'Olive* was enlarged in a second edition from 50 to 115 sonnets.
53. Du Bellay writes: "Voulant donques enrichir nostre vulgaire d'une nouvelle, ou plustost ancienne renouvelée poësie, je m'adonnay à l'immitation des anciens Latins & des poëtes Italiens" ("Préface de la seconde édition: Au lecteur," DO, 12).
54. Peter Hainsworth, *Petrarch the Poet: An Introduction to the Rerum Vulgarium Fragmenta* (New York: Routledge, 1988) 50.
55. In *La Deffence*, Du Bellay asserts that French is a suitable language for poetic expression. Though he is not the first to make this assertion nor the first to write verse in French, many of his contemporaries did favor writing in Latin. French, Du Bellay argues, is no less dignified than Greek or Latin, and though it has been suppressed by Roman occupation and the subsequent preference of Latin as the literary language, great French literature will necessarily be written in French. He writes that: "Tu ne doys avoir honte d'ecrire en ta Langue: mais encores doibs-tu, si tu es amy de la France, voyre de toymesmes, t'y donner du tout, avecques ceste genereuse opinion, qu'il vault mieux estre un Achille entre les siens, qu'un Diomede, voyre bien souvent un Thersite, entre les autres" (*La Deffence et illustration de la langue françoyse*, ed. Henri Chamard [Paris: Didier, 1948] 193–94).
56. Richard Katz examines the Petrarchan devices used by Du Bellay in *The Ordered Text*.

57. Joachim Du Bellay, "Première Préface," DO, 8–9.

58. Arthur Tilley, *The Literature of the French Renaissance*, vol. 1 (New York: Hafner, 1959) 316.

59. Eric MacPhail, "Nationalism and Italianism in the Work of Joachim Du Bellay," *Comparative and General Literature* 39 (1990–91): 49.

60. L. Clark Keating, *Joachim Du Bellay* (New York: Twayne Publishers, 1971) 20.

61. "Celuy donques qui voudra faire oeuvre digne de prix en son vulgaire, laisse ce labeur de traduyre, principalement les poëtes, à ceux qui de chose laborieuse & peu profitable, j'ose dire encor' inutile, voyre pernicieuse à l'acroissement de leur Langue, emportent à bon droict plus de molestie que de gloyre" (DDI 41–42).

62. "Eum vero nemo potest aequare, cuius vestigiis sibi utique insistendum putat; necesse est enim semper sit posterior qui sequitur" (Quintilian, *Institutio Oratoria* [Bk. 10. 2.10–12], ed. H. E. Butler [Cambridge: Harvard University Press, 1961 (1922; rpt.)] 79–80).

63. Petrarch, *Letters on Familiar Matters* [*Rerum familiarium libri* xvii–xxiv], trans. Aldo S. Bernardo (Baltimore: Johns Hopkins University Press, 1985), Fam. 22:2, 214.

64. JoAnn DellaNeva discusses Du Bellay's indebtedness to Quintilian and Petrarch as well as Erasmus in "Du Bellay: Reader of Scève, Reader of Petrarch," 401–11.

65. Joachim Du Bellay, "Préface de la seconde édition: Au lecteur," DO, 14.

66. See, for example, DV, 133–46.

67. Love set out amid the grass a gay net
    of gold and pearls, under a branch
    of the evergreen tree that I so love,
    although it has more sad than happy shadows.
                    (181: 1–4; PRD 326)

68. Bellenger, DO, 161–62 n.

69. Noted by Bellenger, DO, 161 n.:

    It was the day when the sun's rays
    turned pale with grief for his Maker
    when I was taken, and I did not defend myself against it,
    for your lovely eyes, Lady, bound me.

    It did not seem to me a time for being
    on guard against Love's blows; therefore I went
    confident and without fear, and so my misfortunes began
    in the midst of the universal woe. (III:1–8; PDR 38)

70. DellaNeva has noted several poetic theories and practices of the Renaissance which advocated the imitation of minor poets. Erasmus, for example, argues

that "felicities stand out more clearly in (secondary) writers simply because they [do not] occur all at once" (*The Ciceronian: A Dialogue on the Ideal Latin Style*, vol. 28, *Collected Works of Erasmus*, trans. Betty Knott, ed. A. H. T. Levi [Toronto: University of Toronto Press, 1986] 369). The poet who is seeking a striking image can therefore imitate these poems to their advantage. Marco Girolamo Vida, on the other hand, suggests that the works of mediocre poets can and should be reworked and polished to transform them into good literature (*De arte poetica of Marco Girolamo Vida*, ed. and trans. Ralph Williams [New York: Columbia University Press, 1976] 98–99; DV 133).

71. *Rime diverse di molti eccellentissmi auttori nuovamente raccolte*, ed. Gabriel Giolito de Ferrari (Venice: 1545).

72. "L'identification d'Olive avec l'olivier finit par être une obsession: le poète y revient jusqu'à dix-sept fois" (Henri Chamard, *Histoire de la Pléiade*, vol. I [Paris: Didier, 1939] 240). Katz notes that there are actually nineteen (29).

73. Sonnet LIX is a partial imitation of Ariosto's Sonnet XX (Bellenger, DO, 180 n.).

74. The theme of poetic immortality, employed by all of the Pléiade poets, is Platonic in origin (R. V. Merrill and R. J. Clements, "*Vertu* and Immortality," *Platonism in French Renaissance Poetry* [New York: University Press, 1957] 59).

75. Part of Sonnet LVIII is translated from the first quatrain of Petrarch's Sonnet CCV (Bellenger, DO, 180 n.).

76. DD 405. In a similar vein, Sonnet CXIV explores the relationship between the verse and Olive:

> Et vous, mes vers, delivres & legers,
> Pour mieulx atteindre aux celestes beautez,
> Courez par l'air d'une aele inusitée. (ll. 12–14)

Chapter 2

1. In *Don Quixote* (1605; 1615), for example, inquiry tends to lead to "an endless labyrinth" (Miguel de Cervantes Saavedra, *Don Quixote of La Mancha*, trans. Walter Starkie [New York: Penguin, 1979] Part II, Chapter 44, 835). The illusions of the world can "whirl you into a maze of fancies, out of which not even the clue of Theseus could extricate you" (Part I, Chapter 48, 486).

2. Marlies Kronegger, "Games of Perspective in Baroque Art and Poetry," *Papers On French Seventeenth Century Literature* 8.15.2 (1981): 269.

3. Gustav Réné Hocke, *Die Welt als Labyrinth: Manier und Manie in der europäischen kunst von 1520 bis 1650 und in der Gegenwart* (Hamburg, 1957).

4. Saint-Amant, "Préface," *Moïse sauvé*; *OEuvres complètes*, vol. 2, ed. Ch.-L. Livet (Paris: Plon, 1855) 147.

5. The French poet Bouthrays, for example, wrote about the labyrinth of Chartres in a set of Latin verses in his "Histories de Chartres" (1624).

6. Gerald Gillespie suggests that the pilgrimage, the postlapserian rediscovery of Eden through poetry, and the spiritual attainment of the City of God are the three paradigms of quest and discovery revealed by Dante which came to typify the baroque period (*Garden and Labyrinth of Time: Studies in Renaissance and Baroque Literature* [New York: Peter Lang, 1988] 297).

7. One of the most interesting literary labyrinths in terms of maze garden imagery is to be found in Mlle de Scudéry's *Artmène ou le Grand Cyrus* (1649–53). The story of Parthénie (VI, 1) relates how the princess, who has been told by an oracle that she can only be happily wed if she finds someone who will marry her without seeing her beforehand, wins the heart of a young hunter who has become lost in a maze garden. She leads him to the center from behind the hedge. Simultaneously, she frees him, guides him, and makes him a prisoner of her love.

8. A. Bartlett Giamatti, *The Earthly Paradise and the Renaissance Epic* (Princeton 1966). See also Gillespie, 298.

9. Marlies Kronegger, "Mirror Reflections: The Poetics of Water in French Baroque Poetry," *Poetics of the Elements in the Human Condition: The Sea*, ed. Anna-Teresa Tymieniecka (Dordrecht: Reidel, 1985) 245.

10. Gaston Bachelard, "La Grotte," *La Terre et les rêveries du repos* (Paris: Corti, 1948) 183–209.

11. Samuel Borton gives a complete analysis of the phenomenon in *Six Modes of Sensibility* (The Hague: Mouton, 1966). He has identified several commonalities shared by all of these grottoes:

    A. The grotto is an adapted cavern containing one or more spacious, gloomy chambers suitable for retirement, a solitary promenade, and refreshment of mind.

    B. Besides the so-called "piliers rustiques" simulating trees of the forest, there was realistic decoration with ceramic bas-reliefs, inscriptions, and murals showing birds, beasts, monsters, fantastic seascapes, landscapes with ruins.

    C. Streams, fountains, cascades, along with water-operated devices, provide music and the grander sounds of earth and sky.

    D. The numerous statues in the cavern represent elemental spirits and mythic divinities proper to an underground sanctum.

E. Contrasting with the quiet seclusion of the sanctuary, the visitor is made the object of fright at certain junctures by a contrived effect of eery illusion. (51–52)

12. Germain Bazin, *Paradeisos: The Art of the Garden* (Boston: Bulfinch, 1990) 77.

13. BM 56. The French language gained the adjective "grotesque" from the popularity of this element of the Renaissance garden. The first definitions of *grotesque* were actually written by Saint-Amant for the *Dictionnaire de l'Académie française.*

14. André Chastel, *The Crisis of the Renaissance* (Geneva, 1968) 43.

15. Gillespie 297.

16. Du Cerceau was the architect to Catherine de Medici. Among the numerous maze gardens which existed, fine examples could be found at Chateau of Montargi (1550), at De Vries (1583), at Charleval, and in the palace garden of the Archbishop of Rouen at Gaillon. There were also maze gardens in the gardens of Luxembourg and at Tuileries, in the Jardin des Plantes, one at Les Rochers in Brittany, one at Choisy-le-Roi, and one at Sceaux. Belgium, Stockholm, and Germany also had a number of maze gardens. In Spain there was a labyrinth in the gardens of the Alcazar at Seville. Even the pope (Clement X) had a maze in his garden at Altieri (Frank Crisp, *Mediaeval Gardens* [New York: Hacker Art Books, 1979] 71).

One of the most intricate labyrinth gardens was constructed by J. Hardouin-Mansart for Louis XIV at Versailles. In Perrault's book, "Labyrinte de Versailles" (1677) which was illustrated by Sebastien le Clerc, 39 sets of hydraulic statuary based on Aesop's fables are shown to be placed in the labyrinth. At the entrance to the labyrinth, stood statues of Aesop and Cupid (Cupid is holding a ball of thread). Engraved plates on each statue carried a verse by the poet de Benserade. Unfortunately, this labyrinth was destroyed in 1775 (MML 121).

17. Remarkably, over eighty editions of Théophile's works were published in the seventeenth century compared to only 16 editions of Malherbe's works (Guido Saba, "Situation de Théophile de Viau," *Actes de Las Vegas: Théorie dramatique. Théophile de Viau. Les Contes de fées,* 1–3 mars 1990 [Paris: *Papers on French Seventeenth Century Literature,* 1991] 85).

18. Théophile de Viau, *OEuvres poétiques,* ed. Guido Saba (Paris: Bordas-Classiques Garnier, 1990), Ode IV, ll. 31–34.

19. William Howard Adams, *The French Garden: 1500–1800* (New York: Braziller, 1979) 27.

20. Though there is no mention of a maze in the garden at this time, Du Cerceau is well known for his labyrinths, and the possibility should not be discounted.

21. Mark Laird, *The Formal Garden: Traditions of Art and Nature*, photographs by Hugh Palmer (London: Thames and Hudson, 1992) 226.

22. Ernest de Ganay, *André le Nostre: 1613–1700* (Paris: Vincent, Fréal, & Cie, 1962) 79. See note 7 of the "Introduction" for the actual design of the pinwheel labyrinth.

23. Guido Saba, "Introduction," TO, xxvii.

24. In the poem he shares his nightmare and the dire predictions of his friend Tircis, who likely signifies the poet Jacques Vallée Des Barreaux who warned Théophile of his imminent arrest (Saba, TO, 311 n. 4).

25. R. G. Maber, ed. and intro., *Malherbe, Théophile de Viau, and Saint-Amant: A Selection* (Durham: University of Durham, 1983) xix–xx. Obviously the banishment was not well enforced, as he was in Paris when he died. The Duke de Montmorency was himself executed, and his wife, after unsuccessfully pleading for his life, entered a nunnery.

26. *Oeuvres de Saint Amant*, ed. J. Bailbé (Paris: Didier-Société des textes littéraires français, 1971) 3–7.

27. Théophile de Viau alludes to Saint-Amant's lute playing in "La Maison de Sylvie":

> Quand l'Aurore les vient semondre
> Lui donnent un si doux salut
> Que Saint-Amant avec son luth
> Aurait peine de les confondre. (VII: 47–50)

28. Saint-Amant finally retired from his travels and settled in France in 1651. He died in Paris in 1661.

29. Saint-Amant, "Le Contemplateur," *Poésies baroques* (Paris: Vialetay, 1968), ll. 31–32.

30. *La Solitude* has been perceived as the "counterpoint of a complete, complex, and consistent experience in the highly developed architectural phenomenon known as 'la grotte'" (BM 49). Saint-Amant had also written explicitly of a friend's grotto in "Sonnet à feu Monsieur Desyveteaux" (*OEuvres complètes*, vol. 1, 21).

31. Marlies Kronegger, *The Life Significance of French Baroque Poetry* (New York: Peter Lang, 1988) 14.

32. Robert T. Corum Jr., "Response to David Michael Roberts," *Actes de Las Vegas: Théorie dramatique. Théophile de Viau. Les Contes de fées*, 1–3 mars 1990, 39.

33. Marlies Kronegger, "The Growth of Self-Awareness in Saint-Amant's *Le Contemplateur*: A Baroque Vision," *Papers On French Seventeenth Century Literature* 8.14.2 (1981): 135.

34. Imbrie Buffum, *Studies in the Baroque from Montaigne to Rotrou* (New Haven: Yale University Press, 1957) 153.

35. *Webster's Third New International Dictionary of the English Language*, unabridged (Springfield, Massachusetts: Merriam & Webster, 1993).
36. John Ayto, *Dictionary of Word Origins* (New York: Arcade, 1991).
37. Marlies Kronegger, "Mirror Reflections: The Poetics of Water in French Baroque Poetry," *Poetics of the Elements in the Human Condition: The Sea*, ed. Anna-Teresa Tymieniecka (Dordrecht: Reidel, 1985) 245.
38. Buffum 153; Saint-Amant, "Le Contemplateur," Stanza 21.
39. *Dictionary of Word Origins.*
40. *The Barnhart Dictionary of Etymology*, ed. Robert K. Barnhart (New York: H.W. Wilson, 1988).
41. Edward P. Nolan, *"The Forbidden Forest*: Eliade as Artist and Shaman," *Mircea Eliade in Perspective*, 115–16, as previously quoted in note 55 of the "Introduction."
42. Claude Abraham, *Tristan l'Hermite* (Boston: Twayne Publishers, 1980) 60.
43. Erik Michaelsson, "L'eau centre de métaphore et de métamorphoses dans la littérature française de la première moitié du XVIIième siècle," *Orbis Litterarum* 14: 2–4 (1959): 139.
44. Kronegger observes this phenomenon and suggests that Saint-Amant's poetic world hints "at its own irreality in that it changes with altered light or with a shift in the point of view of the observer, it opens, expands space toward the outside or interior scene, reaching far beyond the frame's limitations of representation" (KL 14).
45. A. D. Nuttall, "Ovid's Narcissus and Shakespeare's Richard II: the reflected self," *Ovid Renewed* (Cambridge: Cambridge University Press, 1988) 142.
46. Georges Poulet, "The Baroque Period," *The Metamorphoses of the Circle*, trans. Carley Dawson and Elliot Coleman (Baltimore: John Hopkins Press, 1966) 25, 23.
47. Buffum has asserted that "to feel simultaneously wonder and agreeable terror [. . .] is a state thoroughly congenial to the baroque mind" (157).
48. Lowry Nelson, Jr. has asserted in this regard that: "in order to cope with their complexities and also with the intricacies of human relations, each polarity was expressed in such a way as to take its opposite into account. In other words, the expression of a "unified sensibility" in Baroque literature may actually reflect an uneasy and momentary balancing of disparates, corresponding to the *concordia discors* of the "conceit" (*Baroque Lyric Poetry* [New Haven: Yale University Press, 1961] 14–15).
49. David Michael Roberts, "Théophile's Cygnus and the Vulnerable *locus amoenus*," *Actes de Las Vegas: Théorie dramatique. Théophile de Viau. Les Contes de fées*, March 1–3, 1990 (Paris: *Papers on French Seventeenth Century Literature*, 1991).

50. Icarus and Phaeton are often mistaken for each other and even interchangeable in much of seventeenth-century French poetry, according to J. H. Turner, *The Myth of Icarus* (London: 1976) 74–75; see Stanzas 8–11 of Ode III and the first stanza of Ode IV of "La Maison de Sylvie."

Chapter 3

1. Thomas Corneille, *Ariane*, *OEuvres*, vol. 7 (Geneva: Slatkine, 1970) 592–610.
2. Jean Racine, *Bajazet*, *OEuvres complètes* (Paris: Seuil, 1962) 183–203.
3. Although Voltaire believed Ariane to be the lesser of the two plays, he held it in high enough regard to include a commentary on this play by Thomas Corneille among his essays on Pierre Corneille's works ("Remarques sur *Ariane*, tragédie," "Commentaires sur Corneille," ed. David Williams, *The Complete Works of Voltaire*, vol. 55 [Banbury: The Voltaire Foundation, 1975] 995).
4. "Préface de l'éditeur," to Voltaire's "Remarques sur *Ariane*, tragédie," 978. The play was performed 32 times in Paris between 1679 and 1685 and by 1793 had been performed 258 times at the Comédie-Française alone (Oscar Mandel, "Introduction" to Thomas Corneille's *Ariadne*, trans. Oscar Mandel [Gainesville: University Presses of Florida, 1982] 51).
5. *Companion to Literary Myths, Heroes and Archetypes*, ed. Pierre Brunel, trans. Wendy Allatson, Judith Hayward, and Trista Selous (New York: Routledge, 1992) 122.
6. Oscar Mandel points out that several minor playwrights, including Robert Garnier, had already placed Phaedra on the ship ("*Ariadne* and French Classical Tragedy," MA, 48).
7. Thomas Corneille had indeed translated several of Calderon's works from Spanish to French. There are several similarities between these two texts, including the emphasis on choosing between duty towards Ariadne and passion for Phaedra, and the ending lament by Ariadne (MA 49–50).
8. Voltaire notes that the language used by Corneille is misleading: "*Eviter les détours du labyrinthe en Crète. Thésée n'évita pas les détours du labyrinthe en Crète, puisqu'il fallait nécessairement passer par ces détours. La difficulté n'était pas de les éviter, mais de sortir en ne les évitant pas*" (VR 981).
9. Racine echoes this passage in *Phèdre*, where Phèdre confides to Oenone: "Tes discours trouveront plus d'accès que les miens; / Presse, pleure, gémis; peins-lui Phèdre mourante; / Ne rougis point de prendre une voix suppliante" (*OEuvres complètes*, III:1, ll. 808–10); (MA 20).

10. Ironically it is because she brought one member of her family with her that things go awry.
11. It should be mentioned that Ariane has also betrayed a sibling for Thésée's sake—the Minotaur was her brother after all.
12. Racine's *Phèdre* borrows in turn from Corneille's *Ariane* (MA 56).
13. Maria L. Assad, "Une Réponse classique à la crise de la culture: Phèdre," *Papers on French Seventeenth Century Literature* 13.25 (1986): 50.
14. L. R. Muir, "The Monster in the Labyrinth: The Paradox of Hippolyte," *French Studies Bulletin* 16 (Autumn 1985): 6–8.
15. Nina da Vinci Nichols, "Racine's *Phaedra* and Ibsen's *Hedda*: Transformations of Ariadne," *American Imago* 40.3 (Fall 1983): 237–56.
16. Matthew Senior, *In the Grip of Minos: Confessional Discourse in Dante, Corneille, and Racine* (Columbus: Ohio State University Press, 1994) 193–208.
17. Indeed, Hippolyte does kill a monster from the sea, "described as a bull with scales, a creature that reminds us of the Minotaur" (NP 241).
18. Bryant C. Freeman, *Concordance du Théâtre et des Poésies de Jean Racine*, vol. 2 (Ithaca: Cornell University Press, 1968) 905–8.
19. Racine, "Seconde préface," RB, 184.
20. Susan Tiefenbrun, *Signs of the Hidden: Semiotic Studies* (Amsterdam: Rodopi, 1980) 209.
21. Claude Abraham, "Tristan and Racine: Anxiety in *Osman* and *Bajazet*," *Zeitschrift für französische Sprache und Literatur* 92.1 (1982): 5.
22. It is significant that all of this takes place in a harem. As Roland Barthes says in *Sur Racine* (Paris: Seuil, 1963): "C'est le sérail qui l'invertit; d'abord physiquement même, si l'on peut dire: Bajazet est un mâle confiné dans un milieu féminin où il est le seul homme; c'est un frelon, dont on dirait qu'il est nourri, engraissé par Roxane pour son pouvoir génital même" (96). Bajazet is not the only man in the seraglio, but he is the only man with a sexual appetite.
23. Kathryn A. Hoffman, "The Space of Difference in Racine's *Bajazet*," *Romanic Review* 77.2 (March 1986): 112.
24. BR 100–1. Also, Susan Tiefenbrun has suggested in *Signs of the Hidden: Semiotic Studies* that *Bajazet* is "the poetic illustration of a Cartesian quest for certainty" (209).
25. Maya Slater, "Racine's *Bajazet*: The Language of Violence and Secrecy," *Violence in Drama* (Cambridge: Cambridge University Press, 1991) 142.
26. Variants of "perdre" appear an amazing 26 times in *Bajazet* (FC 905–8).
27. Sylvie Romanowski, "The Circuits of Power and Discourse in Racine's *Bajazet*," *Papers on Seventeenth Century French Literature* 10.19 (1983): 864.

28. Francis Wyndham, "Introduction," *Bajazet*, trans. Alan Hollinghurst (London: Chatto & Windus, 1991) v.
29. Bernet, *Le Vocabulaire des tragédies de Jean Racine* (Geneva: Slatkine, 1983) 36–37. One should also note that *Bajazet* has a small vocabulary even for Racine (Bernet demonstrates that *Bajazet* contains fewer words than all Racine's mature tragedies except *Bérénice* [95]), which makes the huge number of death-words the more notable (SB 144).
30. A variant on this line reads: "Allez, Seigneur: tentez cette dernière voie" (II:5, l. 785; FCII 1382).
31. Bernard Weinberg, *The Art of Jean Racine* (Chicago: University of Chicago Press, 1963) 181.
32. Hoffman asserts that Atalide "fills the space separating Roxane and Bajazet with a fiction that is unstable and untrustworthy" (HS 113).
33. Such imagery prefigures the deaths which are forthcoming (SB 144).
34. Nina Ekstein recognizes three differing accounts of the off-stage meeting between Bajazet and Roxane: those of Acomat, Bajazet, and Roxane (Nina C. Ekstein, "Narrative Reliability and Spatial Limitations in *Bajazet*," *Neophilologus* 68 [1984]: 498–503). However, there is a fourth. Although Atalide's interpretation is based on second-hand information, it has the greatest influence on the dénouement.
35. The first line ironically echoes Bajazet's account of their meeting: "A peine ai-je parlé que, sans presque m'entendre" (Carolyn L. Jacobs, "The Irony of Human Judgment: Act III of *Bajazet*," *French Studies in Honor of Philip A. Wadsworth*, ed. Donald W. Tappan and William A. Mould [Birmingham, Al: Summa, 1985] 56).

Chapter 4

1. Stéphane Mallarmé, *Les Dieux antiques*, *OEuvres complètes*, ed. Henri Mondor and G. Jean-Aubry (Paris: Gallimard, Pléiade, 1945) 1233.
2. Gardner Davies, *Mallarmé et le drame solaire* (Paris: Corti, 1959).
3. Lawrence J. Watson, *Mallarmé's Mythic Language* (Oxford: Tallents, 1990).
4. Mallarmé, letter to Henri Cazalis, February 18, 1869, *Correspondance I*, ed. Henri Mondor (Paris: Gallimard, 1959) 301.
5. Mallarmé, letter to Eugène Lefébure, March 20, 1870, CI, 318.
6. Lloyd James Austin is justified in contending that "créér des mythes nouveaux plutôt que de répéter éternellement des mythes existants fut une des préoccupations constantes de Mallarmé" (*Essais sur Mallarmé*, ed. Malcolm Bowie [Manchester: Manchester University Press, 1995] 226).
7. Mallarmé, "Hamlet," *Crayonné au théâtre*, OC, 300.

8. *Dictionnaire des symboles*, ed. Jean Chevalier and Alain Gheerbrant (Paris: Laffont, 1969).

9. W. H. Matthews, *Mazes & Labyrinths: Their History & Development* (Dover: New York, 1970) 95–96. Also Marcellin Berthelot asserts that the labyrinths found in many cathedrals are known as the *labyrinthe de Salomon*. He describes Solomon's labyrinth as "une figure cabalistique qui se trouve en tête de certains manuscrits alchimiques, et qui fait partie des traditions magiques attribués au nom de Salomon. C'est une série de cercles concentriques, interrompus sur certains points, de façon à former un trajet bizarre et inextricable" ("Labyrinthe," *La Grande Encyclopédie*, vol. 21, 703).

10. Fulcanelli, *Le Mystère des cathédrales et l'interprétation ésotérique des symboles hermétiques du grand oeuvre* (Paris: Jean-Jacques Pauvert, 1964) 63.

11. Nicholas M. Huckle, "Mallarmé and the Strategy of Transformation in *Igitur*," *Nineteenth-Century French Studies* 19.2 (1991): 290–303.

12. Wallace Fowlie, *Mallarmé* (Chicago: University of Chicago Press, 1953) 231.

13. Robert Greer Cohn, *Mallarmé: Igitur* (Berkeley: University of California Press, 1981) 172.

14. Villiers de l'Isle-Adam, letter to Mallarmé, September 11, 1866, CI, 231, n. 1. Paracelsus was the Swiss alchemist who authored *Labyrinthus Medicorum Errantium* (1553).

15. J.-K. Huysmans, Chapter 19, *Là-Bas* (Paris: Gallimard, 1985) 290–98.

16. See also J.-K. Huysmans' "Préface" to Jules Bois' *Le Satanisme et la Magie* (Paris: Chailly, 1895) vii–xxvii.

17. Mallarmé, "Magie," *Variations sur un sujet*, OC, 400.

18. Peter Dayan, *Mallarmé's Divine Transposition: Real and Apparent Sources of Literary Value* (Oxford: Clarendon, 1986) 102.

19. Penelope Reed Doob, *The Idea of the Labyrinth from Classical Antiquity through the Middle Ages* (Ithaca:Cornell University Press, 1990) 69.

20. Jerome, *Commentariorum in Ezechielem prophetam*, *Patrologia Latina*, 25, 447–49; trans. Doob, DIL, 69–70.

21. Grillot de Givry, *Witchcraft, Magic & Alchemy*, trans. J. Courtenay Locke (New York: Dover, 1971) 347.

22. Bertrand Marchal, *La Religion de Mallarmé* (Paris: José Corti, 1988) 452.

23. Louis Bolle, "Mallarmé, Igitur et Hamlet," *Critique* 21 (1965): 863.

24. Jacques Derrida, *De la grammatologie* (Paris: Minuit, 1967) 128.

25. André Leroi-Gourhan, *Le Geste et la parole*, vol. 1 (Paris: Albin Michel, 1964) 272.

26. Jacques Derrida, "The Double Session," trans. Barbara Johnson, *Stéphane Mallarmé*, ed. Harold Bloom (New York: Chelsea House, 1987) 92–93.

27. Mary Lewis Shaw, *Performance in the Texts of Mallarmé: The Passage from Art to Ritual* (University Park: Pennsylvania State University Press, 1993) 165.

28. Jean-Pierre Richard argues that "Comprendre un thème, c'est encore 'déployer [ses] multiples valences': c'est voir par exemple comment la rêverie mallarméenne du *blanc* peut incarner tantôt la jouissance du vierge, tantôt la douleur de l'obstacle et de la frigidité, tantôt le bonheur d'une ouverture, d'une liberté, d'une médiation, et c'est mettre en rapport en un même complexe ces diverses nuances de sens" (*L'Univers imaginaire de Mallarmé* [Paris: Seuil, 1961] 27–28).

29. Despite its incomplete and private nature, writers from Paul Claudel to Wallace Fowlie have considered *Igitur* to be the matrix out of which Mallarmé's later poetry emerges (FM 105).

30. Stéphane Mallarmé, *Igitur*, OC, 375.

31. Jeffrey M. Perl, "Stéphane Mallarmé (1842–1898)," *European Writers*, vol. 7, ed. Jacques Barzun and George Stade (New York: Scribner, 1985) 1588.

32. Speaking of his new project the "Grand Oeuvre" in a letter to Armand Renaud on December 20, 1866, Mallarmé writes that he is not abandoning *Hérodiade*, but that that poem will be "one of the twisted, splendid, and Solomonlike columns of this Temple" (*Selected Letters of Stéphane Mallarmé*, ed. and trans. Rosemary Lloyd [Chicago: University of Chicago Press, 1988] 72).

33. Cohn posits that possibly it is the sound and shape of the letters in "Igitur" which Mallarmé found symbolic—the "I" is especially "'virile,' slim and heroic." Also, in Villiers de l'Isle-Adam's *Elën* (1865), with which Mallarmé was very familiar, the students sing *Gaudeamus igitur*. A further connection is the reference in the song to the river Elbe (CM 22–23).

34. Raphael Patai, *The Jewish Alchemists* (Princeton: Princeton University Press, 1994).

35. Mallarmé, letter to Cazalis, November 14, 1869, CI, 313.

36. Mallarmé, as quoted by Maurice Blanchot, "L'Expérience d'Igitur," *L'Espace littéraire* (Paris: Gallimard, 1955) 108.

37. Mallarmé, letter to Théodore Aubanel, July 16, 1866, CI, 222.

38. This point has already been made by several critics, notably Robert Greer Cohn in *Mallarmé: Igitur* and Nicholas M. Huckle in "Mallarmé and the Strategy of Transformation in *Igitur*."

39. Mircea Eliade, *Rites and Symbols of Initiation. The Mysteries of Birth and Rebirth*, trans. Willard R. Trask (New York: Harper & Row, 1965) xii.

40. Roland Barthes, *Le Plaisir du texte* (Paris: Seuil, 1973) 101.

41. Mallarmé, "Méthode," *Notes, Proses diverses*, OC, 852.

42. Mallarmé, letter to Henri Cazalis, May 14, 1867, CI, 241–42.

43. Mallarmé, "Touches," *Scolies*, OC, 446, 449.

44. Batsdorff, *Le Filet d'Ariadne* (Paris: d'Houry, 1695). This manuscript is also sometimes attributed to Gaston de Claves (FC 104).

45. Nietzsche has employed the image of the spider web to depict the metaphorical tissue produced by man ("On Truth and Falsity in their Ultramoral Sense," *Complete Works of Nietzsche*, vol. 2, ed. D. Levy [London and Edinburgh, 1911] 186).

46. Mallarmé, "Crise de Vers," *Variations sur un sujet, OEuvres Complètes*, 366.

47. "To describe an object in a work is to describe its absence. The real creator is he who disappears so that the work may begin its own truncated and autonomous existence" (FM 116).

48. Shaw 153.

49. If Mallarmé was influenced by any Jewish Kabbalistic texts, it was likely Knorr von Rosenroth's *Kabbala Denudata* (1677–1684), written in Latin but translated into English in 1714, and again in 1894, and into French in 1899. Another book very influential in France was Martines de Pasqually's *Traité de la réintégration des êtres* (1727–1774) which outlined Christian Kabbalah.

50. Gershom Scholem, *Kabbalah* (New York: Meridian, 1978) 94–95.

51. Mallarmé, letter to Cazalis, 14 May, 1867, *Correspondance I*, 240.

52. Mallarmé, letter to Cazalis, May 14, 1867, *Correspondance I*, 243–44.

53. *Le Tombeau de Théophile Gautier*, ed. Alphonse Lemerre (Paris, 1873).

54. Patricia Parker, "Mallarmé's 'Toast funèbre': Some Contexts and a Reading," *Romanic Review* 71.2 (March 1980): 168.

55. "Porphyry" is defined in *Webster's New Twentieth Century Dictionary* (New York: Rockville House Publishers, 1969) as "originally, a hard Egyptian rock having red and white feldspar crystals embedded in a fine-grained, dark-red or purplish ground mass." If one examines the definition of the term "matrix," further parallels can be established: "originally, the womb [. . .] specifically, the rock in which a gem, mineral, fossil, etc. is enclosed or embedded; also, the impression left in such rock when the embedded object is removed."

56. Stéphane Mallarmé, "Toast funèbre," OC, 54–55.

57. Perhaps he is referred to as golden because of his royal parentage.

58. André Peyronie, "The Minotaur," *Companion to Literary Myths, Heroes and Archetypes*, 819.

59. Parker examines the relationship between the torch image in Mallarmé's poem and the ritual funerary torch which was common in Greek sculpture.

60. According to Givry, necromancy had become all the rage in nineteenth-century Paris. One book *Pneumatologie positive et expérimentale* by Baron L. de Güldenstubbe (Paris, 1857) explains the process and explicates the many instances in which the author and numerous reputable witnesses have

succeeded in getting Julius Cesear, Pierre Abelard, and others to write messages to them.

61. Mallarmé, "Préface," *Un coup de dés jamais n'abolira le hasard*, OC, 456.
62. Mallarmé, letter to Léo Orfer, June 27, 1884, *Correspondances II*, ed. Henri Mondor and Lloyd James Austin (Paris, 1959) 266.

Chapter 5

1. Joan Howard, *From Violence to Vision: Sacrifice in the Works of Marguerite Yourcenar* (Carbondale: Southern Illinois University Press, 1992) 2.
2. Jan Amos Comenius, *Labyrint sveta a raj srdce* (VBrne: Barvice & Novotneho, 1912).
3. Marguerite Yourcenar, *En Pèlerin et en étranger* (Paris: Gallimard, 1989) 28.
4. Marguerite Yourcenar, *Le Labyrinthe du Monde, I: Souvenirs pieux* (Paris: Gallimard, 1974); *Le Labyrinthe du Monde, II: Archives du Nord* (Paris: Gallimard, 1977); *Le Labyrinthe du Monde, III: Quoi? L'Eternité* (Paris: Gallimard, 1988).
5. Marguerite Yourcenar, *Le Jardin des chimères* (Paris: Perrin, 1921).
6. Rémy Poignault, "La Légende d'Icare vue par Marguerite Yourcenar," *Retours du mythe: vingt études pour Maurice Delcroix*, ed. Christian Berg, Walter Geerts, Paul Pelckmans, and Bruno Tritsmans (Amsterdam: Rodopi, 1996) 226.
7. Marguerite Yourcenar, *Qui n'a pas son Minotaure?*, *Théâtre II* (Paris: Gallimard, 1971) 163–231.
8. Marguerite Yourcenar, *Les Yeux ouverts* (Paris: Centurion, 1980) 186.
9. For Yourcenar, the relationship between the labyrinth and the cave is taken for granted in *Qui n'a pas son Minotaure?*. In Scene VI, the stage set indicates that Thésée is "dans la caverne" when he journeys into the labyrinth.
10. Marguerite Yourcenar, "Aspects d'une légende et histoire d'une pièce," YQ, 176.
11. *Ariane et l'aventurier* was published along with the stories written by her two friends in *Cahiers du Sud* in the fall of 1939 (HV 10).
12. Marguerite Yourcenar, *Les Dieux ne sont pas morts* (Paris: Chiberre, 1922).
13. Marguerite Yourcenar, "Phèdre ou le désespoir," *Feux* (Paris: Gallimard, 1974) 36.
14. René Garguilo, "Le Mythe du labyrinthe et ses modulations, dans l'oeuvre de Marguerite Yourcenar," *Roman, histoire et mythe dans l'oeuvre de*

Marguerite Yourcenar (Tours: Société Internationale d'Etudes Yourcenariennes, 1995) 199.

15. For an exploration of Racine's *Phèdre*, see chapter 3, pages 88–90.
16. Marguerite Yourcenar, "Aspects d'une légende et histoire d'une pièce," YQ, 178.
17. *Webster's Third New International Dictionary* provides the following etymology of *deviate*: Low Latin *deviatus*, past participle of *deviare*, from Latin *de* from, away + Low Latin *-viare* (from latin *via* way, road).
18. Marguerite Yourcenar, "Avertissement," *Feux* (Paris: Grasset, 1936); C. Frederick Farrell, Jr. and Edith R. Farrell, "Marguerite Yourcenar's *Feux*: Structure and Meaning," *Kentucky Romance Quarterly* 29.1 (1982): 25.
19. *Revue de France* 4 (1935): 491–98.
20. Harry C. Rutledge, "Marguerite Yourcenar: The Classicism of *Feux* and *Mémoires d'Hadrien*," *Classical and Modern Literature: A Quarterly* 4.2 (Winter 1984): 91.
21. Laura Brignoli, "Images du temps et de l'espace dans *Feux* de Marguerite Yourcenar," *Retours du mythe*, 231.
22. In *Qui n'a pas son Minotaure?*, this complicity is seen to also exist in the realm of politics and law. King Minos confides to Thésée in Scene IV that: "Mais le mystère du Labyrinthe est trop compliqué pour que les utopistes, les étrangers, les athées s'en mêlent. . . Les liens qui m'unissent au Minotaure sont [. . .] remarquablement compliqués. En un sens, nous collaborons: son coutelas sert à aiguiser la plume d'oie du législateur" (YQ 200).
23. Marguerite Yourcenar, "Aspects d'une légende et histoire d'une pièce," YQ, 178.
24. Yourcenar constantly uses gender specific attributes: "masculine," "feminine," "like a girl," but even as she offers these constructs, she deconstructs their validity as gender specific.
25. Pyrrhus speaking to Andromaque in Jean Racine's *Andromaque*, 1: 4, 1. 320, *OEuvres complètes* (Paris: Seuil, 1988) 108.
26. Farrell and Farrell have noted a parallel in the use of dance imagery between "Achille ou le mensonge" and "Clytemnestre ou le crime" (FFF 28).
27. Poignault, "La Légende d'Icare," 226.
28. Pierre L. Horn, *Marguerite Yourcenar* (Boston: Twayne Publishers, 1985) 84.
29. Andre Peyronie, "The Labyrinth," *Companion to Literary Myths, Heroes and Archetypes*, ed. Pierre Brunel, trans. Wendy Allatson, Judith Hayward, and Trista Selous (New York: Routledge, 1992) 124–25.
30. C. Frederick Farrell, Jr. and Edith R. Farrell, *Marguerite Yourcenar in Counterpoint* (Lanham, MD: University Press of America, 1983) 49.

31. "After an initial withdrawal, the candidate undergoes transformation and purification by suffering, and, finally, re-birth and re-integration into society with a new perspective" (FFF 30).

Afterword

1. Michel Foucault, *Raymond Roussel* (Paris: Gallimard, 1963) 124.
2. Jacques Derrida, *Of Grammatology*, trans. Gayatri Chakravorty Spivak (Baltimore: Johns Hopkins University Press, 1977) 7.
3. Derrida, *La Dissémination* (Paris: Seuil, 1972) 301.
4. Derrida, "Structure, Sign, and Play in the Discourse of the Human Sciences," trans. Alan Bass, *Contemporary Literary Criticism. Modernism Through Poststructuralism*, ed. Robert Con Davis (New York: Longman, 1986) 488.
5. J. Hillis Miller, "Stevens' Rock and Criticism as Cure, II," *Contemporary Literary Criticism. Modernism Through Poststructuralism*, ed. Robert Con Davis (New York: Longman, 1986) 420.

Works Cited

Primary Sources

Alighieri, Dante. *The Divine Comedy, Inferno*. Trans. Mark Musa. New York: Penguin, 1984.

Ariosto, Ludovico. *Le Opere minori di Ludovico Ariosto*. Ed. Guiseppe Fatini. Firenze: Sansoni, 1915.

———. *Orlando furioso*. Bologna: Carducci, 1960.

Chénier, André. "L'Invention (Poème)." *OEuvres complètes*. Paris: Gallimard-Pléiade, 1958. 123–32.

Corneille, Thomas. *Ariane*. *OEuvres*. Vol. 7. Geneva: Slatkine, 1970. Rpt. Paris, 1758. 592–610.

Du Bellay, Joachim. *Les Antiquités de Rome*. *Oeuvres poétiques*. Vol. 2. Ed. D. Aris and F. Joukovsky. Paris: Classiques Garnier, 1996.

———. *La Complainte du Desesperé*. *OEuvres de l'Invention de l'Autheur*. *OEuvres poétiques*. Vol. 4. Ed. Henri Chamard. Paris: Hachette, 1908.

———. *La Deffence et illustration de la langue françoyse*. Ed. Henri Chamard. Paris: Didier, 1948.

———. *Divers jeux rustiques*. Ed. Verdun L. Saulnier. Geneva: Droz, 1947.

———. *De l'immortalité des poëtes*. *Recueil de poésie*. *OEuvres poétiques*. Vol. 3. Ed. Henri Chamard. Paris: Société des Textes français modernes, 1961.

———. *L'Olive, Oeuvres Poétiques I*. Ed. Yvonne Bellenger. Paris: Nizet, 1989.

———. *Poésies diverses*. Vol. 5. Ed. Henri Chamard.

Erasmus. *The Ciceronian: A Dialogue on the Ideal Latin Style*. Vol. 28. *Collected Works of Erasmus*. Trans. Betty Knott. Ed. A. H. T. Levi. Toronto: University of Toronto Press, 1986.

Mallarmé, Stéphane. *OEuvres complètes*. Ed. Henri Mondor. Paris: Gallimard-Pléiade, 1945.

———. *Oeuvres*. Paris: Garnier, 1985.

Ovid. *Metamorphoses*. Trans. Frank Justus Miller. Cambridge: Harvard University Press, Loeb Classical Library, 1956.

Ovide moralisé. Ed. C. de Boer, M. G. de Boer, and J. Van't Sant. Amsterdam 1931.

Petrarch. *Canzoniere. Canzoniere, trionfi, rime varie*. Torino: Giulio Einaudi, 1958.

———. *Letters on Familiar Matters* [*Rerum familiarium libri* xvii–xxiv]. Trans. Aldo S. Bernardo. Baltimore: Johns Hopkins University Press, 1985.

———. *Liber sine nomine (Petrarch's Book Without A Name)*. Trans. Norman P. Zacour. Toronto: Pontifical Institute of Mediaeval Studies, 1973.

———. *Petrarch's Lyric Poems: The* Rime sparse *and Other Lyrics*. Trans. and Ed. Robert M. Durling. Cambridge: Harvard University Press, 1976.

Racine, Jean. *Andromaque. OEuvres complètes*. Paris: Seuil, 1962. 103–122.

———. *Bajazet. OEuvres complètes*. 183–203.

———. *Phèdre. OEuvres complètes*. 246–64.

Rime diverse di molti eccellentissimi auttori nuovamente raccolte. Ed. Gabriel Giolito de Ferrari. Venice: Giolito de Ferrari, 1545.

Ronsard, Pierre de. *OEuvres complètes de Pierre de Ronsard*. Vols. II and XVIII. Ed. Paul Laumonier. Paris: Lemerre, 1914–1919.

Saint-Amant. "Le Contemplateur." *Poésies baroques*. Paris: Vialetay, 1968. 51–66.

———. "Préface." *Moïse sauvé. OEuvres complètes*. Vol. 2. Ed. Ch.-L. Livet. Paris: Plon, 1855.

Le Tombeau de Théophile Gautier. Ed. Alphonse Lemerre. Paris, 1873.

Viau, Théophile de. "La Maison de Sylvie." *OEuvres poétiques*. Ed. Guido Saba. Paris: Bordas, 1990. 298–338.

Virgil. *The Aeneid*. Trans. Patric Dickinson. New York: Mentor Books, 1961.

Yourcenar, Marguerite. "Ariane et l'aventurier." *Retour aux mythes grecs*. Spec. issue. *Cahiers du Sud* 219 (1939): 80–106.

————. *Les Charités d'Alcippe.* Paris: Gallimard, 1984.

————. *Les Dieux ne sont pas morts.* Paris: Chiberre, 1922.

————. *Feux.* Paris: Gallimard, 1974.

————. *Le Jardin des chimères.* Paris: Perrin, 1921.

————. *Le Labyrinthe du Monde, I: Souvenirs pieux.* Paris: Gallimard, 1974.

————. *Le Labyrinthe du Monde, II: Archives du Nord.* Paris: Gallimard, 1977.

————. *Le Labyrinthe du Monde, III: Quoi? L'Eternité.* Paris: Gallimard, 1988.

————. *En Pèlerin et en étranger.* Paris: Gallimard, 1989.

————. *Qui n'a pas son Minotaure? Théâtre II.* Paris: Gallimard, 1971. 163–231.

————. *Les Yeux ouverts.* Paris: Centurion, 1980.

Secondary Sources

Abraham, Claude. *Jean Racine.* Boston: Twayne Publishers, 1977.

————. "Tristan and Racine: Anxiety in *Osman* and *Bajazet.*" *Zeitschrift für französische Sprache und Literatur* 92.1 (1982): 1–8.

————. *Tristan l'Hermite.* Boston: Twayne Publishers, 1980.

Adams, William Howard. *The French Garden: 1500–1800.* New York: Braziller, 1979.

Allen, Peter. "The Role of Myth in Racine: *Andromaque, Iphigénie, Phèdre.*" *Myth and Legend in French Literature.* Ed. Keith Aspley, David Bellos, and Peter Sharratt. London: Humanities Research Association, 1982. 92–116.

Aspley, Keith. "Introduction: Myth as Proteus. Myth, Legend, and Literature." *Myth and Legend in French Literature.* Ed. Keith Aspley, David Bellos, and Peter Sharratt. London: Modern Humanities Research Association, 1982. 1–23.

Assad, Maria L. "Une Réponse classique à la crise de la culture: *Phèdre.*" *Papers on French Seventeenth Century Literature* 13.25 (1986): 39–51.

Austin, Lloyd James. *Essais sur Mallarmé*. Ed. Malcolm Bowie. Manchester: Manchester University Press, 1995.

Ayto, John. *Dictionary of Word Origins*. New York: Arcade, 1991.

Bachelard, Gaston. *La Terre et les rêveries du repos*. Paris: Corti, 1948.

Barnett, Richard L. *Dynamics of Detour. Codes of Indirection in Montaigne, Pascal, Racine, Guilleragues*. Paris: Jean-Michel Place, 1986.

The Barnhart Dictionary of Etymology. Ed. Robert K. Barnhart. New York: H. W. Wilson, 1988.

Barthes, Roland. *Mythologies*. Paris: Seuil, 1957.

————. *Mythologies*. Trans. Annette Lavers. New York: Noonday Press, 1972.

————. *Le Plaisir du texte*. Paris: Seuil, 1973.

————. *On Racine*. Trans. Richard Howard. New York: Octagon Books, 1977.

————. *Sur Racine*. Paris: Seuil, 1963.

Bazin, Germain. *Paradeisos: The Art of the Garden*. Boston: Bulfinch, 1990.

Benvenuto. *Comentum super Dantis Aldigherij Comoediam*. 5 vols. Ed. J. P. Lacaita. Florence, 1887.

Bersani, Leo. *The Death of Stéphane Mallarmé*. Cambridge: Cambridge University Press, 1982.

Blanchot, Maurice. *L'Espace littéraire*. Paris: Gallimard, 1955.

Block, Haskell M. "The Myth of the Artist." *Literary Criticism and Myth*. Ed. Joseph P. Strelka. University Park: Pennsylvania State University Press, 1980. 3–24.

Blomfeld, Reginald. "André Le Nôtre." *A History of French Architecture: From the Death of Mazarin till the Death of Louis XV. 1661–1774*. Vol. 1. London: Bell, 1921. 164–80.

————. "The Du Cerceau Family." *A History of French Architecture: From the Reign of Charles VIII till the Death of Mazarin*. Vol. 1. London: Bell, 1911. 140–56.

Bolle, Louis. "Mallarmé, Igitur et Hamlet." *Critique* 21 (1965): 853–63.

Boccaccio. *Il Comento alla Divina Commedia*. 3 vols. Ed. Domenico Guerri. Bari: Laterza, 1918.

Borton, Samuel L. *Six Modes of Sensibility in Saint-Amant*. The Hague: Mouton, 1966.

Brignoli, Laura. "Images du temps et de l'espace dans *Feux* de Marguerite Yourcenar." *Retours du mythe: vingt études pour Maurice Delcroix*. Ed. Christian Berg, Walter Geerts, Paul Pelckmans, and Bruno Tritsmans. Amsterdam: Rodopi, 1996. 231–243.

Buffum, Imbrie. *Studies in the Baroque from Montaigne to Rotrou*. New Haven: Yale University Press, 1957.

Buti, Francesco da. *Commento sopra la Divina Comedia*. 3 vols. Ed. Crescentino Giannini. Pisa: Fratelli Nistri, 1858–1862.

Cameron, Alice. *The Influence of Ariosto's Epic and Lyric Poetry on Ronsard and His Group*. Baltimore: Johns Hopkins, 1930.

Cameron, Keith. *La Concordance des Oeuvres poétiques de Joachim Du Bellay*. Geneva: Droz, 1988.

Campbell, Joseph. *The Hero With a Thousand Faces*. Princeton: Princeton University Press, Bollingen Series, 1968.

———. *The Mythic Journey*. Princeton: Princeton University Press, 1974.

Carron, Jean-Claude. *Discours de l'errance amoureuse*. Paris: Vrin, 1986.

Cassirer, Ernst. *Language and Myth*. Trans. Susanne Langer. New York: Harper, 1946.

Cervantes, Miguel de Saavedra. *Don Quixote of La Mancha*. Trans. Walter Starkie. New York: Penguin, 1979.

Chamard, Henri. *Histoire de la Pléiade*. Vol. 1. Paris: Didier, 1939.

Chase, Richard. "Notes on the Study of Myth." *Myth and Literature. Contemporary Theory and Practice*. Ed. John B. Vickery. Lincoln: University of Nebraska Press, 1966. 67–73.

Cipolla, Gaetano. *Labyrinth: Studies on an Archetype*. New York: Legas, 1987.

———. "Labyrinthine Imagery in Petrarch." *Italica* 54 (1977): 263–89.

Claudel, Paul. *Positions et propositions*. Paris: Gallimard, 1942.

Cohn, Robert Greer. *Mallarmé: Igitur.* Berkeley: University of California Press, 1981.

Comenius, Jan Amos. *Labyrint sveta a raj srdce.* VBrne: Barvice & Novotneho, 1912.

———. *The Labyrinth of the World and the Paradise of the Heart.* Trans. Matthew Spinka. Ann Arbor: University of Michigan Press, 1972.

Companion to Literary Myths, Heroes and Archetypes. Ed. Pierre Brunel. Trans. Wendy Allatson, Judith Hayward, and Trista Selous. New York: Routledge, 1992.

Corum, Robert T. Jr. "Response to David Michael Roberts." *Actes de Las Vegas: Théorie dramatique. Théophile de Viau. Les Contes de fées, 1–3 mars 1990.* Paris: Papers on French Seventeenth Century Literature, 1991. 129–130.

Crisp, Frank. *Mediaeval Gardens.* New York: Hacker Art Books, 1979.

Davies, Gardner. *Mallarmé et le drame solaire.* Paris: Corti, 1959.

———. "NarrativeThread in Mallarmé's *Igitur* Drafts." *Rivista di Letterature moderne e comparate* 44.1 (January-March 1991): 45–58.

Dayan, Peter. *Mallarmé's Divine Transposition: Real and Apparent Sources of Literary Value.* Oxford: Clarendon, 1986.

Deacon, A. Bernard. *Journal of the Royal Anthropological Institute* 64 (1934).

Deedes, C. N. "The Labyrinth." *The Labyrinth.* Ed. S. H. Hooke. London, 1935.

Delaney, Susan. "*L'Olive* and the Poetics of Rivalry." *Classical and Modern Literature: A Quarterly* 14.2 (Winter 1994): 183–96.

DellaNeva, JoAnn. "Du Bellay: Reader of Scève, Reader of Petrarch." *Romanic Review* 79.3 (May 1988): 401–11.

———. "Illustrating the *Deffence*: Imitation and Poetic Perfection in Du Bellay's *Olive.*" *The French Review* 61.1 (October 1987): 39–49.

———. "Variations in a Minor Key: Du Bellay's Imitations of the Giolito Anthology Poets." *French Forum* 14.2 (May 1989): 133–46.

Derrida, Jacques. *La Dissémination*. Paris: Seuil, 1972.

———. "The Double Session." Trans. Barbara Johnson. *Stéphane Mallarmé*. Ed. Harold Bloom. New York: Chelsea House, 1987. 79–96.

———. *Of Grammatology*. Trans. Gayatri Chakravorty Spivak. Baltimore: Johns Hopkins University Press, 1977.

———. "Structure, Sign, and Play in the Discourse of the Human Sciences." Trans. Alan Bass. *Contemporary Literary Criticism. Modernism Through Poststructuralism*. Ed. Robert Con Davis. New York: Longman, 1986. 480–98.

Dictionnaire des symboles. Ed. Jean Chevalier and Alain Gheerbrant. Paris: Laffont, 1969.

Doob, Penelope Reed. "The Auxerre Labyrinth Dance." *Proceedings of the Society of Dance History Scholars* (1985): 132–41.

———. *The Idea of the Labyrinth from Classical Antiquity through the Middle Ages*. Ithaca: Cornell University Press, 1990.

Du Bellay, Joachim. *L'Olive*. Ed. Ernesta Caldarini. Geneva: Droz, 1974.

Eigeldinger, Marc. "Le Mythe d'Icare dans la poésie française du 16e siècle." *Cahiers de l'Association Internationale des Etudes françaises* 25 (1973): 261–80.

Ekstein, Nina C. "Narrative Reliability and Spatial Limitations in *Bajazet*." *Neophilologus* 68 (1984): 498–503.

Eliade, Mircea. *Myths, Dreams, and Mysteries. The Encounter Between Contemporary Faiths and Archaic Realities*. Trans. Philip Mairet. London: Harvill Press, 1960.

———. *Rites and Symbols of Initiation. The Mysteries of Birth and Rebirth*. Trans. Willard R. Trask. New York: Harper & Row, 1965.

Eymard, J. "Du Bellay, Icare et le Cygne." *Annales de l'Université de Toulouse-Le Mirail*. NS 14. Special Edition. *Littératures* (1979): 305–13.

Faris, Wendy B. *Labyrinths of Language. Symbolic Landscape and Narrative Design in Modern Fiction*. Baltimore: Johns Hopkins University Press, 1988.

Farrell, C. Frederick, Jr. and Edith R. Farrell. "Marguerite Yourcenar." *French Women Writers. A Bio-Bibliographical Source Book*. Ed. Eva Martin Sartori and Dorothy Wynne Zimmerman. New York: Greenwood Press, 1991. 535–48.

———. "Marguerite Yourcenar's *Feux*: Structure and Meaning." *Kentucky Romance Quarterly* 29.1 (1982): 25–35.

Fenoaltea, Doranne. "Establishing Contrasts: An Aspect of Scève's Use of Petrarch's Poetry in the *Délie*." *Studi francesi* 19 (1975): 17–33.

Foucault, Michel. *Death and the Labyrinth: The World of Raymond Roussel*. Trans. Charles Ruas. New York: Doubleday, 1986.

———. *Raymond Roussel*. Paris: Gallimard, 1963.

Fowlie, Wallace. *Mallarmé*. Chicago: University of Chicago Press, 1953.

France, Peter. "Myth and Modernity: Racine's *Phèdre*." *Myth and Legend in French Literature*. Ed. Keith Aspley, David Bellos, and Peter Sharratt. London: Humanities Research Association, 1982. 227–42.

———. *Racine's Rhetoric*. Oxford: Clarendon Press, 1965.

Freeman, Bryant C. *Concordance du Théâtre et des Poésies de Jean Racine*. 2 vols. Ithaca: Cornell University Press, 1968.

Frye, Northrop. *Anatomy of Criticism: Four Essays*. Princeton: Princeton University Press, 1957.

Fulcanelli. *Le Mystère des cathédrales et l'interprétation ésotérique des symboles hermétiques du grand oeuvre*. Paris: Jean-Jacques Pauvert, 1964.

Ganay, Ernest de. *André Le Nostre. 1613–1700*. Paris: Vincent, Fréal, & Cie, 1962.

The Gardens of Europe. Ed. Penelope Hobhouse and Patrick Taylor. New York: Random House, 1990.

Garguilo, René. "Le Mythe du labyrinthe et ses modulations, dans l'oeuvre de Marguerite Yourcenar." *Roman, histoire et mythe dans l'oeuvre de Marguerite Yourcenar*. Tours: Société Internationale d'Etudes Yourcenariennes, 1995. 197–205.

Gillespie, Gerald. *Garden and Labyrinth of Time: Studies in Renaissance and Baroque Literature.* New York: Peter Lang, 1988.

Givry, Grillot de. *Witchcraft, Magic & Alchemy.* Trans. J. Courtenay Locke. New York: Dover, 1971.

La Grande Encyclopédie. Vol. 21. Paris: Larousse, 1971–1976.

Graves, Robert. *The Greek Myths.* 2 vols. New York: Braziller, 1957.

Griffin, Robert. *Coronation of the Poet: Joachim Du Bellay's Debt to the Trivium.* Berkeley: University of California Press, 1969.

Gross, Mark. "*Bajazet* and Intertextuality." *Yale French Studies* 76: 146–61.

Güntert, Hermann. *Labyrinth; eine sprachwissentschaftliche Untersuchung.* Heidelberg, 1932.

Gutierrez, Donald. *The Maze in the Mind and the World: Labyrinths in Modern Literature.* Troy, New York: Whitston, 1985.

Hainsworth, Peter. *Petrarch the Poet: An Introduction to the Rerum Vulgarium Fragmenta.* New York: Routledge, 1988.

Hamilton, Edith. *Mythology.* New York: Mentor, 1969.

Hawcroft, Michael. *Word as Action. Racine, Rhetoric, and Theatrical Language.* Oxford: Clarendon Press, 1992.

Heidegger, Martin. *What is a Thing?* Trans. W. B. Barton, Jr. Chicago: Regnery, 1967.

Hoffmann, Kathryn A. "The Space of Difference in Racine's *Bajazet.*" *Romanic Review* 77.2 (March 1986): 104–115.

Horn, Pierre L. *Marguerite Yourcenar.* Boston: Twayne Publishers, 1985.

Howard, Joan E. *From Violence to Vision: Sacrifice in the Works of Marguerite Yourcenar.* Carbondale: Southern Illinois University Press, 1992.

Huckle, Nicholas M. "Mallarmé and the Strategy of Transformation in *Igitur.*" *Nineteenth-Century French Studies* 19.2 (Winter 1991): 290–303.

Huysmans, J.-K. *Là-Bas.* Paris: Gallimard, 1985.

———. "Préface." Jules Bois. *Le Satanisme et la Magie.* Paris: Chailly, 1895. vii–xxvii.

Jacobs, Carolyn L. "The Irony of Human Judgment: Act III of *Bajazet*." *French Studies in Honor of Philip A. Wadsworth.* Ed. Donald W. Tappan and William A. Mould. Birmingham, Al: Summa, 1985. 51–60.

Jeanmaire, Henri. *Couroï et Courètes. Essai sur l'éducation spartiate et sur les rites d'adolescence dans l'antiquité hellénique.* Lille, 1939.

Katz, Richard A. "Cliché in Renaissance Poetry: Three Sonnets." *Teaching Language Through Literature* 26.1 (December 1986): 9–16.

———. *The Ordered Text. The Sonnet Sequences of Du Bellay.* New York: Peter Lang, 1985.

Keating, L. Clark. *Joachim Du Bellay.* New York: Twayne Publishers, 1971.

Kern, Hermann. *Labirinti: Forme e interputazioni: 5000 anni di prenzenza di un archetipo.* Trans. Libero Sosio. Milan: Feltirinelli, 1981.

Knapp, Bettina L. *Jean Racine: Mythos and Renewal in Modern Theater.* University, Alabama: University of Alabama Press, 1967.

Kronegger, Marlies. "Games of Perspective in Baroque Art and Poetry." *Papers On French Seventeenth Century Literature* 8.15.2 (1981): 269–93.

———. "The Growth of Self-Awareness in Saint-Amant's *Le Contemplateur*: A Baroque Vision." *Papers On French Seventeenth Century Literature* 8.14.2 (1981): 125–43.

———. "Mirror Reflections: The Poetics of Water in French Baroque Poetry." *Poetics of the Elements in the Human Condition: The Sea.* Ed. Anna-Teresa Tymieniecka. Dordrecht: D. Reidel, 1985. 245–60.

———. *The Life Significance of French Baroque Poetry.* New York: Peter Lang, 1988.

Lacan, Jacques. "Le Stade du miroir comme formateur de la fonction du Je." *Ecrits.* Paris: Seuil, 1966. 93–100.

Laird, Mark. *The Formal Garden: Traditions of Art and Nature.* Photographs by Hugh Palmer. London: Thames and Hudson, 1992.

Lebel, Maurice. "Marguerite Yourcenar traductrice de la poésie grecque." *Etudes littéraires* 12 (1979): 65–78.

Leroi-Gourhan, André. *Le Geste et la parole.* Vol. 1. Paris: Albin Michel, 1964.

Lyons, John D. "Saint-Amant's *La Solitude*: The Rhetoric of Fragmentation." *Orbis Litterarum* 33 (1978): 4–17.

MacPhail, Eric. "Nationalism and Italianism in the Work of Joachim Du Bellay." *Comparative and General Literature* 39 (1990–1991): 47–53.

———. *The Voyage to Rome in French Renaissance Literature.* Saratoga: Amna Libri, 1990.

Malherbe, Théophile de Viau, and Saint-Amant: A Selection. Ed. R. G. Maber. Durham: University of Durham, 1983.

Mallarmé, Stéphane. *Correspondance I.* Ed. Henri Mondor and Lloyd James Austin. Paris: Gallimard, 1959.

———. *Correspondances II.* Ed. Henri Mondor and Lloyd James Austin. Paris: Gallimard, 1959.

———. *Selected Letters of Stéphane Mallarmé.* Ed. and trans. Rosemary Lloyd. Chicago: University of Chicago Press, 1988.

Marchal, Bertrand. *Lecture de Mallarmé: Poésies, Igitur, Le coup de dés.* Paris: Corti, 1985.

———. *La Religion de Mallarmé.* Paris: José Corti, 1988.

Mathews, W. H. *Mazes & Labyrinths: Their History and Development.* New York: Dover, 1970.

Merrill, R. V. and R. J. Clements. *Platonism in French Renaissance Poetry.* New York: University Press, 1957.

Michaelsson, Erik. "L'eau centre de métaphore et de métamorphoses dans la littérature française de la première moitié du XVIIième siècle." *Orbis Litterarum* 14. 2–4 (1959).

Miller, J. Hillis. *Ariadne's Thread. Story Lines.* New Haven: Yale University Press, 1992.

————. "Stevens' Rock and Criticism as Cure, II." *Contemporary Literary Criticism. Modernism Through Poststructuralism.* Ed. Robert Con Davis. New York: Longman, 1986. 416–27.

Minahen, Charles D. *Vortex/t: The Poetics of Turbulence.* University Park: Pennsylvania State University Press, 1992.

Muir, L. R. "The Monster in the Labyrinth: The Paradox of Hippolyte." *French Studies Bulletin* 16 (Autumn 1985): 6–8.

Nash, Jerry C. "Cette 'beauté nompareille': Du Bellay et l'écriture de l'impossible." *Du Bellay: Actes du Colloque International d'Angers du 26 au 29 mai 1989.* Vol. 1. Angers: Presses de l'Université d'Angers, 1990. 15–30.

————. "The Poetics of Seeing and Showing: Du Bellay's Love Lyrics." *Lapidary Inscriptions. Renaissance Essays for Donald A. Stone, Jr.* Ed. Barbara C. Bowen and Jerry C. Nash. Lexington, Kentucky: French Forum, 1991. 45–59.

Nelson, Lowry Jr. *Baroque Lyric Poetry.* New Haven: Yale University Press, 1961.

Nichols, Nina da Vinci. "Racine's *Phaedra* and Ibsen's *Hedda*: Transformations of Ariadne." *American Imago* 40.3 (Fall 1983): 237–56.

Nietzsche, Friedrich. "On Truth and Falsity in their Ultramoral Sense." *Complete Works of Nietzsche.* Vol. 2. Ed. D. Levy. London and Edinburgh, 1911.

Nolan, Edward P. "*The Forbidden Forest*: Eliade as Artist and Shaman." *Mircea Eliade in Perspective.* Eds. David Carrasco and Jane Swanberg. Boulder: Westview Press, 1985.

Nuttall, A. D. "Ovid's Narcissus and Shakespeare's Richard II: the reflected self." *Ovid Renewed.* Cambridge: Cambridge University Press, 1988. 137–50.

L'Olive: A Selection with Notes. Ed. Thomas Thomson. Blairgowrie, Scotland: Lochee, 1986.

Parker, Patricia. "Mallarmé's 'Toast funèbre': Some Contexts and a Reading." *Romanic Review* 71.2 (March 1980): 167–82.

Patai, Raphael. *The Jewish Alchemists.* Princeton: Princeton University Press, 1994.

Perl, Jeffrey M. "Stéphane Mallarmé (1842–1898)." *European Writers*. Vol. 7. Ed. Jacques Barzun and George Stade. New York: Scribner, 1985. 1567–95.

Perry, Kathleen Anne. *Another Reality. Metamorphosis and the Imagination in the Poetry of Ovid, Petrarch, and Ronsard.* New York: Peter Lang, 1990.

Pliny. *Natural History*. Trans. D. E. Eichholz. LCL. Vol. 10. London: Heinemann, 1962.

Plutarch. "Theseus." *Plutarch's Lives of Illustrious Men*. Vol. 1. Trans. J. Langhorne and W. Langhorne. London: Bohn, 1853. 1–18.

Poignault, Rémy. "La Légende d'Icare vue par Marguerite Yourcenar." *Retours du mythe: vingt études pour Maurice Delcroix*. Ed. Christian Berg, Walter Geerts, Paul Pelckmans, and Bruno Tritsmans. Amsterdam: Rodopi, 1996. 211–229.

Poètes du XVIe siècle. Ed. A.-M. Schmidt. Paris: Bibliothèque de la Pléiade, 1964.

Poulet, Georges. "The Baroque Period." *The Metamorphoses of the Circle*. Trans. Carley Dawson and Elliot Coleman. Baltimore: John Hopkins Press, 1966. 15–31.

"Préface de l'éditeur." In Voltaire. "Remarques sur *Ariane*, tragédie." "Commentaires sur Corneille." Ed. David Williams. *The Complete Works of Voltaire*. Vol. 55. Banbury: The Voltaire Foundation, 1975. 978–79.

Quintilian. *Institutio Oratoria*. Ed. H. E. Butler. Cambridge: Harvard University Press, 1961. Rpt 1922.

Reynolds, Deirdre A. "Mallarmé and Hegel: Speculation and the Poetics of Reflection." *French Cultural Studies* 2 (1991): 71–89.

Richard, Jean-Pierre. *L'Univers imaginaire de Mallarmé*. Paris: Seuil, 1961.

Roberts, David Michael. "Théophile's Cygnus and the Vulnerable *locus amoenus*." *Actes de Las Vegas: Théorie dramatique. Théophile de Viau. Les Contes de fées*. March 1–3, 1990. Paris: Papers on French Seventeenth Century Literature, 1991. 123–27.

Romanowski, Sylvie. "The Circuits of Power and Discourse in Racine's *Bajazet.*" *Papers on Seventeenth Century French Literature* 10.19 (1983): 849–67.

Rosenstiehl, Pierre. "The *Dodécadédale*, or In Praise of Heuristics." *October* 26 (Fall 1983).

Rudd, Niall. "Daedalus and Icarus (i) From Rome to the End of the Middle Ages." *Ovid Renewed.* Ed. Charles Martindale. Cambridge: Cambridge University Press, 1988. 21–36.

———. "Daedalus and Icarus (ii) From the Renaissance to the present day." *Ovid Renewed.* Ed. Charles Martindale. Cambridge: Cambridge University Press, 1988. 37–53.

Ruskin, John. *Works.* Vol. 27. Ed. E. T. Cook Alexander Wedderburn. London: George Allen, 1907.

Rutledge, Harry C. "Marguerite Yourcenar: The Classicism of *Feux* and *Mémoires d'Hadrien.*" *Classical and Modern Literature: A Quarterly* 4.2 (Winter 1984): 87–99.

Saba, Guido. "Situation de Théophile de Viau." *Actes de las Vegas: Théorie dramatique. Théophile de Viau. Les contes de fées, 1–3 mars 1990.* 83–95.

Santarcangeli, Paolo. *Le Livre des labyrinthes: Histoire d'un mythe et d'un symbole.* Trans. Monique Lacau. Paris: Gallimard, 1974.

Schnapper, Edith. "Labyrinths and Labyrinthine Dances in Christian Churches." *Festchrift Otto Erich Deutsch.* Ed. Walter Gerstenberg, Jan LaRue, and Wolfgang Rehm. Kassel: Bärenveiter, 1963. 352–60.

Scholem, Gershom. *Kabbalah.* New York: Meridian, 1978.

Senior, Matthew. *In the Grip of Minos: Confessional Discourse in Dante, Corneille, and Racine.* Columbus: Ohio State University Press, 1994.

Sharratt, Peter. "Du Bellay and the Icarus Complex." *Myth and Legend in French Literature.* Ed. Keith Aspley, David Bellos, and Peter Sharratt. London: Humanities Research Association, 1982. 73–92.

Shaw, Mary Lewis. *Performance in the Texts of Mallarmé: The Passage from Art to Ritual.* University Park: Pennsylvania State University Press, 1993.

Slater, Maya. "Racine's *Bajazet*: The Language of Violence and Secrecy." *Violence in Drama.* Cambridge: Cambridge University Press, 1991. 141–50.

Sturm-Maddox, Sara. *Petrarch's Laurels.* University Park: Pennsylvania State University Press, 1992.

Tiefenbrun, Susan. *Signs of the Hidden: Semiotic Studies.* Amsterdam: Rodopi, 1980.

Tilley, Arthur. *The Literature of the French Renaissance.* Vol. 1. New York: Hafner, 1959.

Tucker, George Hugo. *The Poet's Odyssey. Joachim Du Bellay and the Antiquitez de Rome.* Oxford: Clarendon Press, 1990.

Tyard, Pontus de. *Les Erreurs amoureuses.* Ed. John A. McClelland. Geneva: Droz, 1967.

Victorinus, Marius. *Ars grammatica, Grammatici latini.* Vol. 6. Ed. Heinrich Keil. Hildesheim: Georg Olms, 1961.

Vida, Marco Girolamo. *De arte poetica of Marco Girolama Vida.* Ed. and trans. Ralph Williams. New York: Columbia University Press, 1976.

Voltaire. "Remarques sur *Ariane,* tragédie." "Commentaires sur Corneille." Ed. David Williams. *The Complete Works of Voltaire.* Vol. 55. Banbury: The Voltaire Foundation, 1975. 978–1005.

Watson, Lawrence J. *Mallarmé's Mythic Language.* Oxford: Tallents, 1990.

Webster's New International Dictionary. 2nd ed. Unabridged. New York: Merriam & Webster, 1934.

Webster's Third New International Edition of the English Language. Unabridged. Springfield, Massachusetts: Merriam & Webster, 1993.

Webster's New Twentieth Century Dictionary of the English Language. New York: Rockville House Publishers, 1969.

Weinberg, Bernard. *The Art of Jean Racine.* Chicago: University of Chicago Press, 1963.

Weinberg, Kurt. "Language as Mythopoesis: Mallarmé's Self-referential Sonnet." *Literary Criticism and Myth.* Ed. Joseph P. Strelka. University Park: Pennsylvania State University Press, 1980. 141–76.

Williams, David. "Introduction." In Voltaire. "Commentaires sur Corneille." Ed. David Williams. *The Complete Works of Voltaire.* Vol. 53. Banbury: The Voltaire Foundation, 1974. 301–05.

Wyndham, Francis. "Introduction." *Bajazet.* Trans. Alan Hollinghurst. London: Chatto and Windus, 1991. v–x.

Index of Sigla

Primary Sources

CV	Stéphane Mallarmé, "Crise de vers."
DA	Stéphane Mallarmé, *Les Dieux antiques*.
DO	Joachim Du Bellay, *L'Olive*.
DOC	Joachim Du Bellay, *L'Olive*, ed. Ernesta Caldarini.
I	Stéphane Mallarmé, *Igitur*.
OC	Stéphane Mallarmé, *Oeuvres complètes*, ed. Henri Mondor.
OM	Ovid, *Metamorphoses*.
PRD	Francesco Petrarch, *Petrarch's Lyric Poems: The* Rime sparse *and Other Lyrics*, trans. and ed. Robert M. Durling.
RB	Jean Racine, *Bajazet*.
TF	Stéphane Mallarmé, "Toast funèbre."
TO	Théophile de Viau, *OEuvres poétiques*.
VA	Virgil, *The Aeneid*.
YF	Marguerite Yourcenar, *Feux*.
YJ	Marguerite Yourcenar, *Le Jardin des chimères*.
YQ	Marguerite Yourcenar, *Qui n'a pas son Minotaure?*.

Secondary Sources

BEL	Maurice Blanchot, *L'Espace littéraire*.
BM	Samuel Borton, *Six Modes of Sensibility*.
BR	Roland Barthes, *Sur Racine*.
CEA	Jean-Claude Carron, *Discours de l'errance amoureuse*.
CI	Stéphane Mallarmé, *Correspondance I*.
CM	Robert Greer Cohn, *Mallarmé: Igitur*.
CR	Robert T. Corum Jr., "Response to David Michael Roberts."
DD	JoAnn DellaNeva, "Du Bellay: Reader of Scève, Reader of Petrarch."
DDI	Joachim Du Bellay, *La Deffence et illustration de la langue françoyse*.
DG	Jacques Derrida, *De la grammatologie*.
DIL	Penelope Reed Doob, *The Idea of the Labyrinth*.
DS	*Dictionnaire des symboles*, ed. Jean Chevalier and Alain Gheerbrant.
DSS	Jacques Derrida, "Structure, Sign, and Play in the Discourse of the Human Sciences."

DT   Peter Dayan, *Mallarmé's Divine Transposition.*

DV   JoAnn DellaNeva, "Variations in a Minor Key."

ER   Mircea Eliade, *Rites and Symbols of Initiation.*

FCII   Bryant C. Freeman, *Concordance du Théâtre et des Poésies de Jean Racine*, vol. 2.

FFF   C. Frederick Farrell, Jr. and Edith R. Farrell, "Marguerite Yourcenar's *Feux*: Structure and Meaning."

FM   Wallace Fowlie, *Mallarmé.*

FMC   Fulcanelli, *Le Mystère des cathédrales.*

FR   Michel Foucault, *Raymond Roussel.*

GMI   Robert Graves, *The Greek Myths*, vol. 1.

GW   Grillot de Givry, *Witchcraft, Magic & Alchemy.*

HM   Edith Hamilton, *Mythology.*

HS   Kathryn A. Hoffman, "The Space of Difference in Racine's *Bajazet.*"

HV   Joan Howard, *From Violence to Vision: Sacrifice in the Works of Marguerite Yourcenar.*

JI   Carolyn L. Jacobs, "The Irony of Human Judgment: Act III of *Bajazet.*"

KO   Richard Katz, *The Ordered Text.*

KL   Marlies Kronegger, *The Life Significance of French Baroque Poetry.*

LGG   André Leroi-Gourhan, *Le Geste et la parole*, vol. 1.

MA   Oscar Mandel, "Introduction" to Thomas Corneille's *Ariadne.*

MM   L. R. Muir, "The Monster in the Labyrinth: The Paradox of Hippolyte."

MML   W. H. Mathews, *Mazes & Labyrinths: Their History and Development.*

MNI   Eric MacPhail, "Nationalism and Italianism in the Work of Joachim Du Bellay."

NB   Jerry Nash, "Cette 'beauté nompareille': Du Bellay et l'écriture de l'impossible."

NP   Nina da Vinci Nichols, "Racine's *Phaedra* and Ibsen's *Hedda*: Transformations of Ariadne."

PL   André Peyronie, "The Labyrinth."

RM   Deirdre A. Reynolds, "Mallarmé and Hegel: Speculation and the Poetics of Reflection."

RT   David Michael Roberts, "Théophile's Cygnus and the Vulnerable *locus amoenus.*"

RU   Jean-Pierre Richard, *L'Univers imaginaire de Mallarmé.*

SB   Maya Slater, "Racine's *Bajazet*: The Language of Violence and Secrecy."

SDI	Peter Sharratt, "Du Bellay and the Icarus Complex."
SK	Gershom Scholem, *Kabbalah.*
TOS	Thomas Thomson, *L'Olive: A Selection with Notes.*
T P	George Hugo Tucker, *The Poet's Odyssey.*
VR	Voltaire, "Remarques sur *Ariane*, tragédie."
WD	*Webster's New Twentieth Century Dictionary.*
WL	Lawrence J. Watson, *Mallarmé's Mythic Language.*

Index

Currents in Comparative Romance Languages and Literatures

This series was founded in 1987, and actively solicits book-length manuscripts (approximately 200–400 pages) that treat aspects of Romance languages and literatures. Originally established for works dealing with two or more Romance literatures, the series has broadened its horizons and now includes studies on themes within a single literature or between different literatures, civilizations, art, music, film and social movements, as well as comparative linguistics. Studies on individual writers with an influence on other literatures/ civilizations are also welcome. We entertain a variety of approaches and formats, provided the scholarship and methodology are appropriate.

For additional information about the series or for the submission of manuscripts, please contact:

Tamara Alvarez-Detrell and Michael G. Paulson
c/o Dr. Heidi Burns
Peter Lang Publishing, Inc.
516 N. Charles St., 2nd Floor
Baltimore, MD 21201

To order other books in this series, please contact our Customer Service Department at:

800-770-LANG (within the U.S.)
212-647-7706 (outside the U.S.)
212-647-7707 FAX

or browse online by series at:

www.peterlang.com